$6.00

To John
From Joanne &
Jennifer

Leroy A. Battle

Easier
Said

THE AUTOBIOGRAPHY OF LEROY A. BATTLE

D1056572

The Annapolis Publishing Company / *Annapolis, Maryland*

Published by
The Annapolis Publishing Company / *Annapolis, Maryland*

ISBN 1-884878-04-0

Dedication

*I dedicate this book with all my love
to my wonderful wife Alice. Without
her patience, wisdom, expertise,
and encouragement, this book
would not have come to fruition.*

*To the "pros," Rachel and
Philip L. Brown,
I humbly say "Thank You"
for your unselfish guidance.*

Contents

v

Preface

From time to time in recent years, I gave thought to writing a personal account of my life which would chronicle my experiences and also serve as a legacy to my children and their children. But usually, I would abandon the idea almost as quickly as I dredged it up. It wasn't until I was interviewed on Jim Bohannon's nationwide talk show that the idea of writing memoirs again bubbled up. Several people heard the interview, which was centered around my fighting segregation while growing up both in Brooklyn and later in the U.S. Air Corps. Charles and Marion Johnson, my bowling buddies, after hearing the interview, urged me to put something on paper. They said, "Our black youth needs to know about you and your contributions to equality," as did Charles and Melba McMillan and Raymond and Marva Rogers. Frank Hebron, a former principal and a "jolly, gentle giant of a man," said, "Every youngster in Maryland should be privileged to hear that wonderful tape. I had no idea you were with the Tuskegee Flyers. You have some real history with you. It would be wonderful if you would put some of your anecdotes in writing for the younger generation to read." Well, Frank has always been and will always be a champion for youth. All along and sometime before that fateful interview, John and Rosa Davies, long time friends and confidants of our family, have been gently prodding me to document my life... bookstyle. I guess it was the trusting and warm combination of all of the above that finally galvanized me into action. I caution you in advance that these are the memories of a life lived a long time ago, so I only recall the things that had the greatest impact - hopefully they will be the important ones. I have also taken the liberty on occasion, as people of my generation are sometimes inclined to do, to provide instructive commentary on the lessons to be learned from "the good old days" I hope you will indulge me. I have also sought to acknowledge those who have helped, and continue to help me traverse through this life. The results are what follows...

Foreword

One may well ask, "Who is LeRoy Battle? Why read the story of this life?" The answer is that LeRoy Battle is part of a whole generation of black men and women who, within their own communities, have lived quiet and unassuming lives, whose character and achievements now stand in growing contrast to many of the most visible examples of today; that generation needs to find a way of stepping forward as alternatives to the images of hopelessness, anger, and failure that tragically cripples far too many children, and too often infects and distorts public opinion. The troubled black man most people get to see on TV, or on the street corner, or in the newspaper is not the only choice. Neither are the inaccessible superstars of sports. The best heroes are not the ones who go out and achieve the impossible. They can't serve as role models if we are left with the feeling that we could never be that brave, or jump that high, or give that much. The best heroes are the accessible ones, the ones who provide an example of how we can be better than we are, that is within our reach. They live lives that move us and that we can respect, yet they leave us thinking that anyone who really wants to can have these memories, these successes, if they would only try.

Mr. Battle has lived through special times in the history of America, and in the history of black Americans: the passage and the later repeal of prohibiton, the passage of the women's suffrage amendment, the roaring twenties, the gangster era, the Great Depression, the blossoming of the New York jazz scene, World War II, the integration of the public school systems and the subsequent broadening and governmental support of integration. In many ways he was just an ordinary man, but what that meant was significantly elevated by the time in which he lived. The standards of normalcy were more demanding - the personal and social context more straightforward - the level of social consciousness higher. What was largely taken for granted back then - that there was nothing wrong with being good and decent and staying away from drugs, and respecting women, working hard, valuing and working for an education, staying out of trouble – it now takes a Million Man March to affirm.

What Mr. Battle had was; a dream, a commitment to it, and the opportunity to pursue it. It's not the content of the goal that's most important - it's the having of goals at all. With goals come purpose, hard work, achievement, and gratification. They provide a way to measure yourself, a way to be proud of yourself, and a way to earn the respect of others. Purpose, ambition, self-respect, and of course, the enjoyment of one's life, are all enhanced by finding some direction in your life. Without goals, people are unmotivated, aimless, and unfulfilled. They struggle to find some way to be proud of themselves and to earn the respect of others. But instead of having a purposeful goal, they end up picking up their self-image off the street. They adopt what's available, what's easy, what's superficial, and what you don't have to work very hard at to get. And they hurt themselves in the process. Mr. Battle learned so much more than just how to play the drums. He learned self-discipline, he learned an awful lot about human relationships, friendships, cooperation and what you can achieve through it. He learned right and wrong and thereby acquired the strength of moral conviction that enabled him to effectively confront injustices later on. He learned how to handle life. And he has something useful to give back to others.

One of the first things Mr. Battle did when I met him was to provide me with a cassette recording of his band, The Altones. I knew that he had quite an interesting musical career, and I was anxious to hear him play. The next time I saw him he asked me about the tape. I told him that while the band was fine, I was disappointed that it never really featured him on the drums, and that's what I was really looking for. His reply, as well as I can remember it, was, "Yeah, that's what everybody says. But people don't understand what it's all about. Everbody wants to hear me solo. But you know, that's not my thing anymore. I can solo alright, but what I really like about being a swing drummer is just setting that steady back beat - setting the tempo for the band and keeping them together. And then when I want to, you know, I can push 'em. It's like I'm in control, and when I start driving the band and they start responding we really get to cookin' and that's what I like, when we're feeding off of each other like that." In many ways, LeRoy Battle's approach to his drumming parallels what he has done with his life. There's no doubt that he soloed a bit in his youth, but the major portion of his time has been spent trying to "set that steady back-beat" for others. This book is his attempt to continue that effort. I understand what he means, and I appreciate it, but I still wouldn't mind seeing a little bit more of that "solo" side as well.

WTC – Ed.

Part One
My Life

My Mother
Margie Battle - Brooklyn, NY
1940

Growing Up

Early days in Harlem

A last minute addition to the festivities, I was born on New Year's Eve, 1921, the only child of Walter and Margie Battle. I guess this is the one day each year when nearly everyone adopts a naive optimism about the life that lies before them, about what they can do to make it better, and about who they can be. Whether I inherited some of that naive optimism, or came upon it later by other means, I have always had it. I think it has served me well. It seems to have been an optimistic time for most everyone then. My parents and their families were part of a great migration of blacks from the rural South to the cities and industries of the northeast. It was a period of dramatic change in Harlem. In the ten years from 1920 to 1930, 117,000 whites left Harlem, and 87,000 blacks moved in. Many of those who came were writers, artists, and musicians, creating a "Harlem Renaissance." Most of them came in search of a chance at a better life. For my parents, who came separately to New York with their families and met there, that dream, at least financially, must have been modestly fulfilled. As I recall it, our neighborhood was probably what you would consider "middle-class." There was good and bad in there to be sure, but mostly it was just a lot of friendly people looking out for each other. And of course, there was me and the other neighborhood kids, being foolish and trying our best not to survive our childhood.

Though we moved to Brooklyn later, I spent my early elementary school days in Harlem, where my father owned a candy store. We lived on 154th Street and 8th Avenue. It was a long, vague time ago, but some fond images still stick with me. As I recall, those were fast and hectic days, filled with fun, danger, and suspense. The kids all grew up together on the streets and in the surrounding areas. We didn't have television or video games or any of the other things that keep children inside and isolate them from each other today. Between the lack of other things to do and getting on the adults' nerves, we were forced out into each other's care. There, we had a community of our own, though we were never completely out of the watchful view of the adults. We had a "buddy system" then. You picked a buddy, or you were picked, and for the rest of your days in that neighborhood, you and your buddy shared everything. My buddy was a guy named "Choo-Choo." He was

3

my height, about four-foot three. I weighed about ninety pounds, however, and Choo-Choo was about one hundred thirty pounds (hence his nickname). My buddy and I did everything together. We would share the few pennies we had managed to scrounge up by selling bundles of old newspapers to the junk yard man, or from turning in pop bottles for their deposit; we would often pool our change and buy a box of crackers called "Smacks." Then we would go to a local theater and sit through two or three showings of a picture and eat the crackers. I remember our going to the Loews, Brevoort, and seeing "The Werewolf of London" with Henry Hull. Other times, we would go to the corner grocery store and swipe a few potatoes (only then we called them mickies). We would then go to Macombs Park down by the Harlem River and start small camp fires, take coat hangers, pierce the potatoes, and roast them over the fire. It was quite a sight some nights to see seven or eight small camp fires while the air filled with the wonderful smell of roasting potatoes. I recall some of the games we played: ring-a-levy-o, stickball and boxball. Stickball was the city version of baseball. We would use a broomstick and tennis ball. Like most of our childhood games, we made up our own rules to fit what we had to work with. The cars parked on either side of the street would serve as 1st and 3rd base... 2nd base would be two sewer plates from the home plate sewer. The pitcher would stand on the 2nd plate and throw the ball on one bounce to the batter. (Some of those pitchers could make that ball do strange things). We lost many balls which were hit foul five stories up to the roofs of the apartment buildings. Sometimes a window would get busted, which would put an abrupt end to the game. But most of the time, the games ran their course, providing us with endless chances to stretch, challenge, and amuse ourselves. All in all, 154th Street was very exciting and interesting to me - something was always happening.

I spent a lot of time with relatives on my father's side: Aunt Effie, Cousin Lena Bridges, Uncle Morales (who I mainly remember as the first person to introduce me to Spanish rice), and Aunt Fanny. My mother's brothers were always stopping by too, in fact that's how I got my nickname. When I was just a toddler, Uncle Walter stopped by one day on his way out to Long Island to go fishing, and he set down his boots while he went to wash his hands. I climbed into them, and according to Mother, I almost disappeared. When Uncle Walter was ready to leave, he had quite a time extracting me from those boots. From that time on, that's how I was known – as "Boots."

Our street was vibrant and full of life. Actually, it was like one large family. Everybody knew everybody (as you can see, I was related to quite a few of them) and it seemed that at whatever house you or your friends stopped, that's where you ate. No matter where you went on Sundays, the same wonderful, enticing smells seemed to emanate from

4

each apartment: that of roast pork, candied sweets, collard greens and hot rolls. There seemed not to ever be a day where one just did nothing. Of course, it wasn't all just fun and games - there were more than a few rough spots as I was growing up. It was a time when, being very young, we were virtually told by the older boys we hung around with what our place in the "pecking order" was. There wasn't much I could do about the older kids but accept it. My troubles usually started when someone my own age or thereabouts tried to tell me what to do. I had a quick wit as I recall, and my mouth sometimes caused me to have to back up my words with my fists. One of the neighborhood "sports" was called "The Dozens" or "Slips" which involved the exchange of derogatory remarks about each other's mothers, or other convenient relatives. Whether you started the exchange or not, it was usually in front of an audience which was only too glad to provoke the escalation of insults until one you ran out of things to say. At that point the challenge would become more physical, and the two boys woofing at each other would end up fighting. I am loathe to repeat the vile statements that made up "The Dozens" game... take my word, they were very worthy of the fights they precipitated.

Besides my relatives, there were lots of other interesting people to be around. Col. B.O. Davis, Sr., who later became the first black general in the U.S. Army, lived there. It was always a thrill for me to see him come into my father's candy store, dressed in his glittering uniform. (For me there has always been something special about a sharp-dressed man.) I also remember that Buck and Bubbles, a famous black song and dance team at that time, lived on our block, and there were many other entertainers living within several blocks of us. Once or twice a month when Buck and Bubbles would come home after being out on the road, they would line up both boys and girls along the curb on one side of the street and throw fists full of nickels and dimes across the street. Then they would shout "Go", and we would run and try to pick up as many nickels and dimes as possible. This was called "Cock-Scramble". If I was quick I could usually get about forty or fifty cents. My mother would hold it for me until I needed it for a movie. Besides the neighbors, two other characters familiar to our street were the local N.Y.C. police officers - Officer White, who was white, and Officer Dash, who was black. Officer Dash was a very kind man who took a personal interest in the young people. He did not tolerate bullies or any back talk. While Officer White was cordial, he was not as outgoing as Officer Dash. It seemed that Officer White took care of the older boys, and Officer Dash was more concerned with the youngsters.

I also recall that there were some very dangerous moments in my childhood on 154th Street, in fact, two particular incidents have left a lasting impression on me: We lived about two blocks from a part of the

Harlem River that coursed around two steel beams. There the river would swirl and slow down. But unknown to our young minds, there was a fierce, powerful undercurrent there. Actually, a few boys had drowned there. One day I watched as police and fire fighters kept throwing this big hook into the river and dragging it out until they finally caught hold of the body of a young boy from another neighborhood. It was a sight that should have cured me of my interest in jumping into the Harlem River. Even so, in our neighborhood, "follow-the-leader" was a very important part of our tempering... and nobody wanted to be "yellow". So on this very hot day, a gang of the older boys said they were going to take a swim. They said the younger boys could only go if we followed the leader, and we, anxious to fit in, were only to glad to comply. Well, we got to the river's bank and peeled all of our clothes off until we were buck naked (following the leader). Then the older boys started jumping into the river. Despite the fact that I had never learned to swim, the lure of fitting in with the older kids was so great that I was just about to jump when I heard someone shout, "Boots, your mother," and before I could turn around I felt this stinging lash across my backside. I yelped and started running... My mother swung that belt and beat me for two blocks, all the way home, and I was stark naked. Boy, the people laughed and said, "That's right, Margie, get him." Needless to say, that ended my river swimming days. In fact, it wasn't until very late in my adult life that I finally learned to swim.

The other incident involved my playing follow-the-leader again. Right across the street from my father's candy store was a five story apartment building. One fine summer evening my mother just happened to look up and there I was, five stories above the pavement, following a group of the older boys walking on the ledge of the roof on that building. My mother didn't yell because she didn't want to startle me. Instead she sent her brother, Clarance, to get me. I looked out across the roof and saw Clarance approaching, smiling, and waving for me to come to him. I jumped off the ledge and went to him, expecting praise for my "Derring-Do". Instead, I was met with a series of blows and verbal expletives... I beat a hasty retreat down the stairs to the street. The memory of those well aimed blows remained with me for quite a while. Although I continued to play "follow-the-leader," I never "walked" the roof ledge again.

Childhood Adventures

There was another dangerous game some of the older boys from my block liked to engage in. Instead of paying to ride the streetcar to the school block, they would hop on the back of a moving trolley car and hang on to any protruding part to keep from falling... as many as three could be seen holding on for dear life as the trolley sped along. Well, on one particular morning I was spending a little too much time getting myself ready for school. I was admiring myself in the mirror, with my brown corduroy knickers and Mackinaw jacket. I had just gotten a new pair of "Jack Londons" - a popular high-top leather shoe with a pouch and a pocket knife, and was busy checking myself out when Aunt Bert hollered for me to get going. I grabbed my wool cap and book bag and went flying out the door. I was now running a bit late and was about to miss the trolley. As I started for the trolley stop, a couple of boys saw me coming and waved for me to go to the far side of the trolley where the driver couldn't see me in order to hop on the trolley as it pulled off. Well, everything was fine to a point... it was an exciting ride with the wind blowing across my face, the street racing by just under my feet, and me stealing a ride and being a big shot in front of my friends. But my big book bag kept me from getting a good grip on the back of the trolley with both of my hands. Still, I was able to hold on for a block or so before my awkward grip gave way and I fell onto the street. Fortunately, I landed on my stomach with the book bag underneath me, cushioning my fall. Unfortunately, I fell in the middle of traffic. As I hit the ground I heard the sound of screeching brakes and in the next instant felt a terrible pain in my left foot. The tire of a car following the trolley rolled right onto the arch of my foot and was pushing me. Finally, the car and I stopped and a big crowd gathered, including our neighborhood patrolman, Officer Dash. After a quick examination of my condition he said to me, "Son, you are a lucky, dumb fool. The only thing that saved your leg and possibly your life are those lumberjack hightops you're wearing." Then he hoisted me on his shoulder and carried me home. I remember Mother showing both sides of her emotions... she was caught somewhere between laughter from the relief that I wasn't maimed or killed, and anger that I would be so thoughtless to risk my life and safety for no good reason at all, just to save five cents and to be one of the guys. Officer Dash accepted a cup of coffee, checked to see that I did not have to go to the hospital, then left us alone to work out how to make me less of a fool. Mother must have gotten her point across because that was a stunt I never tried again. But in truth she really didn't have to persuade me, I had already scared myself into being a little bit smarter in the future.

Looking back on some of those childhood adventures, I guess I'd have to say all of us were lucky to have survived our foolishness as well as we did. But at the same time, I know that the chances we took and the ways we tested each other were an essential part of our growth, and I wouldn't want children to ever lose the spirit that drives them to explore and conquer their world as best they can. The problem today is with the way that world has changed. The risks some of today's kids are induced to take are profoundly more dangerous, and too many of the adults who are supposed to watch over them often seem to lack the ability or inclination to steer them away from disaster.

Elementary Education

Like our neighborhood, our school in Harlem was segregated, although this was not something we ever gave any thought to. I can truthfully say that I enjoyed school, and I don't think I was unique in that respect. At that time, the most beautiful thing in the world that could happen to me in class was to see a purple star stamped on my homework or seatwork paper. On rare occasions my paper would receive not one but two stars for extra neat work. This was always good for me to hurry home and show my parents. Their encouragement helped me to take pride in my accomplishments in school, and made me want to do my very best. Being a good student also gave me a little notoriety among the other kids, which made me want to do well even more. It was one of the ways a person could stand out. Everybody wanted to be special somehow - it didn't really matter how. For some kids it was being funny, or crazy, or big. Sometimes it was just a stupid hat you always wore. Whatever it was, it just came to you. All it took was for someone to point it out and it was out there for you to live up to or to chase away. I was lucky to be a good student, and for my friends to respect that.

Reading was one skill that came to me because of my curiosity. I like to think that the reading habit came to me during the time that my father owned his candy store located at 272 W 154th Street in Harlem. My particular contribution to the running of the candy store, even though I was just four or five years old, was to assemble the sections of the paper into one unit. The store sold a lot of papers each day. In the morning there was the Daily News; about 2:00 p.m. the Daily Mirror would be delivered to the store, then about 5:00 p.m., the New York Journal was put on sale. While I was putting the papers together, I became curious about the pictures and writings that accompanied them. I literally became a pest, because I asked and begged everyone to help me learn to read. I received a lot of help from my uncles and customers (no one was safe from my queries). By the time I started school, I had quite a vocabulary. More importantly, I was ready to learn as fast as I could to be able to unlock the stories behind all those words.

By the time I was in the 4th grade at PS 35, I was actually reading at a 7th grade level. Without realizing it, at the beginning of my fourth grade, I inadvertently ended up in a sixth grade class. When the teacher finished calling roll, she asked were there any students she missed. I raised my hand and she asked me my name and said that she would check in the office to get my records. Well I guess in the confusion she failed to check on my records. I actually stayed in the 6th grade for two weeks, and I think I would have remained there all year if it wasn't for the fact that I failed so miserably on a math test dealing only with "percentage" problems. The teacher asked me to come to her room after school, there she said to me, "Alright LeRoy, what's going on? You didn't get one answer correct. I even checked your worksheet to see how you approached problem solving." She then went on to say, "You are doing 'B' and 'B+' work in social studies and reading, but your math results puzzle me. Wait here please, I'll be right back." A few minutes later, she returned holding a folder and laughing. She said, "Boy, you almost got me in trouble." Then seeing the look on my face, she quickly added, "No LeRoy, I didn't mean that, it's my fault that I didn't solve this problem on your first day. Tell me, what grade were you in last year?" "Third," I replied. "That's what your records show," she said. The she proceeded to explain that I had to go back to the fourth grade because there were too many skills that I needed to know - mainly in mathematics. Needless to say, I was disappointed. But I took a certain amount of pride back with me knowing that in many ways I was able to keep up with the sixth graders. For the remainder of the year I was fortunate enough to make the Honor Roll. If I ever needed it, extra help was always available from my uncles. To this day I'm forever grateful for their help and encouragement - they were truly "father figures" to me in many ways. Their support of my education made it easy for me to work hard at school.

A Learning Experience

Of course, not all education takes place in schools, some of it is more practical, and I remember at least one case where one of my uncles enthusiastically helped me with this part of my instruction too. Next to the Rockland Palace was a huge laundry, the Hydrox Laundry. Outside of the building there were large baskets on rollers. The laundry trucks would drive up and unload the soiled laundry. Another employee would put the soiled laundry into baskets and roll them inside the building. The baskets were about 4 foot by 4 foot with a canvas body topped by a soft wicker rolled edge all around. The older boys, forever resourceful when it came to thinking up new ways to get into trouble, started cutting off three and four inch parts of the tubular wicker and used them as cigarettes. They would go around trying to act grown-up by puffing on those foul smelling basket parts. One day they decided to indoctrinate me into the smoking fraternity. I had no sooner taken a few puffs on the basket part when I saw my uncle Clarance out of the corner of my eye. He raised his hand and slapped me on my back. I almost swallowed the basket tip. Then Clarance said, "Boots, you don't have to go around smoking this garbage. C'mon.

Let's go hang out on the stoop." Well, I was beginning to feel that at last I was one of the big boys. When we got to the stoop, Clarance told me to wait a second while he dashed into my father's candy store and came out with a fresh pack of cigarettes. He calmly took two from the pack, lit them both and offered one to me. I took the cigarette, put it up to my lips and, trying to act as grown up as possible, took a small puff. "No, not like that Boots," Clarance said. "Take a long draw and hold it in." After three inhales I started to get sick to the stomach. I threw the cigarette away. Clarance said to stay with it and handed me another lit cigarette. In a short while I had gone through ten cigarettes and was ready to pass out. My uncle took me upstairs. I went to the bathroom and threw up. Then I went to bed. Later that afternoon I was awakened by loud laughter. I got up and went into the kitchen where Mother, Clarance and his girl friend were enjoying coffee and cake. As I entered Clarance took out a cigarette, lit it, blew smoke in my face, and started to hand me the cigarette. I bolted from the room and barely got to the bathroom before I threw up, again. Talk about laughing... boy, they really gave it to me. But I haven't smoked a cigarette or anything else since then.

An Awakening

It seems that   was always fascinated with uniforms from an early age on. We lived one block from the Rockland Palace which was located on 155th and 8th Avenue. Rockland Palace was a famous ballroom that Negroes frequently used to hold dances, cabarets, fashion shows, and similar events. It was located on sort of an isolated dead-end street and was the favorite starting point of various Negro organization parades. I remember one sunny day the Knights of St. John were sponsoring a parade. I decided to investigate all the activity that was going on and I soon found myself walking around through the staging area, taking in all the sights and sounds, the confusion and the excitement that are part of the backstage scene. There were about 300 marchers milling around – men decked out in capes, black hats with large white plumes and with many carrying a ceremonial sword at their sides. The ladies were dressed all in white. It was magnificent. You might have thought that I was the Inspector General as I worked my way through each rank and file. I finally got to the group that caused my eyes to pop and my heart to race – It was the sight and sound of those beautiful brass instruments and the tuning and tapping of the drums. Everybody was waiting for the 7 foot drum major to blow the whistle. He seemed to be 10 feet tall with his white bearskin hat. Finally, the drummer said, "Hey Kid - Get to the sidewalk. We're ready to 'break a leg'." I scrambled to the curb but had no idea of whose leg would be broken. Suddenly the drum major thrust his baton upward and seemed to trace some unknown magical symbol in the air - a long blast on his whistle completed the spell as he retrieved his baton. Cymbals crashed, the heavens opened up, and a parade burst forth to the thunderous, crashing cadence of the Knights of St. John Band. It was a magical experience, and in that moment I knew that I wanted to be part of that kind of excitement someday.

On To Brooklyn

During the summer following my completion of the 5th grade at PS 35 in Harlem, we moved to Brooklyn. There I was fortunate enough to stay with my Aunt Roberta, or 'Aunt Bert' as we called her, who owned a beauty parlor at 1544 Fulton Street, and with my grandparents, Isabella and Henry Goldwire who lived nearby at 1616 Fulton Street. These arrangements were made because around this time, Mother and Dad were having their differences and a divorce was imminent. I never really knew why they got divorced, and I don't remember it having much of an impact on me, except for bringing about our move to Brooklyn. I don't recall it having much of an impact on Mother either. My father and I never really spent much time together - he was pretty strict and somewhat distant, and he was always involved in running the store. Most of my free time in Harlem was spent with my relatives and hanging out with the gang in the neighborhood. In Brooklyn I still had my Aunt Bert, who became a second mother to me, as well as several of my uncles to look after me.

It wasn't long before I started making new friends and settled into the neighborhood. Soon you could find me out on the street playing stickball like everyone else. It was during one of these occasions that I was reminded of my dream to get involved in music. We were in the middle of a game and across the way I saw this older fellow, I don't even know his name, but he had a broken down snare drum, and he was sitting down in a doorway rapping on the drum. I was mesmerized by what he was doing and I just left the game - everybody was yelling at me and I just walked over and said, "Man, what are you doing?" It was nothing but this scratch thing, but that was a sweet sound to my ears. And I said, "Man, can I try that?" And he said "No man, you'll put holes in it." But I just sat there watching and pestering, and he eventually let me try it. Once I felt those sticks in my hand, and felt the sound of my own "music" resonating through my body, I was hooked. My general interest in parades and music and marching now had a specific focus - I decided to be a drummer.

My new crusade to become a drummer started at home and I began in earnest. I used to drive my mother and my aunt crazy by beating on the pots and pans and muffin tins with any utensil available; knives, forks, spoons. For some time we were eating lopsided muffins. No cooking pot was safe from my clutches. The roasters were my favorite. The low, ringing tones served as background for my original chants, which I generously called songs, as I marched and banged through the apartment. Soon my love of bands, the trappings of the parade participants, and the "sound of the music" which was awakened in me in Harlem would begin to be nurtured in varied and sundry ways. Music would become the main focus of my life, and if there were any scars from the breakup of my parent's marriage, they must have been washed away by a wave of new experiences, and the steady support of my extended family.

Our New Home

My new neighborhood was in the Bedford-Styvesant section of Brooklyn. Unlike my old block in Harlem, the area where I now lived was integrated. The atmosphere was still pretty much the same; almost all of the families were middle class, and everyone was friendly to each other. We became particularly close to the family of our Italian landlord. At the time I was staying with my aunt, we lived in a small apartment, consisting of three rooms behind the beauty parlor, with a bathroom down a short outside hallway which also led to my favorite place to be alone and use my imagination, our backyard. The entire front part of the yard was under a vine-covered canopy about twelve feet high, fifteen yards across and ten yards deep, all of which was enclosed on three sides by a three foot white trellis fence. Beyond the enclosed portion of the yard was an open area accessible by a three foot wide paved walkway which led to a fig tree on the left, and white and purple grapes on the right along with wild mint. It was wonderful to smell the fruity, tangy odor of the trees and plants. It was here that I spent many hours listening to my Aunt Bert's radio. I would play along with the characters, one moment practicing my quick-draw techniques to help Tom Mix get the best of the Desperados, then fifteen minutes later joining Little Orphan Annie's Punjab in India, fighting back the infidels with my sharp scimitar. It was a great place to escape to, where I was free to ride my imagination wherever it wanted to take me.

The apartment above my aunt's beauty parlor was occupied by her landlord, Mr. Sandora, and his family. Both our families got along very well. In fact, during the summer, when weather would permit, the two families would often eat together under the grape canopy in the yard, gathering about once a month. We would start preparing for our joint dinner early Sunday morning. First we would butt a few tables together, then cover them with oilskin tablecloths. Altogether, we used about ten folding chairs. Mrs. Sandora would prepare the salad, Italian style, with Italian tomatoes, black olives, croutons, and olive oil. In addition, there was veal parmesan. Aunt Bert would usually bake a turkey with all the trimmings. We would drink homemade grape punch along with the meal. It was wonderful eating outside in such a bucolic setting, it was more like being in the country than in the middle of a big city. I still remember those dinners with a great deal of affection; especially the way the Sandora family took us in. I'm certain their hospitality made my transition to the new neighborhood much easier than it would have been otherwise.

The 8th Avenue Subway

I recall how happy I was over the fact that the 8th Avenue Subway (Independent Line) was opening up its station on Throop Avenue. Everybody in the neighborhood was looking forward to this event - it was the main topic of conversation at the beauty parlor for many weeks before it opened. Soon the whole city would be much more accessible to us. Times Square, the big movie houses, and all the boroughs of New York City would be within our reach. The station was just across the street from where I lived. There were about ten of us in the group which I hung with, boys and girls. The day of the big opening they all gathered in my Aunt's beauty parlor waiting for me. I was just finishing my breakfast when someone yelled, "C'mon Boots, we'll be late!" So I gulped down my milk and joined them. "Bye, Mrs. Roderick," they said in unison and we dashed across the street and down the steps of the station. The transit policeman smiled at us (boy, have times changed), and waved us on through the turnstiles. We did not have to pay – the transit authority, in an all out effort to get people used to using the subways, did not charge for any rides up to 4:00 p.m. that day. We laughed and talked as we waited for our first subway ride. Finally, we heard it, a ground shaking low rumble, accompanied by loud screeching sounds as the train rounded a turn to our station. From a short distance we saw the green and white lights on the front car and the large white letter "A". As the front car passed us, we spotted the engineer in his cab on the left side of the car. He waved at us as the car sped past us. I thought the train would never stop - but eventually it did. Then a conductor who was riding between the two coaches yelled, "Stand back, please." The doors opened automatically, and the crowd on the station platform pushed and shoved to get in. I said to our group, "Let's go up to the front car," and we were off, pushing and shoving again. The scary part was going from the end of one car to the next. You had to open and shut the big sliding doors. Sometimes this was a bit difficult if the train was rocking one way and you were trying to open the door. We finally made our way to the front car. There we could actually stand in the front, slide the door back and enjoy the air rushing in. There were numerous chains across the opening to keep you from falling out. Also, it was exciting to know that you could stand right next to the engineer's cab. We rode as far as 125th Street in Harlem. (Yes, this was the same "A" train in Harlem which Duke Ellington and arranger Billy Strayhorn made famous later.) We switched trains at 125th Street and caught the subway home. Everybody slept all the way back. We were exhausted, but very excited. The city had opened up to us in ways that it hadn't before. Though I didn't know it at the time, it wouldn't be long before I was putting this new-found mobility to good use.

A New School

My new school, Stephen Decatur Elementary was at Lewis Avenue and Macon Street. The day I registered was extremely exciting. New teachers, new faces, new challenges. I went to class that same day - I was assigned to section 6A2. My teacher, Mrs. Goodman, asked me if I would introduce myself to the class and tell of my interests. I rose from my desk and moved to the front of the room. Despite my excitement, I was also a little apprehensive about how I would fit in - this was my first experience going to a school that was integrated, and that didn't have any colored teachers. My knees at this stage were starting to feel like rubber bands - so I moved forward and sort of leaned against the desk in front of me. "Thank you, Mrs. Goodman," I said. "My favorite interests are reading and parade music... I like the uniforms and drums." I continued, "I hope to do a lot of reading here." Then I sat down.

Mrs. Goodman said, "Thank you LeRoy. We'll assign someone to be your buddy and show you how to get around the school. She then looked around the room, pointed to a boy in the rear and said, "Louis, you will be LeRoy's guide for a few days. Now everybody take out your civic's book and we'll start the lesson."

After school was out I started walking towards home when I heard my name being called. "Hey LeRoy, wait up." I turned and saw Louis running my way. When he caught up to me, he said, "Back there in class you said that you wanted to do a lot of reading." "That's right," I said. "Well look to your left," he replied. I looked across the street and there was a large, square, red brick structure. "That's the local library. Let's drop in." "That's fine by me," I said. Then we both crossed the street and climbed the steps which led to the main doors. Once inside I was amazed to see a 'million' books. The library was quite full. Many

14

students were gathered around several tables whispering very softly to themselves. Louis looked at me, pointed and said, "The adventure section is over there." When we got to the adventure section, it was all that I could do to control myself. This was my first visit to a library. Everywhere I looked there were stacks of books; the shelves so high that I could barely reach the top. I read title after title and finally settled on a series called *The Green Mountain Boys*. There were seven books in the collection and I had checked out and read all seven within a period of two weeks. After going through that series, I started reading some Sherlock Holmes, Tom Swift, and the *Og, Son of Fire* series. The long and short of it was the fact that I was hooked on reading. There's nothing like getting lost in the adventures of exciting characters in other times and places. However, It wasn't until the 7th grade that my eyes were opened to the full power and beauty of reading and poetry. It was there that my homeroom teacher, Mr. Hirsch (who was a spitting image of the screen star Robert Taylor, and also was built like a Roman gladiator) captured my imagination with poems such as "Old Ironsides," which told about the great sea battle between the two war frigates - the *Constitution* and the *Guerriere*, and the retiring of the *Constitution* by the U.S. Navy; "Annable Lee", which told about Edgar Allen Poe's love for a certain lady who died; "Flanders Field", which was a tribute to the American soldiers who fought and died in France and who were buried in this great field where the "poppies grow row on row..."

Books have remained for me a gateway to wonderful ideas and experiences that would otherwise be beyond my reach. I can truly say that reading has always released my mind and has permitted it to soar in any direction unfettered. Even today, I cannot resist books of adventure, mystery, or especially, police work involving New York City detectives.

Beginning Drums

It wasn't long before I discovered a way to pursue the interest in music that the St. John's Parade had sparked in me. Each Friday there was an assembly for the entire school. It was always a special event, and there was even a special dress code for the day which required all girls to wear white blouses with red kerchiefs and the boys to wear white shirts with red ties. The assembly would start with the Color Guard, students bearing the American flag, followed by the state flag, followed by a snare drummer beating out a solemn, simple rhythm. They would start from the rear of the auditorium and march to the drum cadence down the center aisle, to the front of the auditorium. Then the student body president would lead everybody in the Pledge of Allegiance after

15

which the Color Guard would march back up the center aisle to the cadence of the drum. I made a mental note to one day be that drummer (and to use a snappier, more syncopated rhythm).

With new-found enthusiasm I returned to my self-taught practice sessions, which I must admit produced much more noise than skill. Fortunately for my mother and Aunt Bert, at this point I was permitted to join the Boy Scouts in my church, Bethany Baptist, on the corner of Sumner Avenue and Decatur Street, where I was able to more seriously embark on my "drumming career." Unfortunately, the equipment was not much better than the pots and pans I had been using from my aunt's kitchen. Available to the Boy Scout troop were two battered snare drums, one with no snares and the other with a couple of small holes in the head. With ten boys interested in drumming and such limited equipment, we had to take turns practicing what went for rolls and single strokes. The church's beat up old drums did serve a purpose, however, in that we were able to tie ropes to them, looping them around our shoulders, simulating marching and playing.

In all of this we were under the direction of Mr. Gary Talbert, our Scoutmaster, who was a very kind and caring individual. I would dare say that he was somewhat of a father figure to me. He always seemed so much in control of himself. In all the time I knew him, I never heard him raise his voice. His family was always so kind to me. Some evenings after troop meetings, he would invite several of us to his house for dinner. It was always a lot of fun on these evenings. I recall Mr. Talbert's father giving all of us boxing lessons in the front room, however, our attention strayed when Mrs. Talbert appeared with homemade hot rolls and golden fried chicken.

Mr. Talbert worked with us initially using drum pads and the battered drums. Then it came to a point that Mr. Talbert stated that we were ready for advanced lessons which he could not provide. He subsequently arranged for us to take the subway to the Harlem YMCA to take lessons under Mr. Williams, who was working under a WPA program. We took lessons there each Thursday after school, for a period of six months. Mr. Williams taught us three skills enabling us to be good performers: firstly, the 24 basic drum rudiments, and secondly, how to correctly march while playing our parade drums, and lastly, how to read music. Our last lesson at the "Y" was on a Saturday afternoon. When we arrived back at the church a large committee of church members was there to greet us. They took us to the basement where we usually practiced. The darkness was broken not by the electric lights but by candles on two long white covered tables placed to form a "V", on which were evenly spaced 20 bugles adorned by a connecting, wide, red ribbon, from bugle to bugle. Where the two tables met to form the "V" there were neatly stacked on the floor six brand new parade snare drums with white webbed belts and with one pair of drum sticks placed on each parade drum. On the floor were two large bass drums, each with two beaters and carrying straps. Also included were two pairs of shiny 12-inch Zildjian Cymbals with wooden handles. This was a complete surprise to all of the scouts there. Mr. Talbert had not informed us about his request to the finance committee of the church for drums and bugles and their approval of the same. Following the presentation of the equipment to the scouts by church officials, ice cream and cookies were served to us, the drummers. The buglers were not there at that time. After eating, each of us was assigned a drum of our own. We then formed ranks and played a simple drum cadence. In that instance, when the sound reverberated throughout the immediate neighborhood, the church basement began to fill up with other kids. The enrollment in the scout troop tripled when word got around. After that, it became our regular routine to practice marching and playing those instruments in the basement. All of the kids involved worked hard – they knew that if they wanted to keep their place in the new drum and bugle corps they had better be able to perform. Otherwise, there were other kids waiting in the wings for their opportunity at neighborhood fame and glory.

Anniversary Day

We had our instruments and had honed our marching and playing skills, we were anxious to show everyone what we could do. An opportunity to do so soon arose. The second Thursday in June was called Anniversary Day. As I remember it, it was a day when all of Brooklyn celebrated the founding of Sunday schools. No doubt about it, this day was a very important one to all the church schools, Boy Scout and Girl Scout troops, and other parade participants. But it was more important to the various Drum and Bugle Corps than to any other organized marching group, black or white, because of the competition that naturally arose between them as they performed in front of the crowds. The big parade would kick off in Brooklyn at the same time each year - 2:00 p.m. However, there was a process of meticulous preparation that began much earlier. To begin with, my mother had to wash, starch and iron my suit while I ran out to get a haircut. Then I returned to shine and spit polish my shoes. I'd then take a bath, oil my hair, rub vaseline on my face, hands and arms. I then put on my BVD's, a popular one piece underwear, and ran down to a breakfast, usually of hot cakes, sausage and milk. Afterwards I'd carefully put on my uniform which Mother had laid out on my bed. The pants would go on first because the lower legs had to be laced up first, the part that goes over the calf. My pants looked really neat blousing out on each side like the Canadian Mounties. Then I put on the brown stockings and put a three-inch fold at the top of each stocking. Mother had ironed a sharp crease down the center of each leg. I then put my stiffly starched shirt on with the troop number 197 in white on a field of red, emblazoned with numerous merit badges. Then came my kerchief held together around my neck with the official Boy Scout emblem ring. The last part of my uniform was the stiff, dented crown campaign hat. Man, I was looking so sharp. You couldn't tell me anything. By the time I was dressed there were several other scouts waiting for me downstairs. We greeted each other and, full of self-importance, strutted to the church. We were very mindful of the admiring looks and greetings from men, women, boys and girls. "Go get 'em, fellows. Show them that Bethany is the best." It was the custom for many of the churches to sponsor Boy Scouts and those with the right resources would also have Boy's Drum and Bugle Corps, Drill Teams, or Girl Scouts with drum and bugles too. There was, as I said, quite a bit of natural competition between these groups, and we were ready to do our best.

Altogether, I participated in five of these Anniversary Day parades and each one was a thrill. But none was ever more exciting than the first, when I didn't completely know what to expect. By 1:15 p.m. that day crowds began to gather – everybody was dressed up in their Sunday best. Little girls were dressed all in white, sporting colorful ribbons and showing off their Shirley Temple curls. By 2:00 p.m. the crowd was six or seven people deep, impatient for the start of the festivities. Finally, the drum major blew his whistle, raised his baton, and held it high for a few seconds. Then with a fancy kick, turn-about face, he brought his baton down with a flourish, signalling the drummers to start their cadence. The response was a joyous shout from the crowd. The parade route would carry the corps for two miles in one direction, followed by a left turn, then another two miles. This was repeated two more times and the parade would wind up where it started. Things went relatively smooth for the first leg of the parade. The drummers were crisp. They snapped off their rudiments with army precision. The buglers played with bell-tone accuracy. Our crowd had followed us from the start of the parade, pushing, shoving, and moving the other crowds out of the way. Then we heard them from a distance, something that sounded like distant thunder. In a few moments we saw them, the other parade. These were the "white" groups, consisting of the same units as ours. As both groups approached each other, our Drum Major shouted, "Let's give it to 'em, hard and loud." Immediately, our decibel level went up, arms were raised higher, hands gripped the drumsticks firmer and we drummers began to beat our drum heads unmercifully. Bugles were raised to the sky and all at once both of our Boys and Girls Drum and Bugle Corps struck up "The Muffin Man."

The noise was deafening as both groups were in juxtaposition to each other. Our drum major even marched back to our drum section and urged our bass drummers to keep the solid cadence. As the other group marched beside us, going in the opposite direction, I could see their drummers becoming confused. They hesitated, then briefly stopped to listen and try to pick up their cadence. But, alas, it was too late. We washed them away. As their whole line of musicians and marchers passed us by, we could see that everybody in their group was out of step. It was pure mayhem. They had to stop and regroup. I truly felt sorry for them, but this was the world of competition and we Boy and Girl Scout Drum Corps of the Bethany Baptist Church knew how to compete. Our hearts were light because we met the challenge and won, as we would do each of the following years that I participated. Four more miles of marching took us back to the parade's starting point. After being dismissed, we put our drums and bugles away, then hurried to the main fellowship room where we were greeted with huge bowls of ice cream, piles of sliced cake, slices of pie, cookies and gallons of homemade lemonade. After a few hours, we broke up into smaller groups and walked to the trolley. Destination, Prospect Park.

Prospect Park

Prospect Park was where many of the young people went after the big parade. There we could organize ourselves into teams to play softball, horseshoes, shoot baskets, partake of certain carnival rides, and, in general have a good, old-fashioned time until evening when the fireworks would begin. However, everything was not always peaches and cream with these outings at the park. In some parts of the park, a few gangs would take this time to hold initiations into their particular group. These groups did not mind people checking this ritual out. We would be sure to stand close enough to see, but far enough away to get a good, running start, if needed. We were "privileged," and I use this word advisedly, to observe one of the local gangs there inducting several new members into their exclusive group. Their members formed into two files about four feet apart with each member holding a thick leather belt. The aspiring member, after receiving a resounding whack on his backside, started running this gauntlet. The idea was to run as fast as one could so as to receive fewer blows. If the runner tripped and fell by accident or intention, he was beaten until he either got up and finished the course or ran away. I would like to make mention here that although these gangs were bullies and intimidating, they seldom used knives or guns. Most altercations were settled by fists. However, the gangs odds were four or five to one in their favor.

19

Color Guard

Early in the Summer before the seventh grade I was ready to make good on the promise I had made to myself nearly a year before. Competition for all positions, including drummer, in the Color Guard was scheduled to take place in June. At least six drummers showed up for the competition. The test was really quite simple. Each of us had to strap on the drum, play a simple cadence, mark time in place and then march about 30 yards and turn around. One by one the other drummers were eliminated for one reason or another. Most of the drummers-to-be had two left feet. Others couldn't play and turn around at the same time. My six months with Mr. Williams, all the practicing in the basement, and the experience of performing in public really paid off. I was able to go through the required drills without any problems and was selected to be the new Color Guard drummer. I was so happy – I had set a goal for myself, worked hard to accomplish it, and succeeded. It was one of the most gratifying moments in my young life up to that time.

Starting To Swing

While I was studying and experimenting with the two main arts of drumming for me, parade and concert, mainly with the Boy Scouts, I met a drummer named Ernie Stewart. Now Ernie was a musician whose drumming came to him naturally; he could coordinate both feet and hands beautifully to keep time, however, Ernie could not "read a lick." He was a member of one of the many local neighborhood bands. It was at an afternoon jam session that I first heard and saw Ernie play, and it was at this jam session that I decided to learn this "new" form of drumming. After the session ended, I strode over to where Ernie was starting to pack up his drums. I introduced myself and told Ernie how much I enjoyed his playing. Ernie looked me up an down and said, "You a drummer man?" "Yeah," I replied, but hastily added, "Only parade and concert so far." As it happened, Ernie had not yet broken down his bass drum, pedal or Hi-Hat. Ernie must have noticed my intense gaze at his bass drum and Hi-Hat setup. He extended his hand and as we shook, he said, "Want to try them out?" Then he said, "Wait a second, I'll set up the snare drum for you also." He then went to his drum case, pulled out the snare drum, set it on a drum stand between the bass drum foot pedal and the hi-hat. "Go on, take a seat," he said. I then took the drumsticks he handed me and started playing some drum rudiments on the snare drum. I did a smooth press roll, a bunch of ratamacues and paradiddles. "Use you feet," he yelled. I stopped playing, looked at him and said, "I don't know how." Ernie was silent for a moment and finally said, "Get up, sit in that folded chair next to the bass drum and watch my feet." As I complied, he asked me, "Do you have a set at home?" "No," I replied. "Well," he said, "what I'm going to show you, you can practice and get good at without a set. Now pay close attention to my feet; this is how the basic time-beat is kept, you've got to master this technique." Then he proceeded to demonstrate. "Place the right foot on the foot pedal and slowly beat the bass drum with a steady, nonstop, one-two-three-four, one-two-three-four. Now you do this moving your right foot up and down on the floor."

I did this for about a minute, and Ernie said, "Good, now keep your right foot going as I talk. Now with your left foot, let it beat with your right foot... but only on the 2nd and 4th counts. In this manner you should say to yourself - right, together, right, together." After a few shaky starts and stops, Ernie looked over at my feet, which were in snyc with his and exclaimed, "Hey man, that's it, keep it going." This I did for a full five minutes. Ernie then said, "Boots, that's your name, right? Well, you've got to learn to do that until it becomes second nature to you, so that you don't even have to think about it. Now talk to me and keep your feet going in a steady beat." This I did and asked him about my hands. "Take your left hand and slap your thigh on the 2nd and 4th beats with your left foot." Soon I had all three of my appendages going. "Now take your right hand and play three quick pulses with it starting on the 2nd beat, it should sound like this, Dat-Ta-Dah, Dat-Ta-Dah, etc., so that the "Dat" is always on the 2nd and 4th beats and the "Dah" is always on the 1st and 3rd beats. Soon I had both feet and hands coordinated, yet working independently. "OK Boots, let's go to the set and put it all together." I then sat behind the drums and was just about to start when Ernie yelled, "Don't forget, your right hand plays the Dat-Ta-Dah on that big 'ride cymbal' attached to the bass drum. Soon, I had a very solid rhythm going. Then to my amazement, I felt a reinforced pulse which sounded with my steady bass drum beat. I looked around and there was a bass fiddle player accompanying me. Shortly thereafter, I heard a trumpet player playing very softly and plaintively with a mute (I later learned that we were playing a slow blues). Oh, I was so happy, then all of a sudden I panicked - suppose I get out of rhythm? How do I end the song? I looked over the Ernie and he was smiling and clapping his hands along with several people (some were even dancing). I knew it was ending when the trumpet player, directing us with his left hand while playing with his right said, "Going", and we all ended together and oddly enough, I automatically played a long, soft press roll, holding same until the trumpeter moved his arm with flourish thus signalling the end. Ernie was elated. We both started talking at the same time. Finally, I thanked him profusely and we both exchanged addresses and telephone numbers. Ernie then said to me, "Boots, I can tell by your smooth roll and the other stuff you played that you are a trained conventional drummer and you can read music, right?" "Yeah," I said. "I can read and I just took the test given by the National Association of Rudimental Drummers. I can play 21 rudiments and I know the Army 2/4 solo from memory." "Man," Ernie replied, "I've got an idea Boots. Suppose you teach me how to read, I can't read at all. And in exchange, I'll help you with your swing drumming." "That's a fair deal," I said as we shook hands again. On my way out of the building a young man stopped me and said, "Hi fella, my name is Al Bounds, and I've just started a band. So far I've got a full reed and brass section along with a piano and bass. All I need is a drummer. I heard you a few minutes ago and I know you're just right for my group." I said, "Wow, thanks for the compliment, but I don't even have a set of my own yet." Al said, "Don't worry. For the time being I'll rent a set for your use. I'll have to keep it at my house, however." I said, "OK." Then he told me where and when practice would be. I was thrilled with the idea of joining this community of musicians, and extending my drumming into this new area.

I went home and told my mother and aunt what had happened to me. I then knew what I had to do. I called Mr. Talbert, my scoutmaster, and asked him if I could borrow that old foot pedal the Scouts owned. Mr. Talbert said yes and met me at the church to give it to me. I then went to the local Sheffield Dairy, just a few blocks away, and asked the watchman if he had any old milk crates around with a solid bottom, that he could spare. Again, luck or fate was with me and I gleefully lugged that heavy crate home. Soon I had rigged up a makeshift practice drum set. The crate was my bass drum, to which I attached the foot pedal. I then set my practice pad on a short, small stool between my legs, to serve as my snare drum. And finally, I placed two pieces of wood together for my left foot to hit; this was my hi-hat. On that hot summer day in July, I started out on my personal odyssey to learn swing drumming. I was relentless in my practice. Each and every day, including Sundays, I would practice three, four, even five hours. I would forgo hanging out with the gang. I asked Mother and Aunt Bert not to disturb me or to let my friends interrupt me. At practice time, usually in the heat of the day, I would sit at my "set" in shorts and perspire freely as I whipped my hands and feet into shape.

Several times a week I would get together with Al Bounds and the other members of his band for practice sessions with real drums and real music. It was there that I started reading "Big Band" swing charts. Occasionally I would get together with Ernie Stewart who also helped me with my 'swing' techniques, but most of my time was spent rehearsing with Al Bounds. Songs like *King Porter Stomp*, *Jumping At The Woodside*, and *Moton Swing*, were quite challenging for me. My strength was the driving beat that I had. Nobody, and I mean nobody, can teach you how to swing with the feeling that drummers must have in order to move a big band. This feeling a drummer has flows naturally from his heart through his hands and feet to the drums. The highest praise a swing drummer can get is for the other musicians to refer to him as having "soul" and "can really cook."

The Al Bounds Orchestra practiced with increased intensity in preparation for our first gig at a local recreation center for youth. Finally, "Gig Day" came around. Boy was I nervous and anxious. I arrived at the school in time to see a whole lot of boys and girls milling about laughing and talking – all waiting for the doors to open. "Wow," I said to myself, "all those people waiting for me to play." I was very excited as I made my way around to the side entrance. Al had already set up the drums – he insisted on doing that himself because some other drummer had messed up his high-hat by forcing two pieces of metal together that did not fit. This ruined the high-hat for that performance and the band suffered. Soon, all of the members arrived and we arranged ourselves and started tuning up. We were assembled on a stage in the auditorium and the curtains were drawn. A short while later we could hear the people through the curtains. All of a sudden, the bright lights were dimmed and we were flooded in hues of bright red and blue from the stage lights. An announcer was talking in front of the curtains – then I heard him say very loud, "Ladies and gentlemen, I give you Al Bounds and his Orchestra." With that, the curtains parted and I saw a throng of people gathered in front of the stage – all cheering and clapping their hands. I was mesmerized; I almost missed the downbeat given by Al. We hit that first note of Count Basie's *Jumpin' at the Woodside* with such force that I looked at the snare drum to see if I had put a hole in it. To my relief, I had not. Immediately, the people paired off and started doing the jitterbug. That was one glorious night – I had earned my title as a big band drummer.

All in all I remained with Al for almost a year. Word soon got around that I was an up and coming drummer. It wasn't long before other, more experienced bands, were vying for my services. Soon I left the Al Bounds Orchestra and joined the Harold Cabbell Orchestra. Harold's Band was much more advanced and had a higher level of difficulty – mainly because Harold wrote some wonderful, difficult, original arrangements.

Drums Of My Own

As the year went on, more and more of my time was being devoted to my interest in drumming, and I was getting pretty good at it, but all of my instruments were either begged or borrowed. None were mine personally, so I never had a chance to practice with actual drums at home. Finally, in the spring of my 7th grade year, I was offered a choice between summer camp in Virginia, or receiving a complete drum set which was on sale at the Wurlitzer's Music Company. Both the camping session and the cost of the drum were the same price, one hundred and twenty-five dollars. As fate would have it, I chose the set. I was given permission by both my mother and my aunt to call the music store before going to school, and to my joy and happiness, they promised to deliver the drum set that same afternoon. Needless to say, school was a waste for me that day. All I could think about was getting home to that drum set. Finally, the dismissal bell rang, and I was out of that school like a flash. I ran all the way home. The set was scattered all over the floor. It was a labor of love to assemble it.

Following my purchase of the drums from Wurlitzer's, I began taking private lessons at the store at 25 cents a lesson. It was there that I learned how to coordinate both feet and both hands, and the term, quadridextrous, became internalized in my way of life. At Wurlitzer's they had practice rooms set up for all sorts of instruments, and had a program called "music minus one" which consisted of records of popular songs that included everything but the instrument you were learning to play. You would play along with them, supplying the missing instrument. It was here, by playing along within the context of the other instruments, that I really learned how to play drums with "swing." At home I literally lit up Fulton Street with my all-day practices. I was pounding away in the back of my aunt's beauty parlor for 5 hours a day. Finally, my aunt, to save her sanity, arranged with Mr. Sandora, our building superintendent, to permit me to practice upstairs next door in the Knights of Columbus Hall. Mr. Sandora had a Duckpin Bowling Lane beneath. It was great practicing up there. My drums were set up on a small platform. The large picture windows were open and I was able to "enthrall" the neighbors with my diverse rhythms.

Neighborhood Life

We spent most of our free time out in the neighborhood, which pretty much had everything we needed to amuse and entertain ourselves. The adults left us alone, although we were never completely out of their sight, so we had to learn to work with each other to organize our activities, and we had to learn to settle our own differences. We had fun and we had fights, and we tested each other, and without realizing it, I think we learned a lot about leadership and cooperation in the process. We had the movies to escape to, but even that was a neighborhood activity. It wasn't something that you did alone. I remember in particular the fun we had attending the local movie theaters. The Apollo was our favorite. It was directly across the street from where I lived at the corner of Fulton Street and Throop Avenue. The Art was the theater we would go to if we wanted to see, what we called, "Shoot 'Em Ups" or cowboy pictures. For ten cents we could see three cowboy pictures and a chapter of a serialized adventure or melodrama. The *Apollo* did at least show the class "A" films, even if they were at least seven months late. I recall being treated to the *Apollo* by my aunt when I graduated from elementary school... I saw Clark Gable in *Mutiny On The Bounty*, and there I fell in love with his girlfriend. I never saw her in any other picture, but I'll never forget her face. Going to the movies was an extremely popular activity at this time - which was at the height of the Great Depression. For many people it was a way to take their minds off their problems for a couple of hours and escape from the hardships they were enduring. Of course, for us kids, we didn't really need to escape from anything. The movies were just a great place to have fun and share the adventures of the people on the screen.

The Apollo had a special section for kids which was located in front of the right section and extended about 25 rows back. Needless to say, this was the section which earned the attention of all of the male ushers. No matter what, you would see the ushers come down our aisle and shine his flashlight on some unruly boy or girl. The usual show fare was two feature films followed by the movie-tone news, a chapter of Flash Gordon, then a short comedy featuring the Three Stooges, ending with coming attractions. Usually the children's section was relatively quiet during the first complete show. However, when the picture started repeating, the kids section would erupt. Boys would yell out, "Don't kiss that girl!" or "The guy with the briefcase is the murderer." Thus spoiling the ending for everyone else in the theater. This really kept the ushers busy and I'm loathe to report that they zeroed in on me each and every Saturday. One usher who knew my mother and aunt would shine his flashlight on me and would yell, "Alright, Boots. C'mon with me." Then to hoots and howls of delight, he would march me up the aisle, out of the theater, across the street and deposit me in my aunt's beauty parlor. Now my aunt loved me dearly, but she would not stand for any nonsense from me. As soon as I was in the beauty parlor Aunt Bert would say, "Keep right on walking to the wash room. Get yourself cleaned up. I've got a few things for you to do." So I did a lot of extra work in the beauty parlor – shampooing, washing towels, disinfecting utensils. It also became known among my aunt's customers that I had strong wrists and fingers (from all on my drumming practice), so many of them requested that I give them shampoos because I could be very firm with my fingers and this was good for their scalps. My Uncle Earl also worked with me. Our pay was twenty-five cents each. We would then walk down to Woolworth's 5 and 10 cents store where each of us would get a 10 cent bag of sugar coated peanuts.

The Depression seems not to have had too big an impact on our lives as far as I can tell. My aunt and mother had their own beauty shops that seemed to take care of their needs. And the little bit of money we needed as kids seemed to be available one way or another. But at the same time I do remember some of the things we would do to save what we could. During this time refrigerators were not common. Instead we used ice boxes. Most families bought ice from the icehouse or the truck that came by each day. Some Saturdays when Earl and I went to Woolworth's, we would take a small wagon that we had made. It was a simple wagon made up of four carriage wheels and axles, a wooden milk crate and a piece of two by four. We would go to the Sheffield Milk company which was located three blocks from our home. Each time the milk trucks would return, they would discard the ice on their trucks before going into the garage. People would be lined up trying to get the huge chunks of discarded ice. Usually we were able to bring enough ice back to last us for several days.

Another opportunity to save money was provided by the Tastee Bakery, which was within about ten minutes walking distance. Next to the main entrance was the Bakery's Day Old Store. For a nickel, one could get day old loaves of bread, cup cakes, coffee cakes, etc. For twenty-five cents, one could get enough bread and cake to last a family of four for a week.

There was another way that we youngsters got money. After the subway was put in, grates about four feet by eight feet were placed over the wells, which were dug in the sidewalks. The procedure to follow to secure extra money was as follows: First, you and your buddy had to get the needed items which included a sturdy, wide bottom lock, a 20 foot piece of kite cord, two packs of chewing gum and a book of matches. Both of us would start out looking through the slots in the grates for coins. One would be chewing a piece of gum. As soon as a coin was spotted through the grate, one of us would take the gum , stick it on the bottom of the lock which has the 20 ft. piece of cord attached to it, strike a match and heat the gum. Then the lock is lowered through the slots in the grate until it is over the coin. The lock is then raised slightly and dropped on the coin. Finally, the lock is pulled up through the grate with the coin stuck to the gum. The coin becomes the property of the retriever. Within a mile, if no other team has worked those grates, we could find up to five dollars in change.

Racism

During the hot summer nights in Brooklyn, it often happened that our group, including six or seven boys and girls, just walked around having fun. We would stop and talk with other boys and girls, and, in

26

general have a truly good time. Well, on this particular evening we picked a different route, going nowhere in particular when one of the girls said, "Let's go by Bruggeman's. I hear that they have opened up a new ice cream parlor." We all agreed and now with a purpose, we all headed for Bruggeman's located on upper Sumner Avenue. This was one of the main thoroughfares in the Bedford-Styvesant section of Brooklyn. We could smell the wonderful smells of the ice cream parlor when we were a block away. Boy, we were in the mood for some ice cream. When we reached the store, which was a few blocks into a white neighborhood, we filed in. Some took seats in the wire back chairs which were around quaint, marble-topped tables. Others were seated at the soda bar. The waitresses were adorned with regular uniforms that had short white aprons and each wore a sort of doily in her hair. One of the waitresses came to our table and said, "I'm sorry we can't take your order." This same remark was repeated to our group who sat at the soda bar. Before we could respond, a man came from the back and said to the waitress at the bar, "Serve them soda, then get them out of here." Well, I got up and said, "Let's go gang. We can spend our money someplace else." One of the girls in our group said, "Yeah, we don't want his nasty, old junk anyway." Well, in the meantime, three of the boys with us at the bar put down their glasses. As we walked out of the store we saw Mr. Bruggeman smashing those glasses the three boys had used by throwing them into a large trash can. I cannot begin to tell you the humiliation and hurt I felt. Even to this day when I think back on that night, I can still hear the brittle sound of crashing glasses, all because they had been touched by black boys. That following week, we learned that the local chapter of the NAACP had already filed a complaint about Bruggeman's and was planning to picket the store in protest. Well, we decided in our elementary way to express our displeasure with Bruggeman's. Each evening for about a week we would go to his store and yell epithets through his door. The more daring of us would go to the entrance and yell some remarks questioning Bruggeman's maternal ancestry. Sometimes we would really get to him and he'd come out with a baseball bat raging like a bull. He would chase us for about a half block but we were too fast and went in too many directions. We were not the only group of young people he had offended, and others engaged in similar protests. In the end he eventually sold out to another owner, and we were then able to receive service under the new management, though we went there infrequently. We didn't really care about the store, it's just that we didn't want to see Mr. Bruggeman get away with treating us like that, and to our satisfaction, he didn't. That was a somewhat hollow victory though, because other Bruggemans were always there to be found.

My Sundays

As I recall my youthful days in Brooklyn, I am thankful that the group with which I was connected centered its activities around the church, music and the Boy Scouts. I am not certain that we were all that religious, but nevertheless, the majority of our waking hours involved all of the aforementioned. Not only were we involved in the church on Sundays, we were involved at the Church throughout the week as well. A typical Sunday would require our group being in church or Sunday School five separate times as follows: Morning Sunday school ran from 9:30 a.m. to 10:30 a.m. This was followed by the morning church service with hours from 11:00 a.m. until 1:30 a.m. At this service many of our group sang on the Junior Choir. As for me, I served on the Usher Board. I guess the white gloves, red sash and the usher medallions reminded me of a uniform and I did love uniforms. Also, walking up and down the aisle with my arm behind my back and directing parishioners to their seats was just my style. Then, at 2:00 p.m. several of us met around the corner from the church at Mrs. Flora Douglass' apartment where the Salvation Army held Sunday School. Mrs. Flora had five boys and she was very anxious for them to be our friends and to attend church with us. Now, her five boys were always in some type of situation. I didn't follow them but we treated each other cordially. I must herein confess that I attended the Salvation Army Sunday School for two main reasons. One was that Mrs. Douglass always baked the finest pound cake. This she always served with ice cream at the close of the class which was around 3:00 p.m. The second reason was that the Salvation Army had a wonderful combination marching and concert band, which met every Wednesday downtown. The lure for me with this band was the fact that I was playing with adults and the music was incomparable. Even today I am of the opinion that the Official Salvation Army Band is in a class by itself. Our groups fourth commitment on Sundays was to attend the B.Y.P.U. (Baptist Young People's Union). This was a fun group to belong to. We planned picnics, and did community work like giving food baskets to the needy at holiday times. The meeting would be from 6:00 p.m. until 7:00 p.m. The fifth and last attendance at church would be for the evening service which was held from 8:00 p.m. until 9:15 p.m. So you can see there wasn't much time in our young lives for devilment on Sundays. Our time at church during the week involved scout meetings, drum and bugle corps practice, and choir rehearsals. Also, three other boys and myself, on a dare, formed a religious quartet. We called ourselves the "Golden Leaf Quartet". We only learned two selections, *Take My Hand, Precious Lord* and *Jacob's Ladder*. However, we were asked to sing for every special activity at the church. I convinced the group that we could be even more effective if we marched in from the rear of the church up to the front, singing as we went along. This went over real big with the churchgoers. The announcer would say, "Ladies and Gentlemen, here are Bethany Baptist Church's own, the Golden Leaf Quartet, featuring: Richard Wallace, first tenor, LeRoy Battle, second tenor, Edward Horton, baritone, and Harry Shorts, bass." Then you would see all of the heads turn around in eager anticipation of our procession.

"Teaching" Experience

In addition to working as a beautician, my mother would cook and serve dinner for several wealthy, white families. Mother always carried herself with class and dignity, and was often in demand for these kinds of engagements. One day mother and Mrs. Swanson for whom mother was serving dinner that night, were talking about their sons when the subject of music came up. It seemed that Mrs. Swanson's son, who was also in seventh grade, had aspirations of becoming a drummer and she, his mother, was in the process of looking for an instructor to give her son private lessons. Mother immediately volunteered my services, and must have done a pretty good job selling them on the idea that I was a fairly accomplished drummer myself, because that following Monday after school, I was on the "El" train, headed for my first "professional" teaching job. The family lived in the Bensonhurst section of Brooklyn. At that time Bensonhurst was noted for being the place housing wealthy white people. I must have presented quite a sight to onlookers, as a scruffy little black kid strolling through their neighborhood carrying a drum pad and sticks. I finally arrived at the given address. There was a small metal sign in the grass that said, "Entrance to the Doctor's Suite in the Rear." I continued around the large house until I reached a door which stated, "Ring Bell and Enter." As I stepped through the door, I was greeted with the sight of a room full of patients. All of whose eyes popped out of their heads at the sight of me. The receptionist quickly picked up the telephone, said a few words, and before I could ask any questions, another door opened and a distinguished looking man with a full head of black and silver hair extended his hand and said, "Hello, Mr. Battle. I'm so glad that you could come and give Bobby his lesson. Just go up those stairs to the dining room. I'll be up shortly." The "perplexed looks" hung in the air behind me as I disappeared up the stairs. I dare say that very few of them had ever been invited "upstairs".

When I entered the dining room, a very gracious lady came through some swinging doors and said, "Hello, LeRoy. Your mother has told me all about you and your music. She's very proud of you. Kindly take a seat and I'll send Bobby right down." Then she went to another room, and within a few seconds, Bobby appeared. His mother asked me whether I would like to teach Bobby out on the porch or in the dining room. I chose the latter, because of the very large table on which we could place our drum pads. When Mrs. Swanson left us alone, we sort of looked at each other, sizing each other up. It occurred to me right away that I would have to gain Bobby's respect, and the best way to do this was to execute some flashy drum rudiments. So I started off with a long, hard, fast single-stroke roll. My wrists and sticks were a flying blur. Then, without stopping, I went into single, double, and triple ratamacues. Bobby's eyes widened as he interrupted me saying, "That's great. How can I learn to do that?" I smiled and told him to do a long roll. He gave me a very scratchy, uneven rendition. I stopped him and then laid out a plan for him to practice. I then said to him, "You've got to practice. You know, of late I've noticed that many drummers aren't willing to make the sacrifice and practice really hard." "'Of late'," he said, "I've never heard that. Where did you get that from?" And he went on and on about having never heard the phrase, 'of late'. Just about then, Bobby's father came up from his office and said, "So, how are you boys getting along?" "Dad, get this," Bobby said, "LeRoy used the term 'of late'." "Tell him he's wrong." Bobby's father said, "To the contrary, son, 'of late' is a very sophisticated term used in the place of 'lately'." That answer more than satisfied Bobby. He and I, from that point on, got along fabulously well. I tutored him for over a year and prepared him to successfully compete for and subsequently become a member of his high school band, at the then unheard of, exorbitant fee of seven dollars per lesson, plus carfare. I also learned how gratifying it could be to pass your knowledge and skills onto someone else, and to know the respect and gratitude you could earn from your students and others. The experience opened my eyes to other possibilities for my career – before my only interest in learning was to be able to perform, now I had a parallel interest in being able to teach others what I had learned.

On To Hamilton High

It was a great day for our group when we were all promoted to the 8th grade. This meant that we would attend the Alexander Hamilton High School, located on Albany Avenue and Bergen Street. Hamilton was an all-boys school. At that time, Brooklyn schools were for the most part separated as follows: Boy's High, Girl's High, Boy's Commercial, and Girl's Commercial. The schools would plan coed activities together, and competition between schools was very intense. Hamilton's arch rival was Boy's High. Our school's colors were scarlet and gray. Boy's High colors were red and black. On football days, the stands on both sides were very colorful. There were so many boys enrolled at Hamilton that the school was put on double session. Juniors and seniors would attend classes from 8:00 a.m. until 11:45 a.m. Freshmen and sophomores would attend from 1 p.m. to 5:00 p.m. Special activities such as orchestra and chorus would meet between 11:45 a.m. and 12:45 p.m. One morning as I walked around the top of the auditorium, (the stage was at the bottom with aisles leading up to the top) I noticed the orchestra rehearsing. Wow! There were about 60 students making heavenly music. I was mesmerized, so much so, that I sat down listening for the entire period. (Actually, I cut a class unintentionally.) After rehearsal, I bounded down to the stage and introduced myself to the conductor, Mr. Zeiner, a German from "the old country" as the saying goes. I let Mr. Zeiner know that I wanted to be a part of this group. He looked me directly in the eye and asked, "Do you have any talent? What instrument do you play?" I said, "Sir, I can play the drums." Just then the late bell sounded and Mr. Zeiner said, "Don't worry about being late. I'll give you a note. Now here's what I want you to do. Go to that snare drum and play me five rudiments." Now this was great with me because while a Boy Scout drummer, I had taken lessons from Mr. Williams at the Harlem Y.M.C.A., and continued to develop my skills in the Boy Scout Marching Band. After I demonstrated the rudiments, Mr. Zeiner asked me to read a Sousa march, which I stumbled through. Afterwards he said, "LeRoy, you know we do not have any colored pupils in the orchestra. I don't know why. Are you dedicated? I do not believe in wasting time. I had to literally fight with the administration to get this rehearsal time so our rehearsals must be of the highest quality. LeRoy, I like your style. I think you can make a positive contribution to our efforts." Then he told me to report to rehearsal the next day. Later, a few days after my introduction to the orchestra, a Mr. Chauncey came over to me and asked had I ever considered joining the school's marching band. I said, "No, I haven't thought about it because I've been so busy with the orchestra." Mr. Chauncey then explained that the band met after school from 5:30 p.m. to 6:30 p.m. I told Mr. Chauncey that I would attend band rehearsal after the upcoming orchestra concert. Mr. Zeiner was a very strict director, a perfectionist. Rehearsals really kept one on edge. He kept a small box of broken chalk on his conductor's stand and if you made a glaring mistake, he'd take a piece of chalk and throw it at you and holler, real loud, "You poop. Why can't you understand?" His aim was pretty good, too. It was hilarious to see the French Horn section ducking as they were playing, the chalk flying over their heads to the trombone or drum section.

General Music

The general music classes at Hamilton High were something to behold. The students were not scheduled to individual classes as they are today. At Hamilton, all students who took general music were scheduled at the same time in the auditorium. There we sat by grade level. There was one teacher, Mrs. Carey, who occupied the stage with a Steinway grand piano. Mrs. Carey, as I now think about it, was a great teacher. She controlled that auditorium and there were at least 250 of us students. The first day she had us stand up a row at a time and took us through various vocal exercises. She then arranged our seating according to our voice range, 1st tenor, 2nd tenor, baritone, and bass. The second day she informed us that we were going to give a production of the operetta, *Pinafore*. She passed out a whole outline of the operetta and indicated what special voices she would need to perform the lead parts. Mrs. Carey was also working with the girls at our sister school. Boy, it was beautiful to hear all of these male voices singing the chorus parts. Those students she selected for the solo parts would do so from the stage. For that year we performed *Pinafore* and *Madame Butterfly*. Our success was due to the splendid teaching of Mrs. Carey. She was quite an imposing person. She was tall, platinum blonde and her voice reminded one of Ethel Merman. I'll never forget her. Even to this day I can sing many parts to those two operettas. When it was performance time, the public was seated up in the balcony of the auditorium. The seated chorus members wore blue and white colored clothes. Mrs. Carey said we could mix and match any way we desired. Those main characters on the stage had their costumes which were made by the Home Economics Department of the girl's school. The sets were made and painted by the Boy's Art and Woodworking Departments. On this opening night, jitters were everywhere. The crowd was getting larger and larger. Mrs. Carey was in the lobby shooing the performers to their correct seats. Some students were hawking the programs, and the adults, parents and teachers, were really dressed for the occasion. Suits, ties, shined shoes were the required attire for the men. The ladies wore elegant dresses, gloves and jewelry. One could close his or her eyes and just imagine that they were at the opening of the Metropolitan Opera. Just then the lobby lights flickered, signaling that the overture was about to start. Inside the auditorium the lights were very dim, the stage was dark. However, there was a large spotlight shining on Mr. Zeiner and the orchestra which was on the floor below the stage. Mr. Zeiner raised his arms and the orchestra's response was of one accord. Everything came together. The solos and duets went off without a hitch. Opening night was one grand success.

Neighborhood Bands

While I was now deeply immersed in the study of classical and parade drumming at school with the orchestra and the marching band, I had spent my free time outside of school practicing with some of the numerous neighborhood bands ever since my first introduction to swing drumming by Ernie Stewart. There was a whole subculture of musicians and bands that was a very prominent aspect of the neighborhood. This community of musicians constituted a kind of loosely organized apprenticeship program, where one could hone his skills with groups of similar ability, and move up as you proved yourself ready to go to the next level. We could always go to this neighborhood or that to hear the local bands practice. You didn't have to know the exact address; the glorious thump of the bass drum and the sound of the music would lead you to the crowd and the apartment. My very good friend, Max Roach, who was establishing himself as the premier drummer, would rehearse on a certain night with his group. Usually the apartment would be on the top floor and the teenagers would crowd into the apartment, and cram the staircases all the way down to the street. Each neighborhood had one or two popular bands. The bands from different communities vied for top honors, or just plain bragging rights. Perhaps the best of the bunch was the Clarence Berry Orchestra. This was a full, 18-piece group, which played each Sunday night at the Sea Gull Beach in the Coney Island area. Cecil Payne, baritone saxophone, and Leonard Gaskins, acoustical bass, both from the band, went on to become famous professional musicians. Other local bands with large followings were the Al Bound's Orchestra, the band that I first began with; the Max Roach Orchestra; The Ray Nathan Band; the Harold Cabbell Group; Juancito and his Orchestra; and Eddie Bonnemere and the Manhattan Sextet.

This neighborhood band scene was only one part of the excitement that Brooklyn night life had to offer. On Friday nights in Brooklyn, at the busy intersections, one would find street corner orators talking about Jesus, the end of the world, and politics. We would sometimes wander from crowd to crowd listening to fiery speeches. There was one speaker who wore a long white robe and carried a long staff. He was berating the people and urging them to "Repent or burn in hell!" Well, we didn't stay long with that group. One Saturday night we went to see Prophet Costoni. He always had a huge tent for a week of revival. Prophet Costoni cut a very imposing figure, what with his tall, slender figure. He always wore a white turban with a large crystal in the middle. In addition, Prophet Costoni wore a gleaming white suit with a white satin cape. His tent was always filled and when he spoke you could hear him for blocks around because he had a very effective and loud public address system. We then left the tent revival and went up to see the small carnival on the grounds of St. Phillip's church. We couldn't get in because we didn't have ticket money, however, we found that we could scale the metal spikes which held the twelve-foot canvas walls to keep out prying eyes. We would be able to look down on the other side and see what was going on. Unfortunately for me, the guard came around to chase us away. In my haste to run, I let go of the rail I was holding, but failed to clear my upper inside arm. On my fall one of the spikes nicked that part of my arm and tore a piece of flesh. I was taken immediately to the St. John's Hospital where a new procedure involving a skin graft was performed on me. Needless to say, that incident put an end to my climbing curiosity.

Street Gangs

There was another, less constructive, reality of the neighborhood involving the presence of gangs and gang activities. Even for those who were not personally involved in gangs, it was impossible to avoid dealing with them entirely. It was almost a "rule of thumb" that 7 blocks in the Brooklyn equal one mile so this was one method that gangs used to measure their territory which amounted to approximately one square mile. There were neutral zones, like arteries: Fulton Street, Sumner Avenue, Eastern Parkway, and Nostrand Avenue. Neutral zones were set so a person could go to the grocery store, movies, schools, etc. The strongest gangs would cut across the boundaries for whatever reason. The Forty Thieves were the most feared in West Brooklyn. Snead and his gang were a huge problem in East Brooklyn. As the young people watched out for the gang members, they also tried to find different ways to earn money. The high school shop teacher helped out by letting the students make small shoeshine boxes. We would then go to the 5 and 10 cent store to outfit the boxes for about 50 cents with polish, cloth, shoe polish and sole dressing. Then we would set up our businesses at the entrances to the subway stations. One had to fight for his position. We would be 5 deep at each entrance. Shines were 5 cents. The best deal was to try to earn around $2.00 and then leave because if the Forty Thieves or Snead came around, you could have nothing.

Being a musician was a great help getting along with the gangs. When a group played together, sometimes the drummer would be from one gang, the saxophone player from another gang and the bassist would be from yet another gang. It didn't matter whether you were from this gang or that, or if you were black or white. It's just that you were a musician, and that you were good. Usually, that was enough to keep me out of trouble, but not always. My cousin, Eddie Ogburn, lived in the Flatbush section of Brooklyn. Eddie was a smooth operator. He looked like Bryant Gumbal, only he sported a mustache. He was handsome and very popular with the females. Eddie wasn't a member of the gang, but he had the smooth gift of gab and the gang respected him and his father. His father was an ordained priest in the Episcopal Church. Reverend Ogburn could always be seen talking with boys and girls on street corners, counseling them, urging them to attend church. On this particular Sunday Eddie urged me to attend church with him. Afterwards, we were to have a large family dinner at his house. As we both sat down in the church pew, I couldn't help but notice this sweet-looking, angelic face framed by a mass of flowing, jet-black hair. "My Goodness," I thought. "She's looking at me." My heart skipped a beat, my eyes focused more to be certain that she was looking at me. I risked a slight smile, and yes, I received one in return. I nudged Eddie and started to fill him in and asked questions about the young lady. Eddie looked at the girl, shushed me up and said he would introduce us after the service. Finally, after the longest service I had ever sat through came to an end, Eddie said to me, "She just moved into the neighborhood last month." (I noticed the young lady going with the chorus, probably to put their robes away.) Eddie continued, "Man, all the cats have been trying to get close to her. She's friendly, but will not go steady with any of us. You still want to meet her?" "You bet," I said. So after about five minutes we saw this beautiful angel emerge from a side door, "dressed to kill" as the saying went. We hurried over to where she was and Eddie said, "Hi, Doris. The chorus sounded very good this morning." Doris looked at us both (I thought I would go through the floor) and said, "Why, thank you." Eddie cleared his throat and said "Doris, I want you to meet my cousin, Boots." Doris put out a white, gloved hand and said, "Hi, this is the first time I've seen you around." Eddie said quickly, because he knew I had lost my voice, "No, Boots lives in the Bed-sty section of Brooklyn." Then I asked Doris if she lived far away from the church to which she replied, "No, just one block or so away." Then I said, "It's such a lovely day. Why don't you permit Eddie and me (and I nudged Eddie with my elbow) to walk you home?" To which Eddie spoke up, "No, Boots, I've got to go home to help out. Dad has company coming. Why don't you walk Doris home, if that's okay with you, Doris?" And so, in a few minutes I was on cloud nine walking and talking with a dream girl. Boy, I knew I was looking sharp. I had on my navy blue gabardine suit and was wearing a light gray snap brim hat. A few minutes later we arrived at her stoop. She continued up a few more steps and I remained at the bottom. As I tipped my hat when we said our good-byes, I noticed a concerned look briefly cross her face. Then, as I turned around to start for Eddie's house a few blocks away, I immediately saw the reason for that dark look that crossed her face. There on the opposite sidewalk stood about ten boys who

3 5

weren't in "Sunday Best" dress. I started to skirt them to the right when a voice rang out, "Hey, man. Come here." "This was it," I thought. I couldn't outrun them and here I was alone in enemy territory. I just knew blood would flow and it would be mine. So I turned and walked toward the group determined not to let my fear show. All the boys were standing except one ragged looking dude with his cap askew and with dirty sneakers. I could see that he was the leader. I stood directly in front of him and as I looked down at him, he asked me, "What are you doing walking my girl friend home?" My mind wandered a bit at that because I couldn't picture Doris and this dreg together. A voice to the back of me said, "Why waste time on him, Snake? Let's goop him up." Their leader, Snake, waved his hand to silence the guy. "Where you from, man?" "Bed-sty," I answered. "What's your name, man?" "Boots," I tell him. "Well, Boots," he said, "You're trying to take my girl away from me, so you'll have to take your lumps. We don't have anything against Bed-sty but you're way out of your territory and what's more, you're messing with my girl. Just then one of the gang members said, "Are you the same Boots from Bed-sty who is a musician?" Immediately hope leapt into my heart. I couldn't see who was talking, so I turned and said to no one in particular, but loud enough for all to hear, "Yeah, that's me." "What instrument do you play?" he asked. "Drums," I said. Then I saw this slightly built gang member push himself through the bunch, extended his hand and said, "I know you, man. You play a mean set of drums. We sat in on a jam session at-" And before he could tell me where, I said, "It was at Ralph's Tavern and you play tenor sax. Man, you sure remind me of Coleman Hawkins. We could never figure how a guy so small could coax such a big sound out of that horn." I shook his hand and then he put his arm around my shoulder and said to everybody, "This is my buddy. You mess with him, you mess with me." Everybody laughed, and Snake said, "G'on, Pee-wee, anybody you vouch for is OK with us." Then Pee-wee said, "Where are you going, Boots?" I said I was going to my cousin's house for dinner. Pee-wee turned and said, "Who's your cousin?" "Eddie Ogburn," I replied. At that response, everybody said, "What," in amazement. I said, "Yeah. Rev. Ogburn is my uncle and Eddie is my cousin." Snake got up, came over to me and shook my hand. Then he said softly to me, "Doris isn't really my girl, Boots. You're welcome to come see her all you want."

The thing to bear in mind about my relations with gangs is that they never appealed to me. Gangs operated at the whim of a leader who more often than not obtained his or her positions by brute force. If the leader said, "Let's go over and teach this other gang a lesson," for little or no reason, you had to go and fight. I found this very distasteful. Gangs had to be ready at the drop of a hat. I remember being a member of a "pickup" band that was playing for a black dance. Everything was going along very nicely, that is, until some gang from across town just wandered by to look, when all of a sudden, the group we were playing for started yelling and swinging at the visiting gang. This led to one hectic melee. I didn't bother to stick around. I packed my drums and cut out.

With all my attentions devoted to my study of music, I didn't have any time for or interest in getting involved in the gang scene. There was always somebody in my family reminding me about the dangers of evil. Since mother and father divorced while I was of an early age, my Aunt Bert and Mother worked very hard to see that I would not be hurt by the experience. I had a strong sense of values instilled in me which had been enforced and re-enforced by my participation in the Boy Scouts, church, Sunday School, elementary and high school activities. In all of these groups, the emphasis was always on progress, both individual and group. After the fulfillment I had found in working with others to create moments of excellence and beauty, the thought of robbing a person or a store couldn't hold a candle to the holistic, magnificent chords of a Bach cantata or the beautiful dark tones of a Brahm's chorale.

I have explained all of the above to give one a better idea of what I was about. Yet, sadly, in spite of all the positive values and support, coupled with an honest effort to avoid the evils of the street, there came a time when gang trouble caught up with me anyway. On this particular evening, about four of my buddies and I were returning from a movie. We were approximately three blocks from home, when out of the blue, we were jumped by Snead and his gang. They had seen us from a distance and had hidden in a few doorways. I yelled to our group, "Let's get to the wall." This move enabled us to keep the thugs in front of us. We were swinging and landing punch for punch. "Don't go down," I yelled. It was very dark by now and the gang method of jumping was beginning to take its toll. There were about twelve of them, but they couldn't all get into the fray at the same time. The wall protected our backs, but we were tiring and I noticed my well-aimed punches were landing no more. My arms were just flailing. Just as we were about to be overrun, I felt somebody pull one of my attackers off of me. Then I heard a female voice scream, "Get out of here! Git! Git!" This was followed by a sickening thump. Snead and his gang beat a hasty retreat. Chasing them were my uncle and one of the operators from my aunt's beauty parlor. The operator was swinging a skate, holding it by the leather strap, and she was landing blows. Those guys didn't want any part of what turned out to be our reinforcements. Lillian and Uncle Earl told us that when we were jumped, an onlooker ran to my aunt's beauty parlor to get help, so Lillian and Earl responded as soon as they heard we were in trouble.

We were quite disheveled with torn shirts, scuffed-up shoes, bleeding knuckles, bruises, and whelps. But it was a good fight, even though we were outnumbered, three to one. Word got around that the Glenada Place group were no pushovers. (Glenada Place was where my friends hung out.) I am happy to say that Snead and his group never again attempted to attack us in our own territory. We usually went out of our way to avoid trouble, but, if confronted or cornered, we would fight.

Turning Pro

My first professional nonunion job came when I got a call from Harold Cabbell, who needed a drummer. Being asked to play with Harold represented a big promotion for me from the Al Bounds group I had started with. We played at supper club on 48th Street. It was there that I had my first experience on how music could sometimes cause ladies to express themselves in unique ways. We were playing Duke Ellington's *Creole Love Call* and I was playing a very earthy drum beat on my tom-toms when this lady left her dancing partner on the floor and came over to the bandstand. Never taking her eyes off me, she started to sway right and left, and at the same time, proceeded to raise her skirt with both hands, still gyrating to the drums. She exposed her lingerie, closed her eyes, and then her partner came and got her. That was my first introduction to the power of music over the senses, and I must say, that was quite an introduction for a fourteen-year old. My pay that night was $3.00, which my aunt proudly framed for me. Then I resolved to put in a little extra practice time on my tom-toms. The money and the experience hooked me – I was definitely going to become a professional drummer, whatever it took.

Other older musicians told me that to get "known in the music trade", I had to go where the action was, hence my introduction to the Rhythm Club, located on 132nd Street and 7th Avenue in Harlem. The Rhythm Club was a very important entity to the black entertainer (instrumental musicians, vocalists, tap dancers, etc.). As a person entered the main clubroom, to the left there was a lunch counter with five stools. A special is featured each day, usually chili-con-carne, or fried chicken, or bar-b-que, all served with homemade cornbread at a cost of 40 cents. To the right there were fifteen small round tables, with folding chairs at each table. Seated at the tables were a roomful of musicians playing cards to while away the time. On the back wall was a gigantic blackboard, on which an employee recorded "gigs" as they were phoned in. A typical entry would have said, "Two saxophones needed to play for a show at the Lincoln Theatre," or, "drummer needed for a private party, see dispatcher." In another smaller room one would see tap dancers practicing a dance routine. In yet another room one heard a tinkering piano accompanying voice students.

On Saturdays if I wasn't gigging with one of the neighborhood bands, I would gather up my drums (bass and snare), take the "A" train, and would arrive at the Rhythm Club around noon. I would play cards (usually tonk at 5 cents a game), eat, and watch the blackboard for any gig that could use a drummer. It was at the club that aspirants would get their contacts. Whether I got picked up that day or not, it was always an experience just hanging around the place with all the musicians that would come and go. Being there was an essential part of the training and exposure you needed to make contacts and move on in the business. The Rhythm Club is one of the places where we grew up.

Beating Different Drums

As intriguing as the jazz scene was, I loved parade and concert drumming too, and spent many hours with the school orchestra and marching band. I had an insatiable appetite for all kinds of music, and worked hard to master every aspect of my instruments' range. All my work, which seemed more like fun, really began to pay off when I was in my junior year at Hamilton High. I read about the Philharmonic Scholarship Contest, which was open to all juniors and seniors of high schools in the five boroughs of New York City, and decided to give it a try. Scholarships were offered in each instrumental specialty, and gave the winners an opportunity to study with one of the masters in their field. For drummers, the scholarship consisted of being able to study with the great Saul Goodman, tympanist with the New York Philharmonic Symphony Orchestra. Only one winner would be chosen from each borough. Contestants were instructed to meet at Carnegie Hall in Manhattan on Friday morning. I hit the subways, and they were crowded with rush hour traffic. I was running a bit late already because of the time I took loosening up for the contest. When I finally arrived at Carnegie Hall and found the specified entrance, my heart was beating double time. As I came to a huge glass door, a short, well dressed man emerged wearing a beautiful gray hamburg hat. I said, "Pardon me sir, is this the entrance to where the Philharmonic Scholarship tests are being held?" He stopped and peered at me with sharp, piercing eyes. At the same time, without intending to, I stared at him, eyeball to eyeball, still with the question on my face. He said as he pointed, "Up those stairs to the stage. Take a seat in order." I thanked him and raced up the flight of stairs and entered a brand new world. The stage was huge. In the corner was a chariot and spears. There were banks and banks of lights overhead and on the stage. I gazed up and saw the private boxes that disappeared into the darkness. Only the lights covering the stage were on. To the right of center stage there were groups of chairs filled with students. I made a quick count. There were around thirty students seated, all white, all dressed in suits, and there was one vacant chair. I, dressed in a tee shirt and shorts, ambled over and took a seat, last in line, and feeling more than a little intimidated and out of place. Directly in front of us and to our right there was a complete percussion section set up: tympani, bass drum, snare drum, cymbals, xylophone, and triangles. All of a sudden the lights in the auditorium lit up and there he was, the same gentleman who had given me directions a few minutes ago. He never introduced himself, but I now assumed that he was Mr. Goodman himself. He said, "Good afternoon, Gentlemen. You will find sticks and mallets on the drum trap table. The music I want you to perform is on each music stand." "To begin with, Drummer One, I want you to identify and play the following rudiments." He then listed several. Number One began to play but got all tangled up. Eventually he got through his required selection. He then went to sight-reading and faltered, badly. I was encouraged to see that the competition looked a lot better than it played. This routine went on for each contestant, only everything got harder. By the 25th student, Mr. Goodman had cut down on the number of rudiments he wanted us to do. Instead, he added more sight-reading with new music. In the meantime, it was getting real hot on that stage. The klieg lights were taking their toll. Perspiration was literally pouring off everybody. Finally, everyone before me had auditioned and it was now my turn. I knew I could perform better than the others, but I was still feeling a little shaky, and, to make matters worse, Mr. Goodman left his seat in the audience, came up on the stage and sat on a stool about five feet away from me. I went over to the trap table and picked up several drum sticks, tried them, put them down and tried others. "What are you doing?" Mr. Goodman asked. "I am trying to get a pair of sticks that feel comfortable," I replied. He looked at me and nodded his head. "Play a soft long roll for me." I complied. "Play an open single-stroke roll for me. Now play a double-stroke roll. Now show me a series of Flam-a-cues, then sight-read this section of "Scherazade". I was able to do that with a few glitches. After going through several concert selections and four or five Sousa marches, I was starting to get a bit agitated. He hadn't spent so much time or asked as much of the others before me, and the confidence I had started out with was beginning to wane. He was throwing out challenges to me so rapidly that I was starting to think he was intentionally trying to stump me or unnerve me. Finally Mr. Goodman said, "Okay, LeRoy, I've made up my mind. You will be awarded the Philharmonic Scholarship from the borough of Brooklyn. Meet here tomorrow, dressed in a suit." The next day we met at Carnegie

Hall. There were five of us there, representing each of the boroughs. There were photographers from the all the local papers who took individual photos of each of us. Reporters interviewed us and at the end of the day, our good fortune had been placed in the papers and told over the radio. It was wonderful to hear my name announced by the principal at Hamilton High and to receive the accolades of the students and teachers. I did study with Saul Goodman all of my senior year. Sessions with Mr. Goodman were held at Carnegie Hall twice a week after school.

Encouraged by my success at the Philharmonic competition, I decided to try out for the All-Borough Orchestra. This was where they selected the best musicians in the borough schools to form an "elite" High School Orchestra. Competition was rough. On the day of the selection we had to go to a neutral site, in this case, the Brooklyn Academy of Music. Each section was assigned to a particular room to be adjudicated. My test consisted of playing fifteen rudiments from the N.A.R.D. (National Association of Rudiment Drummers) which was one of the "Bibles" of drumming. Also, I was asked to sight-read charts selected by the examiner. My hard practice in the past served me in good stead for this experience. My orchestra teacher at Hamilton, Mr. Zeiner, had said to me, "LeRoy, the harder you practice, the luckier you will get." With all my practice and application of my studies, my techniques had improved greatly and I breezed through the exam. Finally, those musicians who were chosen filed into the main auditorium and took his or her appropriate position. Well, there was great joy in being chosen, attending special rehearsals and then performing for the Brooklyn Borough President and other dignitaries at a special concert.

Later that year, our school principal, Mr. Jacob M. Ross, received a notice announcing competition for the All-City Orchestra. Tryouts would be held in three weeks – we had to practice a selection and perform it, from memory. Time passed quickly and before I knew it, I was riding the subway to Manhattan. For the first time, I actually became apprehensive about the situation. Maybe it was because I wanted so much to be selected, or maybe after having so much success before, I was afraid everyone would expect me to be chosen again, and I didn't want to disappoint them. There was a stream of anxious high school musicians pouring into Carnegie Hall. I felt at ease a little because of my experience there when I won the Philharmonic Scholarship. As before, we were called one by one to perform in our particular sections. Many of the drummers were eliminated because they could not play more than one percussion instrument. Eyebrows were definitely raised when, after completing my requirements on the snare drum, I calmly went to the tympani, tuned the three of them according to the composition, then proceeded to play sections of Wagner, Berlioz and Copeland. Finally, after several hours, the complete orchestra was in place, and I had been selected to perform as part of the percussion section. There were close to seventy-five musicians sitting on the edge of their seats awaiting the conductor. Meanwhile, from my standing position in the percussion section in the rear, which was directly in front of the conductor's stand, I looked around and was completely awed. Here assembled were the best high school musicians in all of New York City. Yes, I had a very proud, but at the same moment, a very humble feeling. All at once I saw the first chair violinist stand and immediately, all the rest of the musicians stood. I was mildly shocked to see a young look-ing black man stride to the podium. He stood tall, looked at each sec-tion, and said, "Good afternoon, young people. My name is Dean Dixon and I will serve as your most attentive guide as we traverse this musical experience." He then outlined our practice schedule and saw to it that our folders were passed out. He introduced our assistant conductor whose job it was to see that everybody was on the same page. I felt a new feeling of independence with this group. We were performing at the highest level and, as such, we were treated as adults. There were no ifs, ands, or buts. We had our music and we were expected to per-form. Mr. Dixon really put us through our paces. He was a perfection-ist. Each musician practiced hard with the goal of being able to per-form at a higher level. In addition, one of my goals was not to be singled out by Mr. Dixon for failing to observe a rest, or any other minor error. The final concert was like opening night at the "opera". The concert was a black tie affair. The men came in tuxedos and the ladies wore evening gowns. And, to top it off, the mayor and his entourage at-tended. The concert was an unqualified success. It was almost impos-sible to restrain my smile and keep a dignified look on my face with all the applause at the end. I shall be ever grateful for this training and performance under the baton of Dean Dixon. More than anything else, it was an opportunity to be treated with respect and entrusted with responsibility. As such, it was a lesson to us and everyone else on what we were truly capable of if given the chance.

Summer Job

I got my first big-time job the summer after my junior year in high school when I was called to be the drummer of a combo scheduled to play the summer at a resort in upper New York State. I had been play-ing the local neighborhood gigs since I was 13, and for several years had been hanging around the local jazz community, trying to get known to all the right people. They didn't have to ask me twice. "Yes," I said. "When and where do I meet you?" "Hold on young man," the manager said. "Get pencil and paper… You'll need to have your drum set, un-derwear, t-shirts, toiletries, etc., to cover six weeks. We'll play two hours a night, six nights a week. The pay is $18.00 a week. Oh, and you get three meals a day. The limousine will pick the band up at 6:00 p.m. Sunday evening at the 155th Street Station in the Bronx. See you soon."

I immediately told Mother and Aunt Bert. They both were quite excited and happy for me. I had three days to get ready. Mother rounded up a small suitcase for me and supervised the packing and general preparations. She said all I would need in the line of underwear would be 5 pair of shorts, and I should wash them out each day (this was my first real trip away from home on my own, I guess they figured I needed very specific instructions on how to take care of myself). Finally, the day to leave arrived. I said my good-byes and left for the subway. Earl carried my drum case and suitcase. He rode with me to the pickup point. As usual Earl was my true guardian angel.

Gradually, the complete band was present – trumpet, piano, saxophone, bass and drums. We knew each other's faces from the Rhythm Club, but had never worked together.

Around 6:20 p.m. a long black limo rolled up. The driver greeted us and we started packing everything in the limo. It was a tight fit because the bass had to go inside. The ride up was quite interesting. The first thing we did was decide who was going to be the leader. That position went to the trumpet player; he was the oldest and said that he had played many shows and what's more knew how to read music. Actually, all of us knew how to read music.

It was just getting dark when we arrived at the resort. We drove up to the main building, which was a hotel. The manager, a graying man with bushy hair and a leather-like tan, came out to greet us. He was wearing a polo shirt, pastel slacks, and open strap sandals. "Welcome," he said. "First we'll stop by the kitchen, then I'll show you to your cabin." He went to a walk-in refrigerator and returned with a large tray of sandwiches covered over with plastic wrap. He put the tray on a corner table, disappeared into the refrigerator again, and returned with a huge pitcher of lemonade. "Sit down and dig in," he said. Man, we were so hungry we literally wolfed down the sandwiches... ham, chicken salad, tuna. Boy, I was falling in love with this gig already.

After eating we piled back into the limo, drove a few minutes and pulled up in front of a cabin. "OK fellows, this is your home for the duration." All in all, I found that those six weeks were very interesting; I grew up in many ways. For the most part, my time was my own. The only time I was responsible for was from 9:00 p.m. to 11:00 p.m., that's when the guests gathered in the casino for social dancing. As it turned out, that two hours a day was such a small part of the time we spent up there, that it became a minor part of the experience. As far as the music was concerned, I felt like I was just a journeyman musician punching the clock. It was still a good musical experience, though it certainly lacked the excitement I was used to playing in New York. The main thing I discovered was that I had a lot of free time.

After breakfast, on the third day, I went to the library and checked out a book entitled *The Scottsboro Boys*. I then went to the boat dock and signed for a row boat. I rowed to the center of the lake, docked the oars, leaned back against a life preserver and started reading. After two hours I had drifted to shore on the other side of the lake. I marked my page, then set the oars and rowed back to the middle of the lake and resumed my reading. About two hours later, I was aground at another point on the lake shore. I checked my watch and saw that it was lunchtime. I was able to read many books that summer with that routine. After lunch, I wandered over to the archery range and I was hooked after my first lesson. I found there was something very romantic and swashbuckling about releasing an arrow. Earlier, I had seen Orson Welles, Tyrone Power, and Cornell Wilde in an epic surrounding the exploits of an expert archer. I was able to practice a few hours each day until I became quite proficient at hitting the bull's-eye from a distance of 30 yards. In fact, one of the hotel guests had been observing me practice and one day said that he would like to see how I would respond to real pressure. So we talked back and forth and he ended up daring me to try and hit the bull's-eye with him standing beside the center dot. I don't know what the guy was thinking of, it looked to me like all the pressure was really on him, but he was insistent so I said "OK," and he took his stance at the target. I ended up shooting twelve arrows, six of which went in the black (bull's-eye) and six in a tight cluster just outside the black. I don't know what it would have done to my interest in archery (or his) if I had missed the target, but my successful introduction to the sport led me to become one of the charter members of the Mohican Bowmen several years later.

World's Fair

I returned from that resort gig to one of the most memorable events to happen in my lifetime. The 1939 World's Fair was taking place in Flushing Meadows, New York. Despite the crowds and the long lines, there were so many sights to see, and so many things to do that my companions and I made several trips there. Automobile companies had cars of the future there, big cars, chauffeur driven, and all one had to do was get in line and wait for two hours for the comfort ride of a lifetime.

One particular weekend really stood out for me. It was the week the Gene Krupa Orchestra was going to appear at the Jazz Pavilion. He was going to hold a contest to find the best drummer in the New York area. I prepared myself by practicing four to five hours a day. I wouldn't stop those drums for food or drink. Finally, after four intensive days of sweating and drumming, I felt ready.

The next morning I got up early, ate a light breakfast, and practiced a long roll for fifteen minutes, to get my wrists loose. I then took two pairs of my favorite performing sticks, and boarded the subway to the World's Fair. I went alone because I wanted to concentrate and think about my technique. Today the correct phrase would be, "I wanted to stay focused." As I approached the music pavilion, I could hear the Krupa Band playing. When I entered the hall, my spirits were soaring, because all of the seats were filled, and the people were definitely in the mood. After the band completed their selection, Gene Krupa went to the microphone and announced that the contest would begin in a few minutes. He then asked the patrons to gather around a drum set that was set up outside the hall. He asked all the participants to get a number from him. This would decide the order of performance for each contestant. Gene gathered all the contestants around him and offered advice and words of encouragement. Then he added, "Win or lose, gentlemen, You're all going to be famous someday. Just stay with it." The musicians of Krupa's band, five of them, including piano, bass, guitar, trumpet, and tenor sax, were seated around the drum set, waiting for the first contestant. Some gangly kid sat at the drums. Then the piano player leaned over and asked him what song he wanted them to play. The boy looked puzzled, and hunched his shoulders, as if to say, "Why do you need to play? I'm going to do a drum solo." Well, he launched into a torrid solo without feeling or a beat. One could tell that he had studied, but that was all. And so it went. There were about forty-five hopefuls, and as time went by, the drummers got better.

Soon it was my turn. I was a little nervous approaching the set, but once I sat down, I felt right at home. I took a few seconds to adjust the angle of the snare drum. When the piano player asked what I wanted the combo to play, I said, "Just straight blues." He said, "My man! Go ahead; set the tempo." So I tapped the tempo on my drum head and we started swinging. Soon everybody started clapping their hands as I was digging the beat really seriously. At about the third chorus the piano player signalled to me to take a twelve bar solo; then everybody would go out on the last twelve bars. At the conclusion, the audience spontaneously broke into a generous applause. Gene Krupa grabbed me by the shoulders and said, "Bravo, bravo!"

I would like to say that I took first place when the judges cast their vote, but that was not the case. There came a contestant after me who literally brought the house down with an extensive drum solo. I, much later, saw that same drummer playing with the "Tonight Show" band. His name is Alvin Stoler.

School Spirit

By my sophomore year, I had become deeply immersed in my musical studies through my participation in both the orchestra and the Marching Band. Although these two groups shared a number of members, they were quite distinct, and the character of my experiences in each were worlds apart. The orchestra was by nature a much more formal affair, and was focused almost entirely on the music it produced. In its own way, the orchestra provided me with a tremendous amount of enjoyment and was critical to the development of my musicianship. A great camaraderie developed between the orchestra members as we learned to work together to reproduce the works of great composers. There was something sublime and uplifting about the performance of classical works in how it connected you to past centuries of the greatest composers in history. It gives you a reverence for the greatness of their music, and we derived a lot of pleasure from sharing that experience with the audience.

The Marching Band was a little different. In the orchestra, the music was the only thing that mattered - it was music for it's own sake, and the musicians, though essential, were kind of anonymous and remained quietly in the background. In the Marching Band, the music seems to take on a completely different character. In the first place, you take it outside, which changes the feel of things right away. And in the second place, you play it not so much for its own sake, but to make it part of another experience. Another big change is that in the Marching Band, the musicians don't just sit anonymously in the background anymore - it starts with the way you dress. After I had joined the Marching Band I was thrilled when I was fitted for the band uniform. We had West Point style hats which were a light blue-gray color, trimmed with scarlet piping and a large, gold emblem. Also, we had a beautiful scarlet sweater which we wore under a gray cape with scarlet trim. Our trousers were gray with scarlet stripes down the side. To finish our uniforms, we purchased our own white bucks and socks. Obviously, there was more to the Marching Band than just the way it sounded.

During this period, football was more prevalent than any other sport, and football rivalries were more meaningful. Basketball was just starting to come into its own. The high schools were the main supporters of the Evening PSAL (Public School Athletic Leagues). I vividly recall an experiment conducted by the Brooklyn Board of Education regarding the football teams of the Borough of Brooklyn. Instead of each high school playing a game at some designated field, (not all of the schools had their own football field) a schedule was set up involving eight schools on selected Saturdays. All of the games would be played at Ebbets Field, home of the Brooklyn Dodgers. Some of the schools involved were Alexander Hamilton, Boy's High, Tilden High, and Erasmus Hall. The first game was scheduled to start at 10:00 a.m., the second at noon, the third at 2:00 p.m. and the fourth at 4:00 p.m. It was a beautiful sight to see all of the bands, the cheerleaders, and the stands full of each school's supporters. There would be approximately 20,000 people there. It created an unforgettable atmosphere and it was a wonderful thrill for all of us to perform in a professional stadium. It was a fun day filled with bus loads of students and parents, and competing demonstrations of school spirit. All of the bands and cheerleaders would arrive to see the first show and then check out the routines of each of the others. When they announced the name of our schools over the PA system, we stuck our chests out and played our hearts out for dear old Hamilton High. Every student felt that way about his or her school. Alexander Hamilton High School had a very good football team and no matter where we played, our side of the stands was full. Hamilton, in fact, had a very enviable history of fielding excellent football teams.

One of my most vivid recollections was of a league championship game we played at Ebbets Field between Hamilton and Boy's High. That year's Hamilton team was led by two outstanding, but very different, running backs. The first was a tall, black dude named Eddie. Eddie was a ladies man, very popular, very quiet. He was quite manly and handsome, sort of in the Billy Dee Williams image. At lunch Eddie would always tease me and say, "Hey Boots, I thought you said you could play the drums. Well, I didn't hear a thing." Then I would shoot right back at him, "No wonder, after that Vikowski boy from Boy's High hit you, you could hear nothing but bells ringing in your ears," and everyone would laugh. Actually, Eddie was a demon on the field. He played fullback in our single wing formation. Eddie was tireless on the field. Whenever he broke past the scrimmage line, he would plow straight ahead, eating up yards as he kept his legs churning. The other running back was a short, bowlegged, pigeon-toed bundle of energy named Herman Bing. Bing was the sort of happy-go-lucky guy who was very popular with the student body. His trademark was a turned up porkpie hat that he used to carry everywhere. Bing had very wavy hair and a light complexion which showed all of the welts from where he took hits in the game. It was something to see Bing with bandages over or under his eyes. Now Bing was what you would call a scat-back. He was both quick and fast. He would hit the hole before the defense could come up. Then, once through the hole, he would make a cut, left or right, head for the sidelines, then cut up the field toward the goal. This particular game was very competitive, and was being dominated by the defenses on both sides. Neither Eddie or Bing was having much luck moving the ball. Our cheerleaders from our sister school were hoarse from yelling. The fans were on their feet and stomping. The stands on both sides of

47

the field were literally rocking. Both bands were ignoring the courtesy of one playing at a time. Our band was really sending some electric chords over to the Boy's High Band. They could not keep up with us. We sounded like controlled thunder. It was the fourth quarter with just minutes to go, and the score was seven to six in favor of Boy's High. Hamilton had missed the extra point. It was Hamilton's ball on Boy's 45 yard line. The team huddled, the whistle blew, the ball was hiked. Bing got the hand off and started an end-around. Unfortunately, both Vikowski brothers were waiting for Bing. Our blocking had broken down. The brothers put a double whammy on Bing. One brother hit him high, the other brother hit him low. Bing was stopped in his tracks. He just laid there and did not move. Time was called. Eddie walked over to Bing, gently picked him up and brought him over to the benches. The band was nearby and I could see tears streaming down Eddie's cheeks as he handed Bing to the official hands. Eddie then turned in the direction of the band and yelled, "The game isn't over. Boots, get those drums going." We rolled-off and the band played our fight song. Soon the entire stand started singing, waving school colors, and stomping. The whistle blew. It was 2nd down and the ball rested on Boy's High 48 yard line. The ball was snapped but this time it went directly to Eddie and not the quarterback. The left end turned and ran to Eddie for a fake end-around. The Boy's High defense fell for it and charged the end. Eddie rolled outside to the left and it was all over. Two defense players tried to bring him down but Eddie rumbled into the end zone. Time ran out leaving us with an exhilarating and dramatic win. There was a spontaneous celebration on the field and to everyone's relief, Bing, who had only suffered a sprain, hobbled out with a cane to join in. I like to think that the way our band roused our fans rattled the other team while inspiring our own. At the very least, it added immeasurably to the excitement of the moment. It was a victory that I shall never forget, and that as a band member I felt a special part of. It gave me a feeling of pride and accomplishment that never left me, and that I would later be able to pass on to students of my own.

"Taxi Dance" - Times Square

When I wasn't involved with the school bands or orchestra, I was pursuing my professional career. By the time I was a senior I was getting a lot of work. One of the most valuable experiences I recall from that time was at a club called the "Taxi Dance". Now picture a huge room with several chandeliers for lighting. In the middle there was a dance floor surrounded all around by a three-foot rail (sort-of like a race track), and every five feet around the rail were two folding chairs, one on the inside of the rail, one on the outside. Between each chair there was a very small table, barely large enough to hold two drinks.

Seated on each chair inside of the rail (or circle) were young ladies, all painted and perfumed. Around their necks, and hanging down to their waists was a roll of tickets, each ticket marked with a large "10 cents". Lining up to take their seats beside the young ladies would be men, young and old, including many servicemen. The men would take their seats and purchase dance tickets from the ladies. However, the men also had to purchase watered down drinks. There were waitresses on roller skates who responded when someone raised his or her hand. The main idea was for the dancing ladies to keep the men on the floor buying tickets and small shots of the weak whiskey. If a girl was running out of tickets, she would notify a waitress who would have another string ready in seconds. Also, when one couple was dancing, another couple would take their seats, and this would go on all evening long. There may have been over fifty couples on the floor, and another fifty couples at the tables. And just to make sure the customers didn't get the wrong idea, there was one big, electric sign at the entrance which read, "Hostesses may not leave with guests."

The Taxi Dance was where I really learned to drum professionally – playing at the Taxi Dance was like nothing I had ever done before. It was very hard and demanding. Tin-Pan Alley was an area of New York where the overwhelming majority of sheet music was published. The latest songs played by bands, orchestras, or sung by vocalists, came from Tin Pan Alley. Publishing houses like Chappell, and Robbins, would send all of their latest songs to the Taxi Dance Ballroom for exposure.

When I got the call that a drummer was needed at the ballroom, little did I know that I would be in for the musical experience of my life. I trudged upstairs with my drums and was directed to a very small band stand where there was a piano player and a saxophonist waiting for me. "Hurry and get set up! And don't knock that pile of music over!" I was told by the guys. When I set my drums up, and was ready to play, the piano player told me that when we finished each selection, to move it from the right pile start one to my left. The right pile was 24 inches high. There had to have been well over 200 songs included in the pile. Once we started playing, we couldn't stop. We'd go from fox-trot, to tango, to swing, to ballad, to cha-cha, and so on. If my right foot got tired, I'd play the bass pedal with my left foot. We would play for fifty minutes straight out of each hour, then break for ten minutes. It was a business. You had to be back on the band stand before the ten minutes were over. The hours were long; we played from 9 p.m. to 2 a.m. I made the outstanding salary of $25.00 a week playing for six days.

Of all my experiences as a musician, none has been more meaning-ful for me than those "sweatshop" days at the Taxi Dance. When you finished your "internship" there, you were ready for anything because you had played everything. It's a pity there aren't such learning oppor-tunities around now to help the aspiring musicians hone their craft.

The Variety Show

One of the fondest memories I have of my days at Hamilton con-cerned the annual Variety Show. This show played for three nights and was in every sense of the word a variety show. Even though it was spon-sored by the Instrumental Music Department, practically all other de-partments were involved. This particular edition of the show traced the route and influences of jazz, flowing from the deep South up to New York City. We dressed in the style of the times, with the musicians wearing high collared shirts with garters on their arms and pretending to be playing at the Preservation Jazz Society Hall of New Orleans. Other scenes showed boys and girls in the cotton field singing fantastic spiri-tuals in four part harmony. There was one scene very popular with the cast because it involved almost everyone. It depicted a Sunday after-noon as enjoyed by the Negroes in a place in New Orleans called "Congo Square". Musicians were standing on one corner playing jazz selec-tions in the New Orleans style. Couples were strolling, laughing and chatting. The finale involved an eighteen piece dance band and I was the drummer. We were posing as "Woody Herman's First Herd". The shop built special stair-stepped platforms for the band and alone at the top was me. The scene depicted the stage show at Paramount Theater where the band stage slowly rises out of darkness into the spotlight. The audience served as patrons, so it was a show within a show. Our leader played a few bars on the clarinet. I took a two bar solo. Then the whole band fell in with *The Woodchopper's Ball*. The show ended with our version of Benny Goodman's *Sing-Sing-Sing*. During this selection I took a five minute drum solo and when I ended it by hitting the ride cymbal with a resounding crash, the entire band came in with the "go-ing out chorus." From that moment on I was known as the Gene Krupa of Hamilton High.

Graduation Party

The Brooklyn of my youth was a wonderful, open place in which to be alive. In the latter part of June, 1940, my mother and Aunt Bert gave a party for me and my best friend and buddy, Walter Williams, to cel-ebrate our graduation from high school. To me, this was the party of the year. All of our friends, the parents of our classmates, musicians whom I knew, and teachers were invited. To top it off, an invitation was sent to Mayor Fiorello La Guardia. Walter, who's nickname was 'Dickie' and I were dressed like twins. He was taller than I and more slender. Dickie was a nice looking guy. The girls were crazy about his dimples. For the party we both wore dark, navy blue, silk, short sleeve shirts; navy blue trousers and socks; white, rope-like braided belts and white saddle oxford shoes. We completed the outfit with soft, snap-brim, cream-colored Panama hats, each with a navy blue band around the crown. Needless to say, we felt very good about ourselves as the girls gave us the 'eye.' Dickie was a sensitive person who was very good in art. We complemented each other very well.

The party was a huge success. It was held in the Knights of Columbus Hall which was next door to Aunt Bert's beauty parlor. There was a live, six piece band which included the piano, bass, drums, saxophone, trumpet and the singer who was called Little Billie Angel, who patterned her singing after Billie Holiday. We did the slow drag and the lindy-hop (jitterbug), dancing to the songs made famous by Billy Eckstein, Louis Jordan, Duke Ellington and Billie Holiday.

The food was prepared by family and friends. It consisted of fried chicken, hot dogs, potato salad, rolls, soft drinks, cookies, and a large graduation cake with our names on it. We received a lot of gifts.

Several teachers from school did attend our party. Mayor La Guardia did not attend the party, however, he did send two representatives. Reporters from the Amsterdam News (the Negro press) attended also, took pictures and wrote up the affair. Later in my life my buddy Walter became a universally recognized artist. Paris, France was his latest address.

52nd Street

I started getting serious gigs with several organized bands and pickup combos when I became a senior in high school. This made it mandatory for me to join the Musicians' Union Local 802. Once I had done that, I could move up the next step on the ladder. That summer after I graduated I was gigging at the Elks Club in Brooklyn one night when the trombone player, Trummy Young said, "Boots, I'm scheduled to open up at the Three Deuces on 52nd Street next week, and I sure could use you on the skins." "Fine," I said. "Fill me in." He said, "We start next Thursday. We'll play 30 minutes on and 30 minutes off. They will have two bands. You'll need a black suit. Your pay will be eighty dollars a week. We will work six days, and are off one." "Wow!" I didn't hear anything Trummy said to me after he mentioned the pay. That was the most money I had ever dreamed of earning. Though I was only eighteen I had been playing and paying my dues for a long time. Now I felt like I was finally on my way.

Let me tell you about 52nd Street. It was the Jazz Mecca. There were at least six clubs on that one block alone. Such clubs as the Three Deuces, the Spotlight Club, the Onyx Club, and the Downbeat were all extremely popular. This is where such names as Dizzy Gillespie, Big Sid Catlett, Billy Holiday, and Billy Eckstine performed regularly. Each club usually employed two combos. The first combo started playing around 9:30 p.m. The second band rounded up the festivities, playing to around 4:00 a.m. It was unbelievable how crowded each club stayed. After each show, the people would rush to the club next door, or perhaps across the narrow street to the yacht club. Well, I didn't get the chance to open up with Trummy because he had an obligation to fulfill and had to go on the road with a show. I didn't have time to feel disappointment though, because Dave Rivera, a piano player, was also scheduled to open at the Three Deuces, and needed a drummer in a hurry. Dave learned from Max Roach that I was available. Dave called me at home and offered me the gig, with the same conditions: six nights, half-hour on, half-hour off. Only this time the pay was more, at $95 per week. We were to start the next night. Boy, was I excited. Our trio consisted of Dave Rivera on piano, Junior Ragland, previously with Duke Ellington, on bass, and me on the drums. We became the house band for the club, which meant they would engage celebrities who would bring their charts (arrangements) with them, and use us to back them up. I remember when Billy Holiday was engaged for a week. The club really went all out to advertise her. The big facial shots of her were put up on easels outside the club. The Jazz aficionados were lined up for the two hour show. About an hour before the show Big Sid Catlett, a world renowned drummer, came back to the band stand and said, "Boots, this is your first time playing for Lady Day, mind if I offer a hint or two?" This was Big Sid's style, always unselfish, always helpful. "No," I said, happy to have someone to calm me down. Big Sid said, "Billy likes to sing very soft and smooth on her ballads. I suggest you use your brushes, in a circular motion, to give that smooth background." Then he demonstrated what he was talking about. He produced a continuous, smooth sound which reminded me of the steady tearing of a sheet of tissue paper. By then, the club was filled to overflowing. People were crowded around small, round tables. Waitresses were calling last orders before the show. No orders would be taken during the show. Then a warning light came on; waiters and waitresses hastened to finish up their orders and to take their places in the back. The air-conditioners were turned off, and then all of the lights were dimmed. A voice came over the PA system and announced, "Ladies and gentlemen, the one and only, Lady Day!" A single, silver spotlight beam cut through the dark and focused on Billy Holiday's face. She was dressed in form-fitting material that literally seemed to melt to her entire frame. One side of her face was adorned with white gardenias. She turned, looked at Dave, snapped her fingers in a very sexy way, and we moved right into "Them There Eyes". After the show, there was bedlam. Young, white, college girls mobbed the bandstand, then followed Billy into her dressing room. This scene was repeated night after night. Meanwhile, I was making a name for myself. From time to time, other drummers would ask me to fill in for them if they had a record date and couldn't make the club on time.

First Road Trip

It was that wonderful summer of 1940 when I was also chosen to be part of a show that was going on the road for a few weeks. The fellows at the Rhythm Club in Harlem told me that all young musicians should experience this rite of passage into the world of music. Everybody involved was excited because the show would include chorus girls, comedians, a seven-piece combo, and a master of ceremonies. My very good friend, Jack McGuire, played accordion. We would travel by a private Greyhound Bus which thankfully had a toilet and a washroom. We were told not to take too many suitcases because of space required for large instruments, such as the bass fiddle, and drum set. The men were issued collarless tuxedo shirts with stiff breasts. Our collars were separate, and made of rubber. Therefore, they did not need to be washed after each performance. And no matter how wrinkled our shirts were, the stiff breasts, and firm, white, rubber collars looked great under lights. We slept in lounging clothes and used our light jackets as blankets. There were many experiences that made a lasting impression on me. As we rode through the southern towns, we could not stop, rest, or eat, like the average white travellers were able to. Eventually, we found out that the white proprietors loved to ogle the four chorus girls. They were tall, leggy, and, as the saying went in those days, "high yellow." Whenever the need for food came about, a list would be passed around and we would circle what we wanted, and the M.C. would give the list and money to two of the chorus girls. They would go into the restaurant and return shortly with the food, assisted by the proprietors. We would get a big kick out of watching the white owners who were very timid about getting on the bus which had so many "colored people". The girls knew this and would turn and say, "C'mon in, Honey. It's OK. And we do want to thank you for helping us so." And then they would say, "Honey, do you mind going back and bringing us some more ice? It gets so hot travelling." Soon the owner would reappear with a bucket of ice, cups and soda, smiling and saying, "Y'all be sure to stop here on your way back."

Another experience I remember happened when we arrived at our destination, a small town in Mississippi, very late at night. We were scheduled to give two shows in a renovated tobacco barn the next day. It was truly a "one traffic light on main street" town. The bus driver was slowly rolling through the light when we saw the flashing lights of a police cruiser. We stopped, and the officer entered the bus with a bright flashlight. His first words were, "Where y'all going, Boy?" The M.C., using all of his smoothness, said, "Sir, we're scheduled to put on a show at the 'Big Barn' tomorrow." The officer said it was too late to get in, and asked where we were going to sleep. "On the bus," we replied. "Shucks, I can do better than that, if you don't mind, that is." "Just what do you have in mind?" the M.C. asked. The sheriff said, "I'll open the doors of my jail. They're all empty now, and you will be able to shower and sleep." "Solid," we said. "Just leave those doors open," and everybody laughed.

As hectic and tiring as that road trip was, it only heightened my desire to travel with bands and play shows. There have been numerous road trips since. However, all of them followed a northern route.

Keeping Me Straight

These were pretty heady times for a kid my age, and because of that they were pretty dangerous times too. The world of jazz clubs was a lot of things to a lot of people. On the good side it was the center of a powerful, exhilarating, and still evolving art form. And it encompassed a community of musicians dedicated as much to helping each other as they were to the music they were creating. That may have come from the way everyone came up through the neighborhood bands, with the older musicians bringing along the younger ones as they moved through the process. On the bad side, there was the temptation of drugs, alcohol, and dangerous women. Because of the nature of the business it was a late-night party-time world that turned over a lot of money and played to a fast crowd. The underside of this night life usually started after the clubs would close. A number of the clubs seemed to have some Mafia associations. Often we would be asked to stay after closing to play for groups of very well dressed but very secretive men, and their girls, who would come in after everyone else left and stay until morning. This was more of a curiosity to us than a threat – we just minded our own business and played our music. Still, it was a little scary to be so close to the underworld. The real dangers, especially to someone as young and naive as I was, came as part of the social scene surrounding the jazz musician's world.

First there was the temptation of drugs. This was not really a problem for me because the drug of choice among the musicians I knew and worked with was marijuana. Simply put, my Uncle Clarance had cured me once and for all of smoking, and I didn't want any part of it. I hated to be around the fumes because as far as I was concerned, they permeated your hair, skin, and clothes, thus making you smell pretty foul. I was also a little paranoid about it, ever since I met Eddie Stewart as a twelve-year-old. He and I were supposed to get together to help each other with our musical needs, and we did on occasion, but he would walk down the street in the middle of the day smoking a joint. He never seemed to care about it, but I could just imagine getting caught and having to explain it to Mother and Aunt Bert - not to mention what Uncle Clarance would do to me. There was one occasion when I did get high, but through no fault of my own. One Saturday when I was hanging out at the Rhythm Club hoping to get a gig, the dispatcher said he just received a request for a five piece combo to play a wedding in Yonkers. Louis, the trumpet player, told me to get my drums and meet him at his car. Soon five of us were settled in the car and we headed for the gig. It was rather cold and the heat was on, with all the windows rolled up tight. We had motored about half an hour when Greene, the guitar player, opened up a Maxwell House coffee tin – only the container was filled with narrow, rolled marijuana cigarettes. "Anybody want one?" he asked. At that, all the guys took a cigarette, except me." We weren't going to let you have one anyway Boots... you're too young." Everybody laughed and lit up. Soon the entire interior was blue-grey with acrid smelling smoke. Then it happened. Gradually my eyes started closing and for some strange reason I started snapping my fingers and humming some unintelligible song. "What's that you're singing Boots?" someone asked. "Who's singing," I said - indignant. "Boots, what time is it?" I looked at my bare wrist and started giggling. The more questions they asked, the more I giggled. "Hey everybody, Boots is high." So Louis said for everybody to lower all the windows and as soon as that cold air hit me, my head cleared along with the smoke. That was it for me and drugs, including alcohol, but for some of my friends, they didn't get off so easily.

Then there were the women. "Boots, you're prime bait as far as these night crawlers are concerned, they would love to get their hands on you because you're young and a virgin." Sid Catlett was 'waxing eloquently' with me about the prostitutes one evening before a show I was doing at the Three Deuces. He continued, "Man, you've got to be very, very careful. They'll back you in a corner and make your head swim so fast that you will be relieved of your money and honor before you blink an eye." Late one weekend after the gig was over, a tall, voluptuous lady came over to the band as we were packing up. She spoke to our bassist, Junior Ragland, then left. "Say fellas," Junior said, "We're invited to an after-hour party up on 135th Street. Boots, I want you to come and learn." After we had packed up, we piled into our piano player Derrick's car and headed uptown. It was about 3:00 a.m. When we entered the basement door of this brownstone, there was a small blue light that cast an eerie glow over the entrance to the party room, which was flooded in a soft red light. "C'mon in honey," that same tall girl said as she came over and put her arm around Junior. She then looked at me and said, "Hey Babe, I heard you tonight, you were really cookin' on those skins. What's your name Honey?" "Boots," I said, trying to clear my throat. "Well, Hi Boots, c'mon, I'll introduce you to some people." By now my eyes were getting used to the dark and I was able to see several couples in various stages of embraces. "Red, c'mon over here, I want you to meet the drummer." She called to a lady who was standing at a small bar. "Red, meet Boots, Boots, meet Red." She laughed and said, "I'll leave you two to get acquainted."

Now these after-hours parties were money making affairs. Drinks were $2.00 a shot. Dinners of pigs feet, collard greens and potato salad were $10.00, and the juke box was adjusted so that records (all of the songs were slow drag) each cost fifty cents to play. These parties cleaned up. Area musicians along with chorus girls and ladies of the night made for a steady stream of people coming and going.

Well, Red snuggled up to me and said, "I'm thirsty Big Boy, you want to buy me a drink?" "Sure," I said. Then I went over to the bar and ordered a whiskey for her and a Coke for myself. Boy, you could have knocked me over when the girl behind the bar said, "That'll be $4.00." "Wow," I said to myself, "soda costs as much as whiskey." I was in a wild panic because all I had was ten dollars, and that wasn't going to go very far. I took the drink to Red and boy, she was smelling some kind of good. "Let's go over to the couch in the corner," she said. It was then that I started to sweat. I was way, way out of my league and Red was closing in on me like a tiger stalking a lamb. Red leaned her head on my shoulder and said, very low, "Are you married Boots?" At this point, I was feeling quite agitated. Just then I heard a familiar voice say, "Oh, there you are." It was Junior. "Come on, it's four a.m. and Derrick says we've got to be back at the club at 10:00 a.m. Billy Daniels is due in with some new charts." Boy, I was so happy to hear Junior's voice that I jumped up, spilling my Coke on me in the process.

That was just one of the many times the older musicians rescued me. Because I started so young, they were always looking after me, and I guess we all just got used to that relationship. Even when I got older, that still was the way they treated me - they continued to keep me beyond the reaches of the booze and the drugs and the ladies who had improper designs on my innocence. Of course, I knew right from wrong, but in those circumstances knowing isn't always enough. You really need people around you to give you the strength to stay away from trouble. It's not that they wouldn't have let me find my own way into trouble if I really wanted to and thought I could handle it, but they always made me feel comfortable with myself, and in fact encouraged me to stay straight. It's not like today where so many people want to pull you into what they're doing just so they can feel better about themselves, those people are just looking out for themselves. The guys back then truly tried to look out for you first, and I have tried to do the same.

Walter and Margie Battle, the author's parents,
on a Long Island porch in 1923.

LeRoy A. Battle
Graduation from Alexander Hamiliton High School
1940

My mother, Margaret Battle, in the
backyard behind the beauty parlor.
Brooklyn, NY 1935

Roberta G. Roderick, "Aunt Bert"
in 1960

Young "Boots" with his first drum set

Mother's Family

Uncle Clarance

Uncle Robert - "Robbie"

Uncle Walter

*Uncle Fred (with the hat)
and Uncle Earl at Prospect
Park – Spring 1928*

63

Aunt Bert and Uncle Earl
at Prospect Park – 1928

Young Boots Battle playing for Gene Kruppa (in white shirt and tie)
at the 1939 World's Fair in New York

Boots at work in Brooklyn, 1941

Cadet Battle at Tuskegee

Growing Up Again

Military Odyssey Begins

It was the summer of 1943 and my career as an up-and-coming musician was definitely ready to take off. Gigs were coming in on a regular basis; offers to become a permanent drummer with some of the outstanding bands in Brooklyn were in the works. At long last, my career was starting to "flesh-out." Suddenly I was in a position where I had to decide with which band should I play, or what concert I should attend in order to observe certain musicians, and most importantly, which path I should follow regarding my career – concert or jazz performing, teaching music, or some combination of the three. The goals of a lifetime, that had been in front of me since I first saw that grand parade in Harlem with the Knights of St. John, now seemed within easy reach. I knew then that my life would be forever tied to music for as far as that would take me. At this point it seemed just a matter of deciding where I wanted to go.

Such were the vain dreams that all came to an abrupt end when I received my induction notice. I hadn't really given much thought to the possibility of being drafted. My involvement with music consumed nearly all of my attention. If I gave the Army any thought at all, it was nothing more than the vague hope that I wouldn't be drafted. Given the role of blacks in the military, it was not generally a place for black men to become heroes, or leaders of any kind. More often than not, the lot of the black soldier was to provide menial labor in support of the white army. Being drafted into the Army gave me nothing to look forward to, and it plucked me away from my career at the moment when I saw myself on the verge of getting established with some of the prime jazz combos of the time. Of course, I know I wasn't alone in having a change of plans forced on me. Like many others, I suddenly found myself walking away from my drums – my own particular vision of my life – not knowing what the future would hold for me, or if I even had one.

I was inducted into the military in September, 1943 at Camp Upton, Long Island, New York. I met the bus promptly at 6:00 a.m. There were tearful good-byes with my mother and Aunt Bert. I left with one beat-up suitcase which contained various toiletries, a toothbrush, toothpaste, two pairs of socks, a T-shirt, undershorts, candy bars, chewing gum, a comb, a brush, a small tin of vaseline, pencils, one of my favorite books by Henry Ashenfelter, and one pair of drumsticks. The bus ride took several hours, because of stops to pick up other draftees. We finally arrived at Camp Upton around 10:00 a.m., tired and hungry.

There was a beehive of activity all around our misfit group. Some of the men already on base were drilling with rifles. Other groups were involved in close-order drills. A military band was blaring away at a nearby train station, welcoming brass hats, but for the first time in my life, the sound of music failed to move me. We spent our first few hours waiting for someone to tell us what to do. Soon a sergeant came to our group and announced that the Tuskegee Institute, of which I had never heard, was starting a new class of colored aviation cadets the next day, and anybody who wanted "wings" could try out to be a cadet, provided he passed certain tests here at Upton. He then ordered all who were interested to take two steps forward from their group. I can't say that I ever had any previous aspirations to be a pilot, but it sounded like a much better opportunity than anything else than was likely to come along, so I stepped forward with three others. The Sergeant said, "All right. You four follow me. The rest of you freeze on the spot."

We were taken to the dispensary where we were given a most complete physical. We were then taken to an examining room and given special eye tests to see if we were color blind. Meanwhile, I was still hungry and told the sergeant so. He just looked and smiled a wicked smile, and said, "Just hang in there, Son. It won't be long."

We were taken to another part of the building and given a general I.Q. test. Then we were taken to still another room where the sergeant said our eye and hand coordination would be tested. These were called psychomotive tests. One of the tests was right down my alley, so to speak. Picture a record turntable about 14 inches in diameter. Imbedded flush with the surface of the turntable was a round metal object, and about the size of a dime. The examiner handed me a slender rod, about 12" long. This rod had a small module on the tip. About 2" up the rod was a built-in circuit breaker. The test consisted of my keeping the module on the round metal piece, as the turntable rotated. The object was to keep contact, but not to push too hard, as this would break the contact. My experience as a drummer stood me in good stead; the sensitivity needed to keep the module in contact with the dish was no different than the touch required for playing with brushes.

After the tests were completed, we waited for the sergeant to return. He arrived in an Air Force car with my luggage and a brown lunch bag. He said, "Get in, soldier. You're going to the train station. You other three men wait until I return." I was the only one of the four to qualify for the Tuskegee program. Fifteen minutes later, I was on my way to Biloxi, Mississippi. Before the sergeant left the train, he handed me my orders and said to guard them with my life. His last statement to me was, "Congratulations and good luck, future bombardier."

Keesler Field, Biloxi, Mississippi

As the train pulled out, I had such a hollow feeling of helplessness and loneliness. At least at Camp Upton I was among other draftees who were in the same situation as I was. Now I was more isolated than ever. My coach was immediately behind the engine, and I was alone in the car. I took a seat by the window and reflected on the day. It had started out for me at 6:00 a.m., and here I was a 2:30 p.m., headed for God knows where. I had not been issued a uniform, which meant that I was still wearing my same, sweat-soaked clothes. I opened the lunch bag which contained a dry ham sandwich, an apple, and three cookies. I slowly chewed, and looked around. The seats were dirty with soot. There was trash, dried-up rib bones, and other assorted debris, all over the floor. Smoke and soot from the engine was blowing over me and into the train car. The heat was unbearable so the window had to stay open, letting the exhaust wash over me. The trip seemed to take forever, with the stops and layovers in D.C. and the Carolinas.

I arrived at Biloxi, Mississippi about 2:00 a.m. and was immediately abandoned by the train. It was really eerie. Less than 48 hours before I was in the bright lights and crowds and familiar noise of New York City. Now I was like a traveler in a foreign land - in the middle of a humid, noiseless Southern night, the only one on the station platform. But before I could reconsider my choices, an Army car rode up to the station, and a white driver yelled to me, "Boy, is your name Battle?" I said, "Yes, sir." He replied, "Well get your ass in. We ain't got all night." Such was my welcome, and the end of my freedom. Just a few hours later, Tent City, my new home, was awakened at 5:00 a.m.. We were herded to the mess hall for coffee, flapjacks, and eggs. Then we were taken to a warehouse for the issuance of uniforms, from underwear to raincoats. I recall, as we were passing through the line to receive an item, someone said something and we all laughed. This fat, tobacco chewing clerk said in a loud drawl, "Y'all boys, shut yo' mouths. Yo' in Mississippi now." Those simple, uncaring words went through me like a shock. They awakened me to the second class status to which we had been relegated. The disrespect was so arrogant and flagrant and casual, that I knew we were in for some trying times. My morale was pretty low.

One of the good things about this evolving experience was that I can now look back on it with pride because of the men I was associated with. I was assigned as a pre-aviation cadet to Squadron 707. Archie Harris, the famous football player from Indiana University and later the

69

N.Y. Giants Football team, was our squadron leader and one of the first men of note who I shared these experiences with. Each and every morning at 5:30 a.m. precisely, our ears would be assaulted with Archie's booming voice shouting, "Squadron 707, the world is waiting for you. Arise!" This would go on for ten minutes as Archie trudged up and down our designated area of Tent City. Of course, at the time, Archie wasn't yet famous, so I can't say that we entirely appreciated his contribution to our day.

When I made the quick decision at Camp Upton to aspire to be a success in this facet of the service, little did I realize how wide the chasm was between the actual basic training and the glory of pushing a propeller. To put it mildly, life was primitive at Keesler Field. There were no barracks for the new inductees – instead we were billeted in four-man tents. Everywhere a person looked or sat, there was sand - it was white, beautiful sand, like the sand found at Rockaway Beach in New York, but more importantly, it was *everywhere*. The sand worked its way into your clothes, the pores of your skin, and when the wind blew, it was the eyes that suffered. Tightly sealed candy bars, crackers, and the like were the popular food items, because powdered eggs and rations were quite gritty at times. And it was very, very hot in Mississippi. To capture any breeze, we had to roll up the sides of the tent. Then, when it rained, we longed for the sun. It was a chore just to walk from one tent to another. One would sink ankle-deep into the mud. The irony of all of this was the fact that the combination of sand and very tall pine trees made a beautiful, peaceful picture.

The training was very challenging, to say the least, but that was the way it was for everyone, black or white. This was one of the few ways in which the Army treated everyone equally, though separately. This phase of our training was about breaking our individuality down, and rebuilding us as instruments of the Army. There were forced marches with full packs which weighed a good fifty pounds. We would walk at a brisk pace from Biloxi to Gulfport, a distance of around fifteen miles. On our return, we would hump a little faster, because there was serious competition between each squadron to see who made the fastest time. The winning squadron would be free of K.P. (Kitchen Police) duty for one week.

There was one incident during basic training that caused me considerable consternation. We were scheduled to go on bivouac for three days in some desolate areas of the Gulfport area. Then we were to march to the firing range for live ammo indoctrination. We handled the march quite efficiently, because we only had our rifles and a light pack with which to contend. When we arrived at the bivouac area, we were paired up, and immediately set up "pup tents" designed to house two men. At that moment, the skies opened up and a thunderous downpour began. It stormed all afternoon and evening. Our squadron leader said that we could stand down until reveille. With that, my buddy and I gently squeezed ourselves into each side of the tent. The rain was not letting up, but we were dry. Pup tents are like that. They will keep out the rain, that is until one makes the mistake of touching any part of the inside of the tent.

This was my first experience in a pup tent. As I lay there on my back, I noticed a huge bulge caused by the collected rain just above my head. Curiosity got the best of me. I took my index finger and traced a small circle, and, before I could pull my hand away, the water gushed in all over my face and head. Needless to say, that was one miserable, wet night.

The next morning we ate a cold breakfast of corn flakes and headed for the firing range. Once we heard the sound of gunfire, we looked at each other apprehensively. We were directed to an area where we were issued rifles and given instructions on how to carry them in front of us, as we crawled through the grass in special roped off lanes. After a short wait, the range officer ordered us to the prone position, and told us to crab-crawl with our rifles until we heard the all-clear signal. Just before we started, he raised his voice to an unbelievable decibel and warned us to keep our asses down or get them shot off by the machine gunners. As we crawled, I could hear the short bursts of the machine guns, and I swear I could feel the hot air as some bullets passed overhead. After the crawl, we gave the rifles back, and thanks to the powers that be, loaded onto the two-ton trucks, and fell asleep as we were driven back to our base. When we were slowly off-loaded, I beat a path to the shower area, stripped, and stepped under the shower barrel, when I noticed this little bug crawling up my arm. I picked it off, killed it, and then I noticed another one which I quickly dispatched. At this point, I asked another soldier, "What gives?" "Hey man, I'm from the country," he said, "and I swear those are ticks. You don't want them to bury their heads. I tell you what," he continued, "You check me out, and I'll do the same for you." That was my introduction to ticks, and, I have to tell you, that, for a few days afterwards, I was constantly, to the annoyance of some people, checking myself out.

A few weeks later, after our last exercise, we were dismissed, told to shower, to change into dress khakis, and to be ready to fall in on command. We knew that something important was coming our way. We could only guess that "Graduation Day" had arrived. At the appointed time, we formed ranks, were put at parade rest, and waited breathlessly as the names of the pre-aviation cadets were called. The situation was this: if a soldier's name was called, that person broke ranks and formed up in the back of the squadron leader, which meant that you were a full-fledged aviation cadet, and would begin special training at

Tuskegee Institute in two weeks. The down part of this situation was that if your name was not called, you would automatically resort to the status of "Enlisted Man", and be assigned to some "F" Squadron in the Air Corps. The "F" Squadron was, in effect, a service unit designated at all air bases and composed of all "colored troops". These "F" companies were usually composed of many illiterate men, and were given all of the undesirable duties in the Air Corps.

We were still at parade rest as the squadron leader called each name. From the corner of my eye I could use my peripheral vision on both sides of me, without moving my head. I could see the ranks thinning out fast. The squadron leader called what he said was the last name. "What?!" I screamed under my breath. My heart beat faster. I started hyperventilating. "Squadron, Attention!" the squadron leader was saying. "Dismissed," he started to say, then he quickly added, "As you were. PAC (Pre-Aviation Cadet) Battle, step out." Wow, I was so happy I could have cried. The squadron leader dismissed the remaining, downhearted squadron members, then turned to me and apologized because of the snafu. My name had been partially smudged by the mimeograph ink. I had earned the rank of Aviation Cadet.

Tuskegee Institute - Aviation Cadet

After completing my basic training at Keesler Field, I was moved to Tuskegee Institute as a full-fledged aviation cadet. It was here that I took classes along with all the other black cadets, introducing us to the theories encompassing the total flying programs. Discipline was very tough at Tuskegee. We had to learn to focus and suppress any selfish goals we might have had. We had to internalize and practice the phrase, "Anything done must be for the good of the group."

As lower class cadets, we were called "Doe-Does". We had no individual rights, but we were used to that by now. The upper classmen who were flying as basic or advanced cadets were the bosses. We had to do anything they wanted us to do. For example, when the cadets would land after a night exercise, they would head straight for our barracks, turn on the lights, and yell "All right, Doe-Does, bed bug inspection." Of course bed bugs did not exist, but this was the upper classmen's way of bedeviling us. We had to tumble out of our beds, pile our blankets and sheets in one big pile, and then act like we were checking our mattresses for bed bugs. After about ten minutes the upper classmen would leave, but not before one of them would chant, "Lights out!" Thus we would have to use flashlights to find our bedding, make up our beds, then try to get some sleep before reveille.

There was another cute way the upper classmen could make our lives completely miserable. If, by chance during meal time, we earned the wrath of the upper classmen, they would have us eat a square meal as follows: take a fork of food, move the arm out about a foot, move the arm up a foot, move the arm towards the face a foot, then move the arm towards one's mouth. This would have been fine, except that we had only 20 minutes to get in, eat, and get out.

Another favorite practice of theirs was to stop us at random and make us sing one of the Tuskegee Airmen fight songs:

"Contact... Joy stick back
Sailin' through the blue.
Loyal sons of the 99th
Brave, Tried and True.
For we are heroes of the night.
To Hell with the Axis might.
Fight! Fight! Fight! Fight!
Fighting 99th!

I'm also reminded of two questions that bedevilled me as an underclassman. First, the upperclassman would put you in a "brace" (make you stand very rigid at attention), then get right in your face, no further than two inches away, and even if his breath reeked of garlic, you couldn't show it by flinching. Then, at the top of his voice, he would scream at you "How's the cow?" Then I'd belt out in a loud voice "sir," and before I could continue, he would yell "Do you think I'm deaf?" I'd start again in a well modulated voice "sir", and before I could go on, he said "I can't hear you." This went on for a few more minutes and finally I was able to answer the question:

"Sir, she walks she talks
she's full of chalk
the lacteal fluid extracted from the
female of the bovine species
is good for man or beast
of which I am the lowest
to say the least.

The second question which I dreaded was: "What time is it?"

Answer: "Honored upperclassman, I am greatly embarrassed and deeply humiliated that due to unforeseen circumstances over which I have no control, the inner workings and hidden mechanisms of my poor chronometer are in such a state of discord with the Great Sidero Movement by which all time is commonly reckoned, I cannot with any degree of accuracy give you the correct time. However without fear of being too far off or too far afield, I will say it is ___ minutes, ___ seconds, and ___ ticks past ___ o'clock.

All of the above questions had to be recited from memory on demand. While in some ways it seemed a pointless and trivial exercise, it was one of the many shared experiences that bonded us to each other, and to the traditions of military service. It was one of the many things that made us, in our own minds, soldiers, not just "black soldiers." Yet, as we were to learn later, not everyone saw us the same way.

Tyndall Field, Florida

Tyndall Field was my home for six weeks while I took the gunnery program. Though I received the same training as the white cadets who were also stationed here, our group was segregated from them. This was the practice throughout our training, with the exception of the time we spent at Tuskegee, where there were no whites. At Tyndall we would eventually learn to hit and bring down an attacking plane going 400 mph at a distance of 100 yards with a fifty caliber machine gun. That was the theory at least, and the gunnery school instructors did their best to make your fire deadly. In the first phase we had to master was the 24-target turkey shoot. We would individually hop aboard a small flatbed truck which had a 20 inch metal ring anchored with 4 ft. rods to the truckbed. Only one instructor and one cadet were involved with each truck. I stepped inside this waistline ring, which was designed to keep tl e shooter from losing his balance as they traversed the course. The instructor closed the waistline as he handed me a double-barreled, 12 gauge shotgun. The instructor said, "The course has 24 targets, all you have to do is shoot, then hold your shotgun at the ready, and I'll drop the shells in for you. Be sure to lead the target." These were his last instructions before the truck started moving around the course. It was quick fun, "breaking the birds," as we called the pigeons. They would pop out of the ground at all heights, angles, and speeds. Target 24 was the roughest of all to hit because it came straight at me. If I did get lucky and break it up, my face was filled with the mashed pieces. I eventually had to look good missing that shot, because the instructors would take me around four or five times until I could show him that my misses were intentional.

Our next phase of gunnery involved the .50 caliber machine gun. We spent several days and nights learning to disassemble and reassemble the machine gun, blindfolded. One of our lessons with the .50 caliber machine gun was to observe how a single round could travel. We gathered behind a loaded .50, which was imbedded in concrete. One cadet would fire a round which went down range over a cleared swamp. After a very short time you could see the big splash made by the round, four miles away.

The last phase of our gunnery preparation involved demonstrating our marksmanship. Five cadets were assigned to an airship. Each gunner had his tracer bullets painted a different color. The target-towing plane would take off and head for the target area over water. Before he took off, the pilot captain of the target plane met with each cadet and warned us that we had better shoot straight, or else. We all had a laugh at his threat, but the truth was, just as it was when we were crawling under live fire at Keesler Field, that there were very real dangers involved throughout military training. It made you appreciate how much you had to trust your fellow soldiers and how much they relied upon you. It really brought home the seriousness of our responsibilities, and the dangers of the war waiting for us just around the corner. As we rendezvoused with the target plane I could see that there was a distance of at least 100 yards between the plane and the target sleeve. One by one we loaded our special rounds into the machine gun and fired. After all of us finished, we landed and literally ran to the target plane to check the sleeve. An officer was already there, checking the hits. "Calm down, cadets," he bellowed. Then he proceeded to read the color hits. I had blue, which hit 15 times, which was pretty decent.

Not only did we need to rely on each other, but when you're up in the air, your equipment also becomes very important. Unfortunately, with the demands of the war, the planes made available for training, especially for training black airmen, were frequently not in the best of condition. I got the scare of my young life on one of our training missions. We were aboard a B-17. It seems that as we were approaching the field, the landing system went down. That is, the gears were stuck in the "up" position. The pilot said the only thing we could do was to try to crank the wheels down by hand. In the meantime, he said he would circle the field to use up as much fuel as possible, so that if we crashed, the risk of explosion and fire would be reduced somewhat. Two cadets at a time started turning the crank. It was very hard work, and everybody was soaking wet trying to maneuver the crank. Finally, a light flickered on, indicating that the landing gear was down, and the pilot ordered all of us to assume crash positions because he wasn't certain the wheels had locked. Fortunately the wheels held.

On yet another training mission aboard the B-17, I was assigned to the machine gun at one of the side windows. There I was reminded that, despite the dangers and hardships we were enduring in preparation for war, the real thing was a lot worse. What shook me up was what I saw when I looked above my head on the roof of the plane. Starting from midway and continuing in a straight line, stopping at the window, then picking up again at the floor of the plane, was a series of two-inch square metal plates with screws in the middle to form metal patches. What this represented was an American gunner having been machine-gunned by the enemy. It was a pretty sobering thought.

Strange Gig

During my free-time, I discovered a drum set in the recreation room on which I would occasionally practice. Later, another cadet who played the piano joined me, and we began to make music together. Soon word got around about us. The white cadets who were quartered on the other side of the base had planned a dance but needed live music. The group captain asked us to play. We refused at first because no blacks could attend, but finally agreed to play with the stipulation that our entire company be given extra free time. That was agreed upon. On the night of the dance, a surprise scene greeted our eyes when we set up for the affair. Tall palm trees were arranged in front of the musicians. I could only assume that someone didn't want our eyes to see the Southern belles, or maybe they thought seeing us would be offensive to the guests. To those guests, we were the mystery band. Whatever the reason for the arrangement, next time I was asked, I refused.

Midland Texas – Bombardier Training

The final phase of my training to become a U.S. Air Force bombardier took place at Midland, Texas. The training was very intense, tough, and unforgiving. We had to master everything connected with the deadly missiles for which we were responsible. Classroom work involved studying the 100-pound bomb, which was our main armament. We had to learn their make up, how to defuse them, how to fuse them, and how to load them in the bomb bays. Our chief aiming device was the Norden Bomb Sight. Our instructor warned us that when we got into combat, we should never let the bomb sight be captured by the enemy. Consequently, all officers in the combat theaters were issued .45 caliber automatics. Their prime responsibility was to shoot and destroy the bomb sight in the event of pending capture. The training target on which we had to drop our bombs for grades was a 100 ft. radius white circle inside of which were two other circles at a 50 ft. radius and a 25 ft. radius. In the center of the circle was a roughly built little shack. The objective was to hit this shack, which would erupt with very vivid colors. The highest mark one could get was a C.E. (Circle of Error) of zero. If we dropped three bombs and hit within the 100 ft. circle at 50 ft., 20 ft., and 70 ft., our C.E. was 140/3, which came to 46. We tried to keep our C.E.'s less than 50.

I recall one practice run which we flew, but could not complete because, of all things, cows and goats were in and around our 100 ft. target. Our pilot tried to scatter the livestock by buzzing them, to no avail, because some of them just gathered around the shack. We were told to abort that mission and return to the base. The pilot flew us to a restricted area used for that purpose, and we jettisoned all of the bombs. The next morning there were several farmers lined up at the adjutant general's office, demanding money for their livestock which had been destroyed by the training bomb runs. It seemed that this was a regular ritual, and the strange part was that the bombs never destroyed just ordinary, plain livestock, but, rather, they killed prime beef or rare experimental breeds. The day before we had not hurt one cow, but here they were seeking money for the phantom cows.

For our final grade we had to pass a night bombing raid. To make the testing as fair as possible, instructors were switched for this final run. My instructor was as cold as mackerel to me. He didn't even use an oxygen mask as we went up into the stratosphere. Rather, he put the oxygen tube in his mouth and stared at me. We were about 40 miles from the target and, even though we were leveled off at 15,000 feet, where the air was cold, I was sweating, both from the knowledge that this was my final run, and from the instructor's icy stare. I stole a look at him through my oxygen mask and saw that he had a 50 mission crush on his hat and that he was a command bombardier who had just returned from combat. His task was to share his techniques and experiences with the advanced students. At that moment I noticed that we were coming up on the 20 mile check point to the target. The Norden bombsight is equipped so that at a signal from the pilot, the bombardier can take over the plane and fly it straight and level to the point of bomb release over to the target. "I've got it," I said to the pilot. He responded by raising both arms in the air. This signaled that the plane was all mine. I peered intently into the eyepiece of the bombsight and then I saw the target, a brilliant 100 ft. circle, all lit up with electric bulbs. Then things got pretty busy and hairy for me. My eyes were tearing a little, my lenses were fogging, the oxygen was burning my throat, and, as the target loomed closer, a crosswind came up to bedevil me. I finally got a lock on the target and I was doing my darndest to crab in the crosswind with the controls of my left hand. My right hand was busy making final adjustments with the bombsight. Then the moment came, the point of no return, the point where you make the decision to start the rate motor on the bomb sight. I pushed the toggle switch without looking or thinking. The two indicators started for each other, one from the top of the scale going down, and the other from the bottom of the scale going up. When both indicators met, that would automatically send an electrical impulse to the bomb rack which, in turn, would release the bomb and send it on its way. Well, I heard the click and said to myself, "I'm not ready." I had to make another sight adjustment. But it was too late, all I could do was trust that I had made the correct calculation. I closed my eyes and nothing happened. I knew I had blown it. I was starting to feel sorry for myself when all of a sudden, the sky burst into a myriad of red, green and yellow. All of the colors were reflected on the plane. I heard the congratulatory yells from the cockpit and felt a hand on my shoulder, causing me to turn and look into a happy bombardier instructor's face. "Great job, Cadet Battle. You hit the shack. Dinner's on me when we land."

Navigation Training

Our preparation to become bombardiers also included navigation training. "O.C.O.D." was the sweetest sound a training navigator could hear (On Course over Destination.) On this training navigation flight, there were three of us cadets who would take turns guiding the plane through a triangular pattern, each cadet being responsible for one leg of the pattern. Our training ship was the AT-11, which was a twin-motored, single-wing job. The maximum height we could fly was around 9,000 feet. I had the 2nd leg on this flight which would take us through two mountains which we called "The Breasts of Sheba". The Eagle Pass Air Force Base was located at the base of these mountains, but we could not land there, unless there was an emergency. I was doing a good job, but our fuel was running low. Then I noticed that at our present elevation we were headed right for the narrow gap between the mountains. "Can you go over the mountains?" I asked. "Negative," the pilot replied. "This is where your straight line should help us," he said. We entered the gap and then we started getting buffeted all ways, up, down, right, left. It was eerie and scary to see the sides of the mountains on either side of the plane. The natural turbulence created by the winds between the two mountains was difficult to compensate for because it kept changing. I figured that if I could navigate through this then I could navigate through anything, but I wasn't so sure I could get us through this. Then, all of a sudden we broke through to the calm. I looked back and saluted the Breasts of Sheba.

Midland AFB, Texas

One of the most important lessons I received came not from the Army, but from Coleman Young, who is now a former Mayor of Detroit, and was then a lieutenant in the 92nd infantry who had applied to become an aviation cadet. One weekend, during bombardier training at Midland Field, I was getting ready to go to town. Lt. Young offered me a ride. When we got to the gate, the white guard motioned us through. Lt. Young did not move the car. There was a long line behind us, but still we sat there. Lt. Young, said to the guard, "Don't you see these bars?" The guard replied, "Sorry, sir, I thought you were a cadet." "Well, Goddamit, you now know I'm a lieutenant," Lt. Young said in a very loud voice. "So whether you want to salute me or not, salute this bar." The guard turned beet-red and saluted. I'll always thank Coleman for that lesson in manhood and respect. What few rights we had, we needed to insist on being respected if we were going to keep them.

Midland Field at another time served as a focal point for the colored cadets to bond. One Saturday about forty of us were boarded on the army bus for the ride to town. When we got to the gate, the guard, in a "mean" mood, decided to take his sweet time and acted like he was reading a sheaf of papers. A cadet on our bus yelled, "Hurry it up, please!" The guard said, "Who said that?" When nobody answered, the guard came on the bus and selected the first cadet he came to and said, "You. Come with me!" No sooner had they left the bus than all of us decided to egress. The guard's eyes popped open. He ran to the guard shop and came out with a Thompson .45 sub-machine gun. At that moment a colonel was entering the base. We wound up boarding the bus with our liberty canceled, but we were men who had bonded.

The life of an aviation cadet, by design, is a very strenuous one. We did, however, have some occasional free time, though I sometimes think it was only given to us so that the Army could threaten to take it away. The town of Midland, Texas, which offered some recreational opportunities, was about thirty miles from where we were stationed. One had two ways to go to town: by the service bus, or by private car. The first bus would leave the base around 10:00 a.m. Saturday and you could catch a ride to town each half hour until noon. The first bus returning to the base from town left at 5:30 p.m. and for each ensuing half hour thereafter, until the last bus which left at 7:00 p.m.

Well, I was having myself a ball in town. I went to the "colored only" theater, then to the "Greasy Spoon", for ribs and cornbread. I decided to take the early, 6:30 p.m. bus back to the base, because I didn't want to be late for the 9:00 p.m. bedcheck. As it happened, we had a substitute driver who either got lost, or for some reason took the circuitous route to the base, with the end result that I was marked AWOL. The next morning, Sunday, after breakfast, I was summoned to the Colonel's office. Now, this colonel was one tough bird. When I knocked on the door, he literally growled, "Come." I entered, took two steps, and halted in front of a large desk. Seated behind the desk was a stocky, middle-aged man with cold, steel blue eyes. I saluted, remained at attention and focused my eyes on a spot in the wall just above his head. "Cadet Battle," he said. "You missed bed check last night. This is inexcusable. What have you to say for yourself?" I said, "Sir, I took the 6:30 bus because I didn't," he cut me off and said, "You didn't leave early enough." I said, "But I took the early bus so I wouldn't be late." "You didn't leave early enough." Well, this scenario went on for a few more minutes with his response always the same, no matter what I said, "You didn't leave early enough." Then, like a bolt of lightning the thought came to me, "He's right. I didn't leave early enough." I quickly assured the colonel that the point of his philosophy was not wasted on me. To which he replied as he dismissed me, "We'll see."

Later that year, it was rumored that Charlie Barnett and his big band were coming to our base to give a concert, followed by a dance. Boy, I just had to catch that. Well, the rumor turned out to be true. All that week before, I made sure not to get any demerits. Demerits took the form of half hours or hours which had to be marched off by the receiver, usually on Saturday afternoon or Sunday morning. Well, on this particular Saturday we were standing inspection. (We were lined up outside our barracks while the officer of the day was inside wearing white gloves checking for dust and dirt). The OD came out, said a few words to our squadron commander and then departed. The squadron commander called us to attention. Then he said, "The following squadrons are dismissed and free to leave the base: A, C, D, E and F. Squadron B will remain behind and prepare their barrack for a Sunday inspection. Squadron B was my squadron. My spirits hit bottom. I sure wanted to see that "Charlie Barnett Band." They had a very talented drummer with a fantastic back beat. His name was Lehman. To top it off, we still did not know what we had to do to make things right.

When we were dismissed by our squadron commander, we ran through the entrance and were stopped in our tracks by what we saw on the floor. All of our barrack floors were composed of Georgian pine, scrubbed white. What greeted us was a drawn two foot circle of red chalk connected by a red chalk line of four feet to another two foot circle. The first circle had the words, "Not this", scrawled near a small, dirty spot. The second circle had the two words "But this", written in the clean circle. We knew immediately what had to be done. So we stripped to our shorts, took out the scouring powder, got on our knees, and each, with a toothbrush, started scrubbing. This GI party lasted until the wee hours of the morning. We definitely didn't want to flunk the upcoming Sunday inspection.

Midland AAF Graduation

The biggest, most important day of my young life had finally rolled around... November 4th, 1944; this was the day that I would have those silver bombardier wings pinned on my chest. This was the day that I would have those bright and shiny gold bars pinned on my shoulders.

A few days before graduation day at Midland, all senior cadets met in the base theater one morning to prepare for the ceremony. We practiced marching in, sitting and standing together, approaching the stage, walking erectly across same, extending our left hand for the diploma and saluting with our right. Also, we had to take four more strides, come to a halt with both arms by our sides, count to 10 silently (this to account for our wings and bars being pinned on our blouses), then purposely march off the stage and return to our seats.

On November 3rd, 1944, the day before the ceremonies, I was discharged as an enlisted man in preparation for my graduation, a procedure which mystifies me even to this day. That night I could hardly sleep as I reflected on the events of the past year. So many thoughts flashed through my mind. I virtually relived every phase of my training – the ups and downs – the times when I doubted myself – the times when images of my mother and aunt would nudge me to perk up and try harder. Finally, dawn came and the barrack started to come to life with joyous laughter, bantering, and the clatter of shower clogs. I jumped out of bed, grabbed my shower and shaving kit, draped a towel around my shoulders, worked the light switch very fast and yelled, "up and at 'em, cadets, the world is waiting," as I ran for the door, ducking thrown shoes and clothing headed my way. As I hastened to the showers I heard singing emanating from several rooms which caused me to lift my voice and join in, "...For we are heroes of the night, to hell with the Axis might, fight, fight, fight, fight, Fighting 99th." Whenever I sang that song, my heart soared to the outer limits. Shortly thereafter, we dressed, stood roll call and marched to breakfast. This being a special day for us was not lost on the Mess Sergeant. His menu for that morning included orange juice, pancakes, sunny-side up eggs, sausage links, and milk.

At 10 a.m. we filed into the base theater, which was very crowded. The audience included base personnel, underclass cadets, parents, friends, and the press (both service and civilian). The program started with all standing and saluting the flag, followed by the singing of the National Anthem. Several speakers followed, then, at long last, the base commander directed that we, the cadets, as our names were called were to come to the stage to receive our bars and wings. We were then given up to two weeks leave and instruction to report to Godman Field, Kentucky, at the termination of our leave.

As the last of the cadets, now lieutenants, marched across the stage, the theater erupted into deafening applause and shouts of joy. We had reached our first plateau in our quest to become effective, deadly warriors. We cadets then made a slight change in the last procedure. Instead of marching off ramrod style, we broke into a wide grin, faced the audience, raised our diplomas over our heads and shouted "yeah!"

At the end of the ceremony the base commander did a strange thing. Instead of having us stand and file out, he merely said, "Cadets, the rest of the morning is free time for you... Dismissed." Rather than us (cadets) jumping up and running to the exit, we just looked at each other and wondered aloud as we slowly made our way to the exits – we just were not used to extended, unexpected free time. As we pushed open the doors which led to the very expansive lobby, we saw the reason for the rule relaxation. There in a straight line about five yards apart were five mannequins fully outfitted in officer uniforms. Next to each mannequin were two salesmen and a small round table. As we entered the lobby a sergeant announced over a portable P.A. system that these people were here to show and sell us uniforms... that we should shop for our best deal.. that military chits would be provided - two hundred fifty dollars in value with which to purchase our uniforms. The sales pitch was unbelievable - the price for each item was quite reasonable. For example, shoes were fifteen dollars, trousers were fifteen dollars, coat blouses were thirty dollars, visor caps and insignias were six dollars. The scene was free enterprise's finest hour. As it turned out, each company just appeared to offer cut-rate prices to get your business. In the long run, the complete uniform cost the same no matter which company you selected.

Military Experience – Godman Field

On November 16, 1944, I reported to Godman field where I was assigned to the 477th Medium Bombardment Group – 616th Squadron. We were scheduled to do all of our training and fighting in the Billy Mitchell B-25 Medium Bomber. In my mind's eye, I had arrived! I was a Second Lieutenant. Shortly after my arrival on the base, I had my first opportunity to return an enlisted man's salute. I was so happy to salute him back that I almost hit myself in the eye with my thumb. I almost reached out and shook his hand. There were four squadrons in our group – the 616th, 617th, 618th, and 619th. As it turned out, we trained at Godman Field from November 16, 1944 through April 4th, 1945. Our combat training was very rigorous, and seemingly, non-stop. Each morning began with a briefing at 0700 hours, at which time we were given our targets for the day. Records of hits or misses would be kept by gun cameras. Also, navigational problems were built into each assignment by the use of alternate targets. I am loathe to mention my first mission with my permanent crew, however, my conscience insists that I tell it like it was. On this particular morning, our crew learned that we would be flying in formation with two other B-25's. Plane A would take the first leg of the mission by flying 200 miles due southwest of Godman; plane B would take the second leg by flying due north for 200 miles, and my plane (C) would fly the third leg of the mission by flying on a southeast heading back to the base. Theoretically, the squadron was in my hands on the final leg as I became the navigator of the lead ship, with the other two planes following off each wing. The other two navigators guided the squadron without any problem – they jubilantly cried out "OCOD," which means 'on course over destination' when they hit their respective destinations. My pilot maneuvered our plane into the lead and said over the intercom, "OK Battle, you've got it, take us back to the base, I'm hungry."

"Roger that," I said, and proceeded to 'walk' my compass along the third leg. With authority I said, "Our ETA (estimated time of arrival) will be 11:45 a.m. "Great," replied the pilot. We were doing "dead reckoning" navigation (where the exact location of an airship is confirmed by sighting landmarks). After a few minutes, I double-checked my calculations and when I looked out of the window and saw a town whose name was painted on a big red barn, I was both elated and crushed. To my relief, the name of the town was on my map, however, it was twenty miles northwest of my base line. I immediately plotted the new course to the base and pressed my intercom to give the pilot a new heading. "Damn," the pilot exclaimed. "What happened?" he yelled. "I guess crosswinds must have blown us of course," I replied. "OK Battle," he said, "but if this new course heading you gave me is garbage, I'll write you up!" Needless to say, I was one worried 2nd Lt. The next time I looked out the window to confirm our location I was treated to a lovely sight. We were just about to cross the Ohio River and in a matter of seconds we were OCOD over Louisville, Kentucky. Soon the co-pilot radioed to the base traffic controller, "Roger, runway two." After all three planes were taken over by the crew chiefs, I quickly went to each group and apologized to them. The pilot of plane B said, "Forget it Battle, this was your first assignment and mission on a front line warplane with such power and speed, just keep in mind that crosswinds affect us just like it does in the featherweights you were flying at Midland. I strongly suggest that all of you navigators check and go over your calculations every three minutes while in flight."

It eventually came about that the 477th was ready for advanced combat training which would be conducted at Freeman Field. Our "marching orders" came through and on April 5th, 1945, we were flown to Freeman Field.

Freeman Field, Seymour, Indiana

On April 5, 1945, we were transferred from Godman Air Force Base to Freeman Air Force Base for our final training before going overseas to one of the theaters of war. All four squadrons of the 477th Bombardment Group, the 616th, 617th, 618th, and 619th were included in the transfer to Freeman's, ostensibly for advanced combat training. We were on the verge of joining those black airmen who had so recently gone before us and were, despite the scepticism of their white counterparts, distinguishing themselves in combat. As fate would have it, the war would end before we joined them. We did, however, fight one battle ourselves before the end of the war. And in many ways it was a battle of greater consequence than any we were likely to have seen overseas.

Colonel Selway, the base commander, upon learning that an "all colored" unit would be attached to Freeman Air Force Base as of April 5, 1945, had previously issued an illegal order concerning the use of the Officer's Club designed to separate 'trainees' of the 477th Bombardment Group, all of whom happened to be colored, from the supervisory officers, who were white. As an alternative, the Commanding Officer at the airfield would offer the colored officers access to the noncommissioned officers' club on the base. We, the newly arrived officers, did not want that action to be taken because, first, it would have displaced the NCO's, and second, we referred to this building as "Uncle Tom's Cabin," and did not want to be involved in its use.

We, the Negro officers, were very angry. We knew that this denial of our admission to the Officer's Club was arrogant, blatant racism. We knew that our commission gave all of us the right of access to the club, as stated in Army Regulations 210-10, paragraph 19, dated 1940, which opened the Officers' Clubs on all posts, bases, and stations to all officers. The regulations clearly stated that being an officer entitled one to membership in Officer's Clubs. This was one the pleasant perks that made military life comfortable. This also gave one access to the swimming pool, dinner specials, bar and locker privileges, dances, weekly out-of-town shows, and so forth. As a practical matter, we were not about to accept accommodations inferior to what the white officers enjoyed. As a matter of principle, we were not going to allow the Army to violate clearly stated regulations in an effort to enforce the racially motivated segregation of our unit. And as a matter of pride, we were not about to endure the disrespect for ourselves and what we had accomplished, inherent in this attempt to prevent our free association with the other, white, officers. We had trained the same, been tested the same, and achieved the same as our white counterparts. And we were prepared to fight and die if necessary to preserve the freedoms upon which our country had been founded. We were determined not to accept this intolerable violation of our rights and the disregard for our dignity that Col. Selway's order represented.

I was one of the officers from my squadron who decided to take a stand against segregation at Freeman's Field the day of our arrival, April 5, 1944. After attending a movie at the base theater, we decided to enter the segregated Officers' Club. I was among the first 19 to test this unlawful order by Col. Selway. We lined up by two's and approached the main entrance. We were met there by the Assistant Provost Marshall and several military police who refused us entrance into the club. We looked at each other in disbelief. During the interim, 2nd Lt. Roger C. Terry, and officer whom we all admired and respected, passed by the Assistant Provost Marshall, inadvertently brushing up against him. For that Lt. Terry was arrested, charged and eventually convicted by general court-martial. The rest of us in that particular line were placed under 'barrack' arrest. Word spread like wildfire throughout the 477th. Within two or three days, the figure of those arrested rose to 101 plus 3. The '3' included Lt.'s Terry, Thompson, and Clinton. Altogether, 104 Negro officers were taken into custody for this act of defiance.

We were very cognizant of the fact that, theoretically, because this was during wartime, we could be brought up on charges of treason, or mutiny, and consequently executed. There was a very real danger that this could happen. The idea of people taking aggressive civil rights actions was not yet established in the public mind, much less in the context of the military with its far greater restrictions on personal liberties. Bear in mind that our actions came 10 years before Rosa Parks refused to give her seat to a white man in Montgomery, Alabama, and more than 20 years before Martin Luther King, Jr. marched on Washington. Still, we were committed to our cause, and believed that whatever the outcome, we had no choice but to proceed as we did.

We were released from barracks after about a day and a half, at which time we were asked to read, and acknowledge by our signatures, that we understood Base Regulation 85-2, which was the illegal memorandum placing the Officer's Club off limits to us. The entire group of us who had been arrested for entering the club in the first place, refused to comply with this request, and were subsequently rearrested. We continued to be confined to our barracks where we were subjected to extensive and very intense interrogations. I remember being interrogated three times. Senior officers from the Adjutant General's Office in Washington, D.C. came to the base for that particular purpose. Their sessions with me would start around 2:00 a.m. and continue until daybreak. I was transferred from Freeman Field back to Godman on April 28, 1945, still under barrack arrest and still under interrogation by the Senior officers from Washington. During the interrogation sessions, each protester was called into a small room and questioned relentlessly. Actually, they were trying to find out who our leaders were; they were very anxious to identify them and make examples of them. They tried to break our spirits, but we bonded together. The interrogators urged us to sign a form saying that we would not attempt to reenter the club, and further, to admit that we had disobeyed direct orders. We were told that if we signed the form, all charges would get dropped. We refused and subsequently remained under arrest. Below I have included some of the transcript from one of my interrogations.

Excerpts from the interrogation of Lt. LeRoy A. Battle
by Col. John A. Hunt, IGD

Q *... You were told that you were going to be put under arrest by order of the Commanding Officer if you went into the club, isn't that correct?*

A Yes, we were told we would be put under arrest.

Q *Yet you did violate the order and you were placed under arrest, isn't that true?*

A Well, that wasn't in the form of any order. That was just a statement by them, sir.

Q *You didn't understand it to be an order?*

A No, sir.

Q *A superior officer told you that that was the case and that you would be arrested if you went inside. That didn't indicate to you that you were not supposed to go in, is that it?*

A Well, he didn't explain anything, sir.

(Later, on the issue of whether or not Lt. Battle understood the content of the order)

Q *Well, if I say that you are an officer undergoing training and that you were not to enter Club Building T-930, would you understand it?*

A Well –

Q *Would you understand that you were to remain out of Club Building T-930?*

A Well, I don't understand why, sir.

Q *I'm not talking about why. Do you understand from the language in here that you are not supposed to enter Building T-930?*

A I don't understand why, sir.

Q *If I told you that I did not want you to enter that closed door over there, would you know what I meant?*

A Well, yes, sir.

Q *As your superior officer, if I ordered you not to leave this building, would you understand what I meant?*

A Yes, sir.

Q *If I told you that, as your commanding officer, I forbade you to enter that building across the street, would you know what I meant?*

A Yes, sir.

Q *And if I were at Freeman Field and told you that Building T-930 was assigned to other personnel and that you were not to enter it, would you understand what I meant?*

A Well, no, sir.

And so it went.

There was a public outcry. The "colored press" was behind us all the way; the Afro-American Newspaper, the Amsterdam News and, mainly, the Pittsburgh Courier, just to mention a few. The parents of each officer became involved. My mother wrote President Truman regarding my being held under barrack arrest. She received a reply from the President in which he stated that the problem would be investigated.

As a direct result of my having taken part in protesting the practice of segregation by insisting on entering the Officer's Club set aside for white officers only, I received an Administrative Reprimand, alluding to my stubbornness and noncooperative attitude. Specifically, the charges of "mutiny in the time of war" were reduced to "conduct unbecoming to an officer, failure to obey a lawful order, and breech of good order and discipline." This was the strongest injunction that could be taken against the 101 officers by the base commander. Said reprimand was placed in my 201 file. No further action was taken against me. I was released from barrack arrest. At Godman, the second time around, following our release from barrack arrest, we continued with our training as bombardiers and navigators.

I was, and still am, proud, very, very proud, of the part I played in our fight against racism and segregation... this fight was started at Freeman Field in Seymour, Indiana and played out at Godman Field, Kentucky, makes me happy to have been one of the original 101 plus 3 who threw down the gauntlet and openly challenged segregation in the armed forces. We fought the good fight, and won on many fronts. This experience definitely contributed to my tempering. Eventually, I am happy to report, President Truman abolished segregation at all military installations in 1948.

As further vindication of our actions, more recent exciting events have occurred which I am very happy to report:

1. August 12, 1995, fifty years later, Rodney A. Coleman, Assistant Secretary of the Air Force, announced that the Court Martial conviction against 2nd Lt. Roger C. Terry, who is now president of the Tuskegee Airmen, Inc., has been set aside and that all rights, privileges, and properties have been restored.
2. The 101 plus 3 officers involved in the so-called mutiny would have their letters of reprimand removed upon written request.

Walterboro Air Force Base, Walterboro, SC

Our training continued, but more as a formality, or perhaps just as a way of occupying us until they decided what to do with us. Though we were ready for combat assignment, I don't think anyone really wanted to send us overseas at this point. We were subsequently assigned to the Walterboro A.F.B., apparently for over-water training which should have included air-to-air gunnery, dead-reckoning navigation, and drift reading. Our training at Walterboro was to have been top quality, however, our complete complement of B-25's never arrived. In the final analysis, the effectiveness of our training was definitely compromised by the incompleteness of the program.

The immediate working conditions also tested our mettle. Walterboro was an anathema to me. Seemingly, the humidity was always higher than the temperature, which always lurked around the 100 degree mark. A good night's sleep just wasn't to be. For example, as soon as I laid down, one could see my body outline on the cot in sweat. We were billeted in tents at times, and had to be constantly wary of bugs and snakes. Through it all, however, we kept focused and made a pact that, with all we had gone through together, we would do whatever was necessary to help each other to ensure that no one would fail.

Shortly thereafter, word came down that the 477th would be disbanded and that all non-pilot officers would be able to continue in the service by taking pilot training a Tuskegee.

Tuskegee Army Air Field

I immediately enrolled in the primary class at Tuskegee and was making good progress in learning the skills of flying. However, the vagaries of war did not wait for me to become a pilot. On August 6th, 1945, the United States dropped the atomic bomb on Hiroshima. Three days later a good friend and I were flying in formation over the main campus of the Tuskegee Institute when a news flash came over our headphones stating that another atomic bomb had been dropped on Nagasaki. About one half hour later an announcement came over the radio stating that all officers who were classified with certain MOs and points could immediately file for honorable discharge. – File for discharge, wow! I couldn't believe it. Lights started going on in my head. "Could this be true?" I asked myself. "Battle," Harmon said, "C'mon, straighten up and fly right." I looked over to Harmon and saw that my daydreaming had caused me to drift away from our tight formation. I laughed, waved my hand then pulled up beside him. I was so excited, now I could get back to my first love, music. I really missed my drumming, oftentimes I would imagine myself at a club swinging away with some combo, and going back to school. There were so many things that popped in my head; "Where was I going to enroll? What subjects? Who was I going to study with? What about my music contacts? Would I get any gigs?" "Boy," I said to myself, "now I can continue my dream of becoming a musician and a teacher and help young minds to develop."

Any question I may have had about my ability to lead was dispelled long ago by the Air Corps when I became an officer. My friend and I each made the decision, at that point, to take advantage of this new "early-out" situation. After landing and clearing the flight line, we took a jeep and went directly to headquarters and filed for honorable discharge. This we were able to do because we had fulfilled our active duty requirements.

Following completion of all of the necessary paperwork, I was transferred to Maxwell A.F.B in Alabama for my final clearance, and was discharged from the Army Air Force on November 7, 1945.

HEADQUARTERS
MIDLAND ARMY AIR FIELD
Office of the Commanding Officer

Army Air Forces
Instructors School (Bomb.)

Army Air Forces
Bombardier School

Midland, Texas

November 4, 1944

Mrs. Margie Battle
1544 Fulton Street
Brooklyn, New York

Dear Mrs. Battle:

     Today I had the pleasure of seeing your son, who has been with us for four and one-half months as an Aviation Cadet, receive the silver bombardier wings that mark the beginning of a new career for him in the Army Air Forces.

     It is no easy task to complete successfully the eighteen week course at this Army Air Forces Bombardier School, the world's largest. I want to take this opportunity to tell you that you have every reason to be proud of your son, and of the record he has made here.

     As a bombardier-navigator, your son will play an extremely vital role in achieving the final victory for which we all are striving. He will be entrusted with great responsibility. He will be called upon to use his carefully acquired skills, and the skills of the men who have designed and produced American bombsights, planes, bombs and guns, to hasten the ultimate defeat of our enemies. I am more than confident that he is worthy of that trust.

     As a training school, we naturally take keen interest in learning how our graduates put into practice the lessons they have learned here. I hope that you and your son will write from time to time, keeping us informed of his progress.

     My heartiest congratulations to both you and your son. Good luck and Godspeed.

Sincerely,

CHAS. H. DOWMAN,
Colonel, Air Corps,
Commanding.

*Letter of congratulations to my mother upon
my completion of bombardier school.*

Lt. LeRoy A. Battle on leave in Brooklyn
following graduation, reunited with his mother (left),
and Aunt Bert. His officer's uniform had not yet arrived.

2nd Lt. LeRoy A. Battle

Some of my 'comrades-in-arms'

CONFIDENTIAL

HEADQUARTERS
FREEMAN FIELD
SEYMOUR, INDIANA

N-6

201-Battle, Leroy A. (0)   24 April 1945.

SUBJECT: Administrative Reprimand.

TO   :   Second Lieutenant Leroy A. Battle, "E" Squadron (Trainee), 118th Army
           Air Forces Base Unit (CCTS-M), Freeman Field, Seymour, Indiana.

           THRU: Commanding Officer, "E" Squadron (Trainee), 118th Army Air
                   Forces Base Unit (CCTS-M), Freeman Field, Seymour, Indiana.

     1.   On or about 11 April 1945, at Freeman Field, Seymour, Indiana, you
displayed a stubborn and uncooperative attitude towards the reasonable efforts
of constituted authority to disseminate among officers and flight officers of the
Command, information concerning necessary and proper measures adopted in the
administration of the Officers' Clubs of that station. This action on your
part indicates that you lack appreciation of the high standards of teamwork
expected of you as an Officer in the Army of the United States, and a failure to
understand that you should so conduct yourself at all times so as to be a credit
and a source of pride to the military service. In these respects, you have
failed definitely in your obligations to your Command and your country. It is
hoped and expected that you will consider this reprimand as a stern reminder of
the absolute requirements of prompt and willing compliance with the policies of
superior authority, and that there will be no repetition of such regrettable
actions on your part.
                                    made
     2.   This reprimand will be/a part of your official record.

     3.   You will acknowledge receipt by indorsement hereon.

                                            ROBERT R. SELWAY, JR.,
                                            Colonel, Air Corps,
                                            Commanding.

201-Battle, Leroy A. (0)   1st Ind.   N-6
HEADQUARTERS, "E" Squadron (Trainee), 118th Army Air Forces Base Unit, (CCTS-M),
Freeman Field, Seymour, Indiana. APR 24 1945

TO: Second Lieutenant Leroy A. Battle, "E" Squadron (Trainee), 118th Army Air
      Forces Base Unit (CCTS-M), Freeman Field, Seymour, Indiana.

      For your information and compliance with paragraph 3, basic communication.

                                            ANTHONY N. CHIAPPE,
                                            Captain, Air Corps,
                                            Commanding.

                                     - 1 -

*Letter of reprimand placed in 201 file of Lt. LeRoy Battle, as
punishment for refusing to sign and acknowledge Base Regulation 85-2,
the unlawful order which prohibited their use of the base Officer's Club.*

93

Men Crashed Clubroom For 'Whites Only'

Commanding Officer Threatened Court Martial of Men Who Busked Jim Crow Practice

WASHINGTON — Secretary Stimson's office in the War Department clamped down a complete blackout on any news regarding the reported arrest of 60 Negro officers at Freeman Field, Ind., charged with "invading the sacred precincts" of a club set apart for white officers.

FREEMAN FIELD, Seymour, Ind. (ANP)—Sixty Negro officers were placed under arrest at this field Friday for defying a ban on colored officers at the swanky and modern officers' club at this post by order of Col. Robert Selway, Jr.

...mass arrest, which is being unprecedented in the history of the army, has this post in uproar and has disrupted the ...re training program of the ... Bombardment group. This ...p is the first of all Negro Bombardment group—that is, all Negro for training—put whites for command and ...otion.

K-5

HEADQUARTERS
FREEMAN FIELD
SEYMOUR, INDIANA

11 April 1945

SUBJECT: Disciplinary Action.

TO : All Concerned

1. Pursuant to authority conferred by the 69th Article of War, the following named commissioned and flight officers are ordered into arrest in quarters, effective 2245 hours, 11 April 1945.

NAME	RANK	SERIAL NO.	SIGNATURE
Robert S. Payton Jr.	2nd Lt.	01174678	
Theodore O. Mason	2nd Lt.	0858167	
Adolphus Lewis Jr.	F/O	T-140136	
Luther Oliver	2nd Lt.	0841272	
Edward E. Tilman	2nd Lt.	02080957	
Frank V. Pivalo	F/O	T-136681	
Leonard E. Williams	2nd Lt.	01054447	
Norman A. Holmes	F/O	T-141212	
Roy M. Chappell	2nd Lt.	02068895	
Leroy A. Battle	2nd Lt.	02076525	
Charles E. Malone	F/O	T-136247	
Walter R. Ray	2nd Lt.	02058902	
Charles R. Taylor	F/O	T-136723	
Roger Pines	2nd Lt.	02058901	
Roland A. Webber	F/O	T-136696	
Samuel Colbert Sr.	2nd Lt.	02082500	
Rudolph A. Berthoud	2nd Lt.	02082576	
Clifford C. Jarrett	2nd Lt.	02075547	
Marcus E. Clarkson	F/O	T-138615	

2. It is ordered that each commissioned and flight officer acknowledge receipt of this order, by placing his signature opposite his respective name.

ROBERT S. SELWAY JR.,
Colonel, Air Corps
Commanding

Lt. LeRoy A. Battle – one of the original 19 officers to be formally charged.

Officers in Mass Arrest

Special

While the country mourns for Franklin D. Roosevelt, approximately one hundred Negro officers are being held under Gestapo tactics for upholding the principles of democracy for which he fought—and died. Three of the officers, members of the 477th Bombardment Group, are under technical arrest at Freeman Field, Seymour, Ind., while approximately 100 more were transferred last week to Godman Field, Ky., from whence they came, for refusing to sign a statement issued by the camp commander, declaring that they would follow orders to keep away from an officer's club, at the camp, which is used by whites only.

The three officers who were arrested Wednesday of last week, and scheduled for court martial for demanding entrance into the officers' club, are a part of a group of 61 who were originally arrested. They are Mardsen A. Thompson of Los Angeles, trainee adjutant; Shirley R. Clinton of Camden, N. J., trainee intelligence officer, and Roger C. Terry of Los Angeles, trainee co-pilot. The other 58 were released shortly after their arrest.

Later in the week, however, the commanding officer, Col. Robert Selway, requested all of the Negro officers to sign a statement, which he issued, declaring their intentions to obey the jimcro orders. Of a total officer personnel of the 118th Base Unit, of which the bombardment group is a part, approximately one hundred refused to sign the paper and they were shipped back to Godman Field and held in detention.

Despite efforts to hold the men incommunicado, tapping telephone wires, and barring them from telegraph offices and post offices, the men have found a way to communicate with relatives and friends and to tell the unseemly story of their plight.

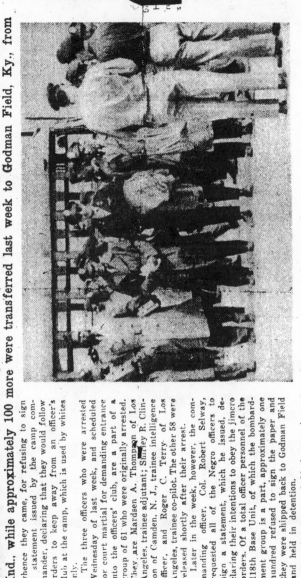

They're Fighting Jimcro. A few of the 101 officers at Freeman Field, Seymour, Ind., just after their arrest for refusing to sign an agreement that they would not enter a "white" officers' club. These men were given only one hour's notice to pack up before being flown to Godman Field, Ky., near Fort Knox, where, quite unexpectedly they were rearrested.

Army to Shift Colonel From 'Jim Crow' Field

By PAUL SANN
Post Staff Correspondent

Washington, Apr. 19—The War Dept., it was learned today, is taking steps to relieve Col. Robert R. Selway Jr. of duty as commandant of Freeman Field, Ind., at least until the investigation of the arrests of 101 Negro officer trainees as the field is completed.

The Inspector General's office has several men at the field at Seymour, Ind., and nearby Goldman Field, Ky., interviewing the officers who were arrested for refusing to sign a form pledging themselves not to attempt to use an officers' club reserved for white instructors.

Orders relieving Col. Selway were reported on the way to the base from Washington. When a somewhat similar incident occurred two years ago at Selfridge Field, Mich., the commanding officer was similarly relieved and Col. Selway succeeded him.

104 Face Courts Martial

The Post, which first revealed the mass arrests, also learned that the 101 men, as well as three Negro officers previously arrested, will face courts martial regardless of the results of the in-

Washington Bureau
Special to The Post

vestigation, because charges were quietly filed against them before the War Dept. took over the case.

The charge is violation of the 64th article of war—refusal to obey a direct command of a superior officer. It was learned that the 101 men were taken individually before a superior officer and in the presence of witnesses ordered to sign the indorsement of the Jim Crow policy.

Although Negroes were barred from the instructors club at Freeman Field on the pretext that it was Air Force policy to maintain separate recreational facilities for teachers and trainees, it was learned that no such distinction is drawn at other air fields where both teachers and trainees are white.

Action Against... Officers Halted

61 Ignored Color Bar at Officers' Club

3 FACED TRIAL

War Dept. Probe May Hit Biased Policy

WASHINGTON

Punitive action against 61 Air Force officers accused of violating jim-crow regulations at Freeman Field, Ind., has been suspended pending the outcome of an investigation now under way, the War Department announced Monday.

The announcement was construed as indicating that the officers might be sustained in their defiance of a post regulation which itself violates a War Department order against segregated recreational facilities.

It is understood that all the men involved are to remain at liberty during the investigation.

Attorney Retained

Meanwhile, Dr. William H. Hastie has been retained by the NAACP to represent the officers in any court-martial proceedings which may be held, with the assistance of Theodore M. Berry, president of the Cincinnati branch of the association.

Army Clears Negro Officers

 PM's Bureau

WASHINGTON, Apr. 26.—The War Dept. has dismissed charges against 101 Negro flying officers who had been arrested at Freeman Field, Ind., for refusing to sign a Jim Crow order issued by the commanding officer, the NAACP (National Association for the Advancement of Colored People) reported today.

At the same time, Rep. Helen Gahagan Douglas (D. Cal.) wired Secretary of War Stimson urging that charges also be dropped against three additional Negro officers who were arrested earlier for "jostling" a superior officer who sought to deny them admission to the officers' club.

Mrs. Douglas said in her wire that a total of 162 Negro officers had been arrested at the field since Apr. 5, with "all arrests predicated upon an invalid and wrongful order of the field commander." She added that the arrested men had not been furnished charges or permitted to consult counsel.

Leslie Perry, Washington representative of the NAACP, said the release of the 101 officers "is clear proof of the fact that the War Dept. has been able to see through the flimsy attempt of Col. Robert R. Selway, Jr., commanding officer, to segregate Negro officers at the field."

Negro Named Air Unit Head In Race Clash

Washington, D. C., June 21 (U.P.) —The recent conflict between white and negro Army Air Force officers over use of an officers club at Freeman Field, Seymour, Ind., prompted the War Department to place Col. Benjamin O. Davis Jr., a negro, in command of the 477th Composite Group, it was disclosed today.

Largely composed of Negroes, the 477th formerly was commanded by a white officer, Col. Robert B. Selway Jr., and had other white staff officers. It had been stationed at Freeman Field until its recent transfer to Godman Field, Ala.

Eaker Goes to Field.

Davis, accompanied by Lieut. Gen. Ira C. Eaker, flew today to take over his new assignment. He formerly commanded the 332d fighter group in Italy which flew as part of the 12th Fighter Command under the overall command of Eaker. A West Point graduate, he is the son of Brig. Gen. Benjamin O. Davis Sr., only Negro officer of star rank in the Army.

The Freeman Field incident arose when the officers club was reserved for use of the base staff and instructors. This, in effect, reserved it for white officers and barred Negro officer trainees.

97

IN REPLY REFER TO:
AGOB-C 291.2
(25 Apr 45)

WAR DEPARTMENT
THE ADJUTANT GENERAL'S OFFICE
WASHINGTON 25, D. C.

7 July 1945

Mrs. Margie Battle
223 W. 145 Street, Apt. 20
New York, New York

Dear Mrs. Battle:

This is in further reply to your letter of recent date concerning the arrest of your son, Lieutenant Leroy A. Battle, at Freeman Field, Indiana.

An investigation of conditions prevailing at Freeman Field discloses that Colonel Robert H. Selway, Jr., the Commanding Officer, directed that all officers of his command read a recently published regulation and certify that they had done so. The majority of the officers, including Negro officers, promptly complied. Approximately one hundred Negro officers, however, refused to obey the order and were thereupon placed in arrest. As you have perhaps learned by this time, they were subsequently released with a reprimand, there being a reasonable doubt that they understood the implication of their actions and it having been established that, as recent arrivals at the station, current base regulations had not been explained to them.

Sincerely yours,

EDWARD F. WITSELL
Major General
Acting The Adjutant General

LORs removed from Tuskegee Airmen's records

By MSgt. Merrie Schilter Lowe
Air Force News Service

Retired Air Force Lt. Col. James C. Warren and 100 other black Army Air Force officers stood against an unlawful order at Freeman Field, Ind. in 1945 and each received a letter of reprimand for his actions.

The men had tried to enter the base officers' club, which had been integrated by War Department policy, but again segregated by the local commander.

Fifty years later, on Aug. 12 in Atlanta, the Air Force vindicated Warren and 14 other Tuskegee Airmen members by removing the letters of reprimand from their permanent military records.

Rodney A. Coleman, assistant secretary of the Air Force for manpower, reserve affairs, installations and environment, announced the Air Force decision during the Tuskegee Airmen annual banquet.

He also announced that the Air Force set aside a court-martial conviction against another former Army Air Forces officer, Roger C. Terry, who is president of the Tuskegee Airmen, Inc. Additionally, the service restored all the rights, privileges and property Terry had lost because of the conviction.

Air Force Chief of Staff Gen. Ronald R. Fogleman, who was the banquet's guest speaker in Atlanta, presented the official documents to Warren and Terry.

"With this action, a terrible wrong in the annals of U.S. Air Force and U.S. military history has been righted," said Coleman. He said the Air Force will remove the letters of reprimand from the other 89 former officers' records as soon as it receives their requests.

The most recent of such requests were signed at Bolling last week.

During an informal ceremony Sept. 13 at the Bolling Officers' Club with the presence of Col. James Robertson, 11th Support Group commander, and Gerald

Tierney, officers' club general manager, two local Tuskegee Airmen filled out their DD Forms 149, application for correction of military record.

Earlier in his remarks, Coleman called the Freeman Field incident a "bellwether for change with respect to integrating the U.S. military."

He said the men who took part in the actions had taken "a giant step for equality" nine years before Rosa Parks refused to sit in the back of the bus in Montgomery, Ala., and paved the way for changes "in the soon to be brand new service — the U.S. Air Force."

Warren, who had been a flight officer in training at Freeman Field, started the letter removal process by writing to Coleman and asking the Air Force to consider correcting the records of everyone involved in the Freeman Field incident.

Coleman said his office worked with the records correction board to investigate the circumstances of the 50-year-old incident, which Warren describes in his book the "Freeman Field Mutiny."

"The 104 officers involved in the so-called 'mutiny' have lived the last 50 years knowing they were right in what

(Left) Alfred U. McKenzie and (above) Leroy A. Battle, Tuskegee Airmen, fill out DD Forms 149 in order to have LORs removed from their military records. (U.S. Air Force photos by SSgt. Joan Anderson-Brown)

they did — yet feeling the stigma of an unfair stain on their records because they were American fighting men, too — and wanted to be treated as such," said Coleman.

The Freeman Field incident began April 1, 1945, when the base commander issued a letter segregating trainees from base and supervisory officers. At the time, all the trainees were black and all base and supervisory personnel were white, said Coleman.

"The actual effect of the letter was to segregate the officers' clubs on the basis of race and authorized discrimination in violation of War Department policy," said Coleman.

Four days after posting the letter, the commander heard that some newly arriving black officers would try to enter the club so he ordered all doors locked, except the main entrance. He then posted military police at the club to keep out all "non-members."

That night, April 5, 1945, numerous groups of black officers tried to enter the club, Coleman said. Terry, who was a second lieutenant, brushed against a superior officer to gain entrance and was subsequently charged and convicted by

general court-martial of assault. Two other officers were also court-martialed but were later acquitted of all charges, said Coleman.

Those given letters of reprimand were charged with "conduct unbecoming an officer, failure to obey a lawful order and breech of good order and discipline." At the time, the letter of reprimand was one of the strongest administrative actions a commander could impose on service members, said Air Force legal officials who also worked on the LOR removal process.

Normally, requests to correct military records must be filed within three years of an incident. However, in the Freeman Field incident, the Air Force waived that ruling.

Other officers whose records have already been corrected are:

James B. Williams, James W. Whyte Jr., Alvin B. Steele, Frederick H. Samuels, Wardell A. Polk, Charles E. Malone, Edward R. Lunda, Adolphus Lewis Jr., James V. Kennedy, Edward V. Hipps, Mitchell L. Higginbotham, Lloyd W. Godfrey, and Roy M. Chappell.

"Boots" Battle reunited with
Junior Ragland and Dave Rivera
back at the Three Deuces Club, 1945

Growing Others

Transition From Discharge Back To Brooklyn

After two years away I wasn't sure what to expect when I returned. My mother and my Aunt Bert of course were still there. After my re-union with them, I went straight for my drums. I played a fast and furious single stroke roll to loosen up my wrists. Then I settled in to some of the old swing numbers I used to play. During my two years in the service, I kept a pair of sticks with me. I couldn't carry a drum pad so I had to drum on chairs, tables, and, when frustration set in because of studies or classes or heavy winds when I was navigating, I would drum on the floor. I literally drove my roommates batty. One time I remember they even hid my sticks for a few days. But there was no one to stop me now, and I was anxious to catch up with the latest music.

I hitched a ride home on a mail plane flying to Fort Dix, New Jersey, so I was able to save quite a bit of the cash the service allowed me for travel expenses. That, coupled with my "departure pay" meant that I had over seven hundred dollars in my pocket. The week after I got home I went downtown and got myself a complete outfit from the Lewis & Thomas Saltz clothing store. I bought several popular knit sport shirts in various colors; I also purchased three pairs of pastel colored gabardine slacks, a half-dozen argyle socks and two pairs of suede sport shoes – brown and tan.

I had Mother and Aunt Bert fill me in on who of my friends were still around. They always knew what was going on from listening to the ladies who gathered at the beauty salon. As luck would have it, all of my group were still away and involved with the services. A few days later I hopped the subway and made my way to the Rhythm Club on 132nd St. The employees were elated to see me. I couldn't pay for anything – they treated me to drinks and meals. They said I could work that very day if I had my set, because gigs were plentiful. It was a musician's dream, "Gigs-a-plenty."

Soon word got around that I was back in the circuit and it wasn't long before I started gigging again on 52nd Street. For a while I got back together with Junior Ragland and Dave Rivera, and played at the Three Deuces. That summer I returned to the resort I played at follow-

101

ing my junior year in high school. Later, Oscar Smith, a bassist with whom I gigged occasionally prior to my stint in the military, and I hooked up again along with a keyboard player to form a swing trio.

When the winter term came around, in January of '46, I matriculated at the Julliard School of Music, my goals being to study the classics and to seriously start on my path to teaching. I never lost that "fire-in-my-belly" to teach in the high school. I studied at Julliard for three semesters under the G.I. Bill of Rights. It was wonderful being associated with my former instructor, Professor Saul Goodman, again. Things were back almost to the way they were when I left for the military; I was going to school during the day and gigging at night.

During my time at Julliard my goal to become a high school teacher started gaining momentum, but it seemed elusive. Juilliard was geared more toward those individuals who aspired to be professional performers. As much as I enjoyed performing, I knew that if I wanted to teach someday, I would have to go somewhere else to complete my education. So when Oscar Smith mentioned Morgan State College in Baltimore as a school which could effectively prepare me for a teaching career, my ears perked up.

Oscar Smith was a very erudite musician. He had it all, the theory, the technique, and the soul. One evening during a break, Oscar said to me, "Boots, this is my last week here. I am leaving to fill a position at Morgan State College." This news affected me a great deal because Oscar and I had been playing together for some time. As part of the rhythm section, and members of the "trio" we worked in tandem to drive this group to new heights.

Eight months after he left 52nd Street, Oscar wrote me a letter. In short, he stated that he could use me at Morgan to help with his percussion section. He said if I came down he would see that I got financial aid. He also said that I could get work gigging at the local clubs.

I showed the letter to Mother and Aunt Bert. Both agreed with my decision to enroll at Morgan. This is what I have always loved about Mother and Aunt Bert. They never stood in my way if I wanted to spread my wings.

Morgan - Orientation to Campus and City

The letter from Oscar arrived during the month of August. Within a week after receiving the letter, I had tendered my resignation from the gig on 52nd Street, packed my bags and was on my way to Baltimore. Oscar met me at the station and we took the long ride out to the campus. We went to the registrar's office where I was eventually enrolled. Afterwards Oscar said he had some business to see to and would meet me at the registration building around 4:00 p.m. I decided to forgo using the student guide to shepherd me around, and take the more adventurous way of wandering around the campus alone. As I emerged from the registrar's office, I heard the glorious thump and boom of an orchestra's rhythm section in the distance. I followed the beat until the trumpets and reed section became clearer. I hastened my step and finally stood in front of a rehearsal hall. Classes had not begun yet, but this was preregistration week and all freshmen had reported early. There was large crowd of them gathered around the entrance, and some were looking into the windows. I became very excited when I heard the strains of Count Basie's "Swingin' the Blues," emanating from that room. There were more students gathered around the orchestra. There, in the middle of the room, was Morgan's Stage Band, consisting of four trombones and a full rhythm section consisting of piano, guitar, bass, and drums.

Everything and everyone was informal and casual. Some band members wore pork pie hats, caps, and "T" shirts. Their instructor sported an open collar sport shirt with short sleeves. In comparison I must have looked a little out of place. I was wearing a rust colored cardigan sport jacket which had no buttons, held together with a belt which I had casually tied in front. My slacks and shirt were cream colored and I wore black rayon socks and ox-blood colored loafers. To say that I was the best dressed student on campus was putting it mildly. Between selections, Mr. Strider, chairman of the instrumental music department, came over to me and asked if any of my relatives were in the band. I told him no, then I explained why I was there at Morgan. I told him of my professional background experience on 52nd street, and, also, told him about my special relationship with Oscar himself. Mr. Strider's eyes lit up and he introduced himself. He had a broad grin when he said to the band, "Ladies and gentlemen, I want you to meet our newest addition to our music department, Mr. LeRoy Battle, who comes to us directly from 52nd Street." Then he turned to the drummer and said, "John, would you mind sitting out a few numbers and let Mr. Battle have at it?" I quickly told Mr. Strider what my nickname was and that they could feel free to call me the same. I then went back to the drums, shook John's hand and thanked him. Mr. Strider then asked if there was any special number in the stack on the drummer's stand that I wanted to play. I shook my head. Mr. Strider then said, "Well, let's swing one," and he called Basie's "Moton Swing". Mr. Strider set the tempo by stomping his feet four times, then I took it from there. I dug deep into that bass drum, set a sizzling rhythm on the 20" Ride cymbal, all the while my left foot was accenting the 2nd and 4th beats, while my left hand was doing some syncopation. Immediately, eyes turned my way. The band members in front were trying to keep one eye on their music and the other on me. Students started clapping their hands.

Others got up and started dancing. I got deeper and deeper into the chart. Perspiration was running down my face and all I could think of was how to further build upon my driving beat. Finally, the song ended and the room erupted into a thunderous volley of applause. I got up from the drums, handed John the sticks and said "Nice set of skins. Thank you." But John was having none of that. He pushed the sticks away and said, "Boots, its been a privilege to hear you. Play to the end." I really appreciated hearing that from a very good drummer. John Saunders and I were to become very close friends in the ensuing years.

After practice I said good-byes to the band. We knew we would be seeing each other when classes started. As I was about to leave, a few of the male students came over to me and asked about my clothes – where had I gotten the jacket, where had I gotten those soft pastel colors? I laughed and told them that what I was wearing was one of the combo uniforms I wore on the 52nd street gig. I told them about London Tailors in Times Square. This was where all of the bands in New York went to get their uniforms made.

I then left and made my way back to the registrar's building. Waiting for me on the steps was Oscar, who was bowing in my direction. "Hail to the chief," he said. "May I carry your bags, sire?" I just stopped and looked at him with a bemused look on my face. Oscar said, "You've already got the campus buzzing about your prowess on the drums. Boy, you just wait until the upperclassmen arrive next week. They take a dim view of freshmen stealing the spotlight." I said to myself that I would worry about the upperclassmen when they were on campus. For the present, I kept myself occupied by purchasing textbooks, meeting with my class advisor, and, in general, familiarizing myself with my upcoming class schedules. Morgan was the perfect place for me to pursue my interest in teaching. My advisor and I laid out a program setting me up to become an instrumental music teacher. With the credits I received for my classes at Juilliard and City College, I was only three short years from my goal.

That weekend, Oscar made it a point to introduce me to the night life of Baltimore. Pennsylvania Avenue was the main artery running through the black part of the city. The lights, the cacophony of sound, street noises and music, brought back fond memories of 52nd Street. Clubs such as The Comedy Club, Gamby's, The Sphinx Club, and The Alhambra, all contributed to the glorious profusion of crowds, bands, and bar-b-que. Before that weekend was over, I had managed to sit in with about four combos. All of the groups were curious about my Gotham beat. Each club provided music 6 days a week – Tuesday to Sunday. They were also open on Mondays, but none had bands or entertainment. This same setup was practiced in New York, except that in some cases, relief combos played on Monday nights. Before long, I made this suggestion to one of the club owners and he said to let him think about it. Well, by that following Monday I had talked myself into a job. I had to really hustle to make some local contacts and find musicians who could carry their weight, but I soon had a swinging quartet. Later, after the upperclassmen returned, we hit it off together really well. We reorganized the quartet and made it a quintet, naming it the "Mo-Bops," taking the prefix Mo (Morgan). This was really a tight group. Some of the names and instruments I recall are Walt Dickerson on vibes, (Walt was a very gifted musician whose brother sang on the Arthur Godfrey Show with a group called the "Mariners"), Henry Baker, on tenor sax. (Henry loved music but he became a national salesman and opened up a men's haberdashery). Our pianist was named Charlie Bakerville. Now Charles could tickle some ivory. Nothing ever bothered Charles. If he didn't know the channel of a song, he would substitute blues changes. Standing out above all the rest was Monty Paulson, who was an excellent bassist. Monty could pull those strings. He always rode around in his big Cadillac, and he was the first person I ever saw who had a car telephone. We finally got our act together and landed a gig at Jones' Cafe on Monroe Street in Baltimore. We were getting paid peanuts, but, by being able to play and hone our skills several times a week, we were able to send a message to other groups.

Pledging

During my three years at Morgan I always lived off campus, missing, I am sure, much of the interaction that took place outside the classroom. For some persons one of the most interesting and apprehensive times at college was that of being "tapped" by a certain fraternity or sorority to become a pledgee. The parent group looked for certain qualities in individuals which they felt would enhance their particular group. For some reason, I was sought by the Q's or the Omega Psi Phi's. This group usually went after the varsity athletes on campus, but since I was friends with many of those athletes, I guess that qualified me. Everything associated with pledging pointed towards "Hell" week. We had to meet with our upperclassmen to learn the Do's and Don'ts of every situation. We had to get white tams and wear them everywhere so that the whole school could recognize us and, subsequently, heckle us. Even visiting upperclassmen who were bona fide Q's had their swing and sway over us

I remember the eve of a very important game between Morgan and North Carolina A & T, our arch rivals. The most feared player on A & T was named "Stonewall Jackson." They didn't call him Stonewall for nothing. He was a great full back who would punish you if you tried to tackle him. As I think back he reminds me of Earl Campbell. Stonewall

105

decreed that all Q pledgees assemble in the gym ASAP. As an associated chapter of the Q's, they had this authority, which put a quick end to any plans I may have had for that Friday. We gathered in the gym. Finally, Stonewall and the rest of A & T's football team filed to the front of the room, took their seats and looked at us menacingly. Stonewall said, "I want all of you dogs to rise, one by one, introduce yourselves and sing your high school song. If we don't like it, you're gonna git whacked." Over in the corner was a huge A & T football player with a long, heavy, paddle. "Number one," Stonewall yelled. A very scared neophyte stood up and had just started to say his name when Stonewall roared, "Out of tune, 10 whacks," and the poor pledgee leaned over the chair. After the fifth stroke, he started to bawl. The guy with the paddle kept punishing. "Next," Stonewall yelled, and the scene was repeated. The neophyte didn't even get a syllable out. Boy, it was rough. There were three more to go before my turn. When they got to the next neophyte before me, something came over me. I looked at all those A & T football giants. I looked at Stonewall who had a permanent frown etched on his face. I looked at the hopeless pledgee who was about to be beaten. This was a bad situation. Usually, when they plan to swing and sway with the paddles, we were allowed to put protection over our buttocks, such as pillows, or the like, but tonight we did not have anything. Now, I was willing to tolerate a lot as part of fulfilling the "rites of passage" associated with joining the fraternity. I understood about the tradition and the bonding that came from going through this experience and these rituals. But I also knew that there's a limit to what should be required of us, and as far as I was concerned, we were well past that limit. I don't know what got into me but I stood up, and looking directly at Stonewall, I said, "This is wrong." He said, "Sit down, dog, and stay sat until I tell you to jump." The front of the room howled with laughter. Well, it was all or nothing at all with me and I said, "No, I will not sit. What you are doing is wrong. You came in here and told us what you want us to do, which in itself is O.K., because I know that when Morgan's football team travels to your campus, our Q's more than likely hold similar sessions with your neophytes. So to that I say fair is fair. What's good for the goose is good for the gander." No one stirred. One could have heard a pin drop. I could hear them thinking, "Who is this upstart talking like that? Doesn't he realize that we are the mighty A & T Aggies? I turned my head and looked into every hostile eye. "You marched in here, you set up the rules as follows: Each of us was to rise, introduce ourselves, tell something about our life, and sing our high school fight song. Then and only then, if you did not like what we said or sang, we would be stroked. Starting with the first neophyte, you had him across the chair before he could really open his mouth. You don't even know his name. I fact, you never gave any of us a chance to give you what you requested. Well, before you lay wood on me, you're going to know what I'm about. My name is LeRoy A. Battle. They call me Boots. I'm from Brooklyn, New York. I went to Alexander Hamilton High, I'm a professional musician, drummer by trade." Then I sang the Hamilton High Fight Song. After I finished there was a smattering of applause from the cowed neophytes. Before I sat down, I said, "One more thing I learned at home. Right is right, even if nobody's right, and wrong is wrong even if everybody's wrong."

This time the entire room exploded with applause. Stonewall got up and apologized to the group of us on behalf of his team. He then, just as a courtesy, asked each of my group to stand, and to give his name and hometown. Then he dismissed us all. He came over to where I was and said, for all to hear, "We could use you at A & T."

Out of State Scholarship

While a student at Morgan, I learned of the Out-of-State scholarship offered by the state of Maryland to black students, undergraduates and graduates. At this time, "colored" students and educators could not enroll at any institutions offering Masters or Doctors degrees in Education in Maryland. The "black colleges" did not have graduate programs, and the other state schools were closed to us. To compensate for not allowing blacks into their own graduate programs, Maryland offered out-of-state scholarships to enable blacks to receive graduate training elsewhere. This restriction seemed very stupid to me, albeit the colored students and educators did not hesitate to take advantage of this situation. Witness the fact that during the summer break, students from Morgan would matriculate in colleges all across the United States. Now, my home was Brooklyn, NY, and just to illustrate how stupid this out-of-state scholarship program was, I applied to take two special courses in music at Columbia University in New York. To keep me from going to summer school at the University of Maryland, I was given close to one thousand dollars to take care of my tuition, room, and board. So, in effect, the state of Maryland paid me to go home. In one respect, it was disheartening to run up against another racial injustice, but at least in this case, for a change, it cost them and benefited me.

Graduation

The last phase of my training required me to student-teach at one of the local high schools. It was there that I confirmed to myself that I had made the right decision for my future. I enjoyed it right from the start. It was a very special feeling being able to help others pursue their interests. I especially enjoyed working with the perscussionists. In fact, it was so rare to find someone as well trained on the tympani as I was

107

that several other schools would send their students to receive instruction from me. It was also a good opportunity for me to learn some of the practical skills that go along with handling the day to day business of public education. I learned a lot about the administrative tasks that are an integral part of teaching, and it gave me a chance to evaluate some of the factors that go into designing and implementing a successful band program. Most importantly, it gave me a chance to evaluate my ability to relate to the students and communicate what I had to offer. My style was to approach them honestly and respectfully, to let them know that they needed to be serious about their work, but that I wanted it to be fun for them too. I let them know that if they did their best, that was all I expected from them. This wasn't an approach I had learned or decided to implement, it was just the only way I knew how to be. Fortunately, it seemed to work.

Finally, that magic day rolled around – I was a graduating senior at Morgan State College. It was a very, very, hot June day, and the cap and gown made it seem as though I was in an oven. But I didn't mind. I was getting ready to "Go forth" into the world and seek my fortune. It was a challenge filled with sweet anticipation. Student-teaching had given me a brief taste of the gratification one can get from sharing your knowledge and experience with others. That was all I needed to assure myself that I had made the right decision about what course to take in my life. Now it was just a matter of finding the right place to put my ambitions and training to work.

The "Lakeside Philharmonic," back together again.

*Back in town after
the war – trying out
a drum set at
Mannie's Music store
– 120 W. 48th St.*

*Practicing by the lake
Upstate New York
Summer of '46*

FLASH GORDON   CHARLES BASKERVILLE   HENRY BAKER   WALT DICKERSON   BOOTS BATTLE   MONTY POULSO

Two sides of LeRoy Battle at Morgan State:
with The Mo-Bops (above), and with the Marching Band
at the Polo Grounds in NY for a game against
West Virginia State College (below)

110

*On the campus of
Morgan State with Joe
Black, future pitcher with
the Brooklyn Dodgers
(left), and on the way to
class (below)*

LeRoy A. Battle, Band Director

The Douglass Experience
The Fruition of My Dream

Following my graduation from Morgan, I was called into my advisor's office where he told me about teaching openings in Charles County and in Prince George's County, Maryland. I wrote to Prince George's County and an appointment was set up for me to meet with the principal, Mr. Frisby, at the Frederick Douglass Jr.-Sr. High School located in Upper Marlboro. I truly did not know what to expect during my interview. This was my first formal application or interview for any job. Mr. Frisby conducted the interview in a very informal manner. He encouraged me to talk about my background and through it all I imagine that my concern for the students was quite evident. Since early in my childhood, I had been preparing myself to be a teacher. I knew I wanted to share my enthusiasm for learning with others. Later that week, I was informed by mail that I had been chosen to be Douglass' new band director. I was awed, apprehensive, anxious, and happy. For the first part of that summer I stayed busy in professional music, gigging with several combos. I received several offers to go on the road and to play music full time. The offers were tempting, however, I declined, but not before I told each leader that teaching was my heart and soul. Around the first of August I went down to Douglass to check the band room, and, to my delight, my office. Seeing that I had my own office, I knew I had officially arrived at my new profession. However, my enthusiasm was somewhat dampened by the fact that the band room was empty. At this point the instrumental music department had no instruments, no piano, no music stands, nothing.

I went to the main office to get a list of the students who would be in my classes. The secretary, with pity in her eyes, said "Mr. Battle, you have no students - this is the first year that we've ever had instrumental music or a band, although I think they tried to have one about fifteen years ago." Needless to say, I was both perplexed and dumbfounded. "Well, where am I going to get the students from?" I asked. My voice was rising. "I don't really know, Mr. Battle. All of the students are scheduled in regular classes, five required and two electives."

Right then, I knew what I had to do. I had to find some way of prying a few of the students away from the other electives they had chosen. I just wasn't sure how to go about giving myself that opportunity. As I left the office I heard a voice say, "Hi, are you the new music teacher?" I turned and looked into the eyes of a man who became a godsend for me. He said, "I'm Cleo Whitley. I'm the vocational-agriculture teacher here." Whitley was a mature individual. As we shook hands,

I introduced myself and we bonded immediately. Whitley said to me, "You had a worried look on your face as you left the office. Anything I can help you with?" "Boy," I said, "You got a few hours?" Then I proceeded to explain my predicament. When I finished Whitley said, "I think I can help you out. Why don't you come with me - I've got a few errands to run." With that we began my introduction to the area that was about to become my home, and which was home to the students who were about to become my charges.

Frederick Douglass Jr.-Sr. High School was located in the town of Upper Marlboro which was in the heart of what used to be "tobacco country." Practically all high schools in this rural, agriculturally oriented county had clubs dealing with the farming theme. The Negro clubs were called the Future Farmers of America. During the summer, each member of Whitley's group (FFA) would be responsible for a farming project. That meant that Whitley would periodically visit each student to check on his project. On this particular day Whitley suggested that I ride with him as he made his rounds. It was quite a ride for a city boy from New York. Whitley knew every dusty back road in the county; he had to in order to get to all the kids in his program – they were all over the place. It was nothing like New York where most of the school lived within walking distance or a short subway ride of the school.

It was quite obvious that Mr. Whitley had good rapport with the students and their parents. Each home we visited was a welcome stop. We were offered lemonade or iced tea. After everyone said their hellos, Whitley would go out in the garden to check on the fruits or vegetables, or in some cases to the barn for those students who had projects involving livestock. Meanwhile, the parents would talk with me, questioning me about the upcoming music program. I would then let them know that this was my first teaching experience and I would appreciate any support they could give me. I think we visited more than forty homes that August and I met as many students plus other brothers and sisters. Wherever we went, my program was well received by the parents, and I was even able to recruit several youngsters who were interested in beginning drum instruction. Getting these first recruits was the hardest part. Since a music program had never been offered to these students before, it had never entered their minds as something they might have wanted to do. And with the community being so closely tied to farming, I was asking them to give up some of the time they would otherwise spend helping the family. But we had made a start, and I knew that once the other kids saw what we could do, and the fun we could have, more recruits would follow.

A Special P.T.A. Meeting

In early August before my first year as a teacher, a special PTA "Get Acquainted Meeting" was held. All teachers were required to attend as well as new students and parents. The auditorium was packed, and for this meeting, Mr. Doswell Brooks, the Negro supervisor of "colored" schools and Mr. Frisby, were both present. Mr. Frisby asked the new teachers to stand up, introduce themselves, and explain something about their goals for their students for the upcoming year. When it came my turn, I stood up, told my name, and began to outline my program. Even though we were starting from scratch, I felt that if we all worked together, the program would succeed, and then exclaimed that I would like for every student in my program to learn to play an instrument. This was unusual for music programs in the area. Usually, the majorettes, flag corps, banner carriers, and color guard, would only have marching responsibilities, but I felt it was important for everyone of them to get instruction on some instrument. We had a rather small budget, so our ability to purchase new instruments was limited. I reassured the parents that we would find ways of working that out. First I told them that I would start with the students making drum pads. I held a drum pad that I had purchased from the music store up for them to see. I told them that the drum pad cost seven dollars, but that the students could make them by using discarded inner tubes and scrap lumber. I could tell by their faces that this was the kind of thing they wanted to hear and that I had won them to my side. Before I sat down, I said, "I'd like to leave this thought with you: Let me teach your child to blow a horn and I promise you he'll never blow a safe." I knew from my own experience that once you get involved in something like music, just the way it occupies your time can go a long way toward keeping you out of trouble. And once you start to produce positive results for yourself, as you learn to play your instrument - even if it's just squeezing out that first note, that success gives you such a feeling of accomplishment and pride that you don't need to go following others into trouble, just because you have nothing better to do, or because you're trying to belong.

Setting the Record Straight

When I first reported to Douglass, I was shown where the Music Department's mail slot was located. It was stuffed with advertisements, magazines, and brochures. Most of the mail we were addressed to: Douglass Colored High School. This offended me very much. I reasoned that since Douglass had not had an official instrumental music department for awhile, that part of the mail had been ignored, or perhaps, although I could not see how, simply not noticed. I took the mail to my office and separated the "offensive-to-me" mail into one pile, and the acceptable mail into another pile. I rummaged through the desk and came up with a few sheets of composition paper and envelopes. I then cut the paper into nine slips, addressed eight envelopes and placed a note in each explaining that the term, 'Colored High School,' was offensive, that there was only one Frederick Douglass Jr.-Sr. High School in Upper Marlboro, and that it would be appreciated greatly if they addressed any correspondence to us in that manner, and that, furthermore, we were not accepting any more letters addressed where we were identified by race. I then signed the communication to each, "Sincerely yours, LeRoy A. Battle, Chairman, Instrumental Music Department."

I felt good. That was my first official, independent act as a teacher. About a month later I started receiving letters from these companies, each addressed as requested and all were accompanied by a letter of apology.

Visit to Pomonkey

As a new band director one of my objectives was to prepare my students for performances. Another objective, after they were prepared, was to find places where they could perform. It was my over-enthusiastic pursuit of this second objective which almost cost me my job.

In the early 1950's, the colored schools (as they were called) in Prince George's and Charles counties did not have varsity football teams as we now know them. Rather, they had what were called "Flag Football Teams." There were only six or seven players on each side, and there was no tackling. Instead the object was to stop the opposing offensive player by snatching away the flag snapped to his waist band. Late in October, Douglass' team was scheduled to play at Pomonkey High School in Charles County for their Homecoming. I found out from Ben Cumbo, our physical education teacher, that he had received an invitation to the team and cheerleaders to be included in their celebration. They were almost ready to go that morning when Ben told me about the invitation. I asked Ben to please take me, my eight drummers, and my seven majorettes with him. The drummers were performance ready because I had had some of the summer and the early fall to prepare them. The other instrumentalists had to wait until after the P.T.A. meeting before they could get started. Ben said, "Fine, but you'll have to get Mr. Frisby's approval." I went directly to Principal Frisby who immediately told me no. Well, I didn't back down. I proceeded to plead my case. Mr. Frisby just looked at me. When I finished he firmly said, "No." Well, at that time I was young, foolish, and filled up with the idea of putting on a show with my drummers and majorettes. I left the office, contacted the majorettes and drummers, via the grapevine, instructed them to make a quick change, get their drums and meet me at the bus ASAP. The bus was parked down at the end of the school building, not readily visible by the general school population, and we left, I thought, without being seen.

It was a crowded, exciting trip to Pomonkey. The performers were nervous, as was I, but not for the same reasons. When we pulled onto the playing field, we were met with cheers as the student body was already outside. At two minutes before the half, I lined Douglass' drummers and majorettes up to await the start of the halftime show. When the referee blew the whistle signalling the end of the second quarter, the various queens and their escorts strode from the sidelines to the center of the field. They were met by community dignitaries, and were presented with plaques and trophies. Then, to the accompaniment of recorded music, they made their way off of the field.

As soon as the field was cleared, our drummers took up a very rhythmic, soulful cadence. Our majorettes strutted and performed high kicks, all while twirling their batons. The routine only lasted about five minutes, however, the Douglass majorettes, accompanied by the drummers, high stepped and swirled themselves right into the hearts of the Pomonkey High School faculty and students.

The ride back to Douglass was filled with a joyous noise. However, my personal joy was replaced with instant fear and regret, because no sooner had our bus pulled up to the school's entrance when I spotted Mr. Frisby with his arms folded and a most dour look on his face. I thanked Ben for the ride and hustled the bandsmen to hurry and change so they could catch their rides home. Mr. Frisby looked at me and started out by saying, in a slightly raised voice, "Battle, you've got a lot of explaining to do." Just then Mr. Frisby's secretary came to the door and yelled outside to him, "Mr. Frisby, you have a long distance telephone call. They sounded like it was important." Mr. Frisby turned around in annoyance and said he'd be right there. He told me to wait, that he wasn't finished with me yet. I sat down on the bench in the foyer feeling quite alone. I feared that my career was about to come to a grinding halt. Fifteen minutes later the secretary came and beckoned to me to come into the office. Before I went in, she said to meet her in the faculty lounge after Mr. Frisby had finished with me. I winced at the word "finished."

When I entered the office, Mr. Frisby said, "Sit down, LeRoy. Tell me, how did our team do?" "They won." I replied. My mind was racing. Mr. Frisby then inquired as to how our majorettes and drummers enjoyed their first performance. By this time I was completely perplexed. As Mr. Frisby ended the meeting, he rose up from his chair, offered his hand, cleared his throat, and said, "Well done."

117

I left the office and went immediately to the faculty lounge where Mr. Frisby's secretary awaited me. She laughed and said, "Boy, that was one upset individual. You should have seen his face when he learned that you had gone with your bandsmen to Pomonkey in spite of the fact that he had forbidden you to go." My throat was very dry so I went to the dispenser, got two sodas, offered Mrs. Ruth one, sat down, and said, "Fill me in, please, because right now I don't know if I'm coming or going. A few minutes ago when we first got here, he was starting to ream me out pretty good. Then just now back in the office he was congratulating me, I think."

"Well," she said, "Remember that phone call he got when you both were outside? It was the principal of Pomonkey High. He called to say how happy he was that Mr. Frisby had sent the drummers and the majorettes. He said that our appearance shook up the entire student body. They want to sign up and take music. To top it off, the chairman of the County Commissioners was there along with members of the Board of Education. They were very impressed and promised to seed a program for Pomonkey High to get started in instrumental music."

I thanked the secretary and said, "Mrs. Ruth, if you are around whenever I get a dumb, stupid, idea again, kindly shut me up anyway you can. I'm not sure I can count on being so lucky the next time."

A Plan Evolves

Back at the beginning of the school year, I met the general music teacher, Oliver Davis. We got along very well, and I explained my problem to him of getting students into my program. At the time I had about twenty aspirants for the Drum and Bugle Corps from my summer recruiting, but I was also interested in putting together a stage band – a small ensemble built around a jazz orchestra, playing contemporary music – to capture the interest of other students and ultimately involve them in a larger program. Together we arrived at a possible solution. The trick was to get the students to drop one of their electives and take instrumental music. Davis gave me permission to visit each of his classes and take volunteers to my classroom to screen them for the instrument which would best suit them, be it trumpet, trombone, woodwind, flutes, percussion, etc. At the end of two weeks I had my band, at least on paper.

The next step was to get the instruments we needed. One of the first problems was finding a way to pay for the fifteen bugles I had ordered for the Drum & Bugle Corps, and it was here that I really began to rely upon the parents and the community. To meet this obligation, the parents formed the Band Boosters Club to raise the needed funds. Next came the problem of getting the remaining instruments for our newly formed stage band. The school had a very limited budget for the band, and we were virtually starting from nothing, so we had to be resourceful. We were able to arrange to share a piano with the music department, and we acquired a bass that had been "surplused" by one of the white schools' band directors. I scavenged up some drums, and some of the kids had their own guitars. This filled out the rhythm section which formed the heart of the jazz ensemble. We still had a ways to go, however, since we needed at least two trumpets, three saxophones, and two trombones to round out the ensemble. Fortunately, we were able to get each student into the rental-purchase program offered by the local music stores. This was the procedure where a student would rent a horn for a period of three months with the option of buying it. The rental fee paid by the student would go toward the purchase of the instrument. Everything was falling into place, the jazz ensemble was nearly complete; to supplement my teaching I brought in some of my professional friends to encourage, inspire, and demonstrate to my charges the correct way to interpret the charts. The last piece of the puzzle was to find the right person to be my drummer.

Many boys tried out, including my drummers from the Drum & Bugle Corps, but I was not overly impressed. Then one day this young girl approached me and said, "Mr. Battle, I would like to try out to be the swing drummer." I said, "What is your name young lady?" "Rose Weems," she replied. I then said, more to find out where her heart was than anything else, "Do you realize what is involved? Both feet must do separate things while your hands must act as though they have a mind of their own." I went on to explain other difficulties involved, but she was not dissuaded. I finally said, "OK, young lady, report here after school today and we'll take it from there." To my pleasant surprise, Rose showed great aptitude for the drums... her hands and feet worked well together in coordinated independence. In the end, after a good solid two weeks of intense lessons, Rose beat out all of the competition and became the drummer. With all the pieces in place we set about rehearsing. At first I was splitting my time equally between the Drum and Bugle Corps and the stage band, but that changed when we received an invitation from Mr. Strider, head of the music department at Morgan State. They were hosting their first annual music festival, to be held on their campus, which was open to local high school bands. We weren't quite in the category of a high school band yet, but as small as we were, we still wanted to go and represent our school. Now that we had a specific performance commitment ahead of us, the stage band rehearsals received a much greater emphasis as we prepared for our first public appearance.

Finally, spring arrived and the jazz ensemble was ready for its first trip to Baltimore. For some students it was their first trip anywhere beyond Upper Marlboro, and for everyone it was their first big performance, so the bus ride to Morgan was filled with excitement and anticipation. As the bus pulled onto Morgan's Campus, the musicians were glued to the windows taking in the sights of the big, beautiful buildings, not to mention the latest in student styles. When we pulled up to the parking lot a uniformed guide from Morgan's band met us. He was splendidly attired in his navy blue tunic, adorned with gold braid, epaulets, and white gloves. He introduced himself to us and asked where the second bus was. We laughed and told him, "This was it." I explained to our guide just what type of group we had and what we would need – mainly a piano and about fifteen folding chairs. Once inside the foyer, our guide spoke to a few maintenance people, and it wasn't long before I saw the grand piano headed into the performance hall, followed by a rack of folding chairs to be set up in our assigned position. I showed Rose where to set up her drums, and the other musicians arranged their instruments. Once everything was in place, we went off to do a little sight-seeing around the campus.

When we reassembled in the foyer, the guide pointed out where we were to enter the performance hall. As we opened the huge doors, we were greeted by a dazzling sight. On the polished floor of the auditorium were five bands, seated in concert position, with uniforms that were beautiful combinations of blue and gold, maroon and silver, and red and black. We were dressed in white shirts and blouses, with black trousers and skirts. I looked back at my students as I was leading them in and told them to look and appreciate, but not to be disheartened, because next year, we would have uniforms of our own. The stands themselves were packed with students, many of whom had been bused in by the participating schools to cheer on their bands. The judges' stand was immediately opposite the center band. There were three judges, all colored, who were music teachers at area colleges. It was a pretty intimidating moment for my young students and I wasn't quite sure how they would respond.

Finally, Mr. Strider strode to the standing microphone and greeted all the visiting bandsmen and their instructors. He offered greetings from the college president, Mr. Jenkins. Then he introduced the judges, and ended his remarks with a dramatic, "Let the music begin! The first band to play will be the Bates High School Band from Annapolis, Maryland, under the direction of Mr. Weldon Irvine." Their rendition was outstanding and received a very warm round of applause. Then the second band gave a rendition of a selection by Wagner, and it too received a well-earned enthusiastic reception. This procedure continued until all five bands had performed. At long last it was our turn to play.

Mr. Strider introduced both me and my group. Then he said, "This young group will give their rendition of, and I hope I'm pronouncing it correctly, Wham-A-Lam." At those words a loud murmur swept through the crowd. I faced the band and asked with my eyes whether they were ready or not. All eyes were on us; it seemed as though everyone in the auditorium was holding his or her breath. Then I pointed to Rose, as if to communicate to her to dig in and drive this band to new heights. She nodded back that she was ready. I held my arm out for a few more seconds, then, sweeping my eyes over each and every player, I stomped the tempo off .The air suddenly seemed to part as the music swept over me and out into the crowd at my back. Rose set a terrific back beat while the trombones and saxophones set a solid dirge for the trumpets to play obligato on the melody. In a moment the crowd was on its feet, clapping, stomping, and chanting the riffs. This was a tune they knew, and they kept their response up through the entire song. When we ended with the final chord, bedlam broke out. Over the cheers and the applause, Mr. Strider, laughing, nodded to me to render an encore. My charges gladly obliged, reveling in the kind of moment that sometimes only happens once in a lifetime, if at all, and rarely to black farm kids from Upper Marlboro. I couldn't have been prouder.

Year Two

The successes of the band during my first year had established our program in the school. It generated a lot of interest among the students, which greatly helped us in recruiting the additional players we would need to form a full-scale concert band. Equally gratifying for me as a teacher, was the way we had also been embraced by the local community - we were starting to become a source of pride for them too. During the course of my first year I discovered that, as spread out as the black families were because of their agricultural orientation, there were several things that brought them close together and enabled them to develop a real sense of community identity. Tobacco was the leading product which provided a living for the majority of families, and Upper Marlboro served as the economic center around which that crop revolved, for both black and white farmers. They all had to come to town for seed, fertilizer, and other supplies, and most importantly, the tobacco warehouses were there. This was where they would auction off their crop each year. Still, as important a focus as Upper Marlboro was for the black community, it was a white man's town in most other respects. For example, while blacks were allowed to join the St. Mary's Catholic Church, the "colored" parishioners had to sit in the back, and when they took communion, they had to wait until the white parishioners had been served. The only theater in Upper Marlboro employed similar practices. The white patrons of the theater sat downstairs, while the colored patrons had to climb an exterior stairway to get to the balcony of the theater, where they were permitted to sit. Wherever they went, blacks were able to carry out their business, but almost always with some restriction or other that served to isolate them from the white population, or give the white customers preference. The only thriving black business in town was Tolson's - but as the one place where the blacks felt welcome and were treated fairly it was extremely important.

Tolson's was a combination bar, lunchroom, pool room, and most importantly, it was the only public place where the Negro patrons could bring their lady companions and be seated at a table. It became the social center for the blacks whenever they were in town, and was sometimes the only reason they went to town. The busiest day at Tolson's was Saturday. Three Negro "special" policemen (Nelson Lee, Thomas Curtis, and "Son" Gray) were hired by the town to police the place. Now these policemen's uniforms were all black, with black Sam Browne belts. These uniforms were entirely different from those of the regular county police. They did carry holsters with loaded .38's, however, they could only arrest other blacks.

About noon people from miles around, mostly farmers, would start pouring into Tolson's. They came prepared to spend the rest of the day. In the back room pool tables were set up and there were continuous games of '9 ball' and '5 ball'. Those who weren't playing joined in on the wagering. The main item of food, and the most popular, was the hot fried chicken sandwiches served by Mr. Emory Tolson's daughter, Ruth. Ruth was married to Ben Cumbo, our physical education teacher. Ruth was also an elementary school teacher and, along with many other teachers, would stop by regularly to eat and have conversations with the parents and friends of their students. This provided some relief from the inevitable discussions about tobacco farming. Now, the conversation was starting to include discussions of the school band as well.

One of my goals for the band this second year was to march in the traditional Memorial Day Parade in May. It was customary for the white high school, Frederick Sasscer to be featured at the Memorial Day Parade and at the county fair. The Memorial Day Parade, I was told, was not attended by too many Negroes. However, when word got around that Douglass' band would participate that year, the parade route was jammed. For several weeks we had been a favorite topic of conversation at Tolson's. It was something special to have their "colored" school finally represented in the festivities. Spectators were 10 deep and hundreds of Negroes attended. For this parade, Sasscer, as usual, was the lead band, followed by floats. Bringing up the rear of the parade was the Douglass Band. I told the bandsmen to keep their chins up and to look at it like they were saving the best for last. That really got a big laugh. Well, when it came our turn to march through the center of town and by the receiving stand at the courthouse, the streets erupted with cheers. They had never heard a drum cadence like ours. I used four bass drums, which at that time was an innovation. That was the first and last time we brought up the rear of the parade. Thereafter we were the permanent lead-off band.

The Prince George's County Fair was and still is a very big deal. The fair lasted four or five days and featured musical groups, singing groups, country western dancing, cooking contests, and the other typical fair activities. After we had participated for several years as one of the secondary performers, the County Fair committee finally asked my principal to let the Douglass Band lead the parade. The parade was held at the race track. There the participants would march around the oval until they came to the grandstand where each unit would stop and perform for the judges. My band was, as usual, well prepared for the competition, but on this day we faced an additional opponent.

We were getting ready to fall in and lead our section when I saw two clowns prancing in front of a fire engine. There were lots of fire companies in the parade. They would have contests against each other later in the day. What struck me about these clowns was the way they were dressed. One had the usual tiny hat, big nose, and long fins on his feet. However, his face was painted black and his lips were extremely large and painted white. Across his shoulder was a string holding huge dice. The other clown had the same black face and string over his shoulder holding two large whisky jugs. Their attire was torn and tattered red coats with large black and white knickers. Well, after they and the fire truck passed, the parade marshall ran up to me and yelled in a not too friendly voice, "C'mon, get the band going." I shot back, "This band stays put until you get those clowns out of the parade." The marshall looked at me and I stared him down. Meanwhile, the fire chief, county officials, and the crowd were clamoring for the parade to start. The marshall checked his watch, turned and hustled towards a special tent set up for registration. After about ten minutes I saw several "dignitaries" talking to the clowns. Meanwhile, the bandsmen close to me said, "Good, Mr. Battle. You sure told him."

Finally, I saw the clowns, and the offensive racial stereotyping they represented, step out of their parade spot and wander off until they were lost in the crowd. I then turned to tell my lead drum majorette, Barbara Parker, to show our colors, but she had already whistled the band to attention. We were now ready to put the show on the road, but the most important victory of the day had already been won.

Band Boosters Club

When I first came on board at Douglass, the yearly allotment to Douglass' Music Department was around six or seven hundred dollars. At the most, we could only purchase a set of tympani, or a sousaphone, or maybe two baritone horns. Our yearly allotment did not increase much during the ensuing years. However, our band enrollment grew by leaps and bounds. This meant we needed many additional instruments. This was where the Douglass High Band Boosters Club took an active part. They were an organization composed of parents of band members, and friends who, although they didn't have a child in the band, were willing to contribute time, money, and encouragement to the Douglass "Eagle" Band, took an active part. They would sponsor bake sales, school dances, and started the tradition of selling Thanksgiving dinners each November. The town of Upper Marlboro looked forward each year to these dinners. The bandsmen would scatter all over town taking orders. These Band Boosters Club members who were not involved in the cooking of the dinner would use their cars to deliver the dinners to homes and offices. The dinners were cooked in the school cafeteria and the public could walk in, purchase a dinner, and eat at the cafeteria tables. The bandsmen who so desired served as waitresses or waiters. All of the food was raised or grown by the band boosters who happily contributed the food. It was a most happy sight to see parents coming in with bushels of fresh greens, sweet potatoes, or white potatoes. Some parents contributed huge turkeys that they raised. One year I remember a parent donating two large hams from hogs that he had just prepared.

The Band Boosters Club stayed active all year. During the summer when the rest of the school was on vacation, the band boosters were raising money or serving as chaperones as we participated in parades sponsored by the fire departments, or giving community concerts. It was at this time that I sponsored the summer music program. Aspiring band members who were scheduled to be promoted to high school the following fall rented instruments and vied for future membership.

I'll forever be grateful and indebted to the Douglass High School's Band Boosters Club. It would have been impossible to accomplish all that we did without their support.

Once a Douglass Bandsman, Always...

There were many former Douglass bandsmen who unselfishly offered their time and talents for the benefit and advancement of the Douglass "Eagle" Band. The bandsmen were and are proud of their motto, "Once a Douglass Bandsman, Always a Douglass Bandsman." I would like to relate my experiences with one bandsman in particular whose action exemplified the true sense of the motto. His name is Gilford Tolson, but we knew him as "Groucho."

Groucho was one continuous burst of energy. He was very popular and well-known in the Douglass area. His parent's owned the most prominent black business in town. I have nothing but fond memories when I think of Groucho's induction into the Douglass Band when he was in the 7th grade. He was a lovable rascal who never failed to test me and keep me sharp trying to stay a jump ahead of him.

Groucho grew up certain that his parents would get him out of whatever trouble he might get into. He had many positive attributes to his credit, two of which were his ability to talk and charm. Groucho played the Alto saxophone and it wasn't long before he blew his way into the "A" Band. That is where we would butt heads regularly. Groucho had his own agenda concerning the times he was going to come to rehearsals or when he was going to stop honking on his horn between selections. It finally came down to just who was in charge. At one rehearsal, I had had it with his antics. I took Groucho's horn, put it in the case and literally grabbed him by his ear and marched him up to his father's place of business.

All the while Groucho was frowning, saying, "Ow, that hurts, Mr. Battle." I replied, "Good, I want it to hurt." When we got to the building, I took him right in to his father and said, "Here, Mr. Tolson, there can only be one leader in this band." At that, the customers burst into laughter, one saying, "That's the way Mr. Battle. I've got two at home I wish you could do something with." The father said, "Thank you, Mr. Battle. I guarantee he won't give you any more trouble."

Well, Groucho and I from time to time still had our differences. However, I can truthfully say that there never was anything done by Groucho in meanness. Rather, it was always his trying to get the advantage, and he could really make you laugh.

Through it all, I began to appreciate the leadership qualities he exhibited. It was after he graduated from Douglass that his qualities of communication, leadership, and the gift of gab came into play to help the Douglass Band. We were talking together one day at his home and I said, "Groucho, the Band Boosters Club is really struggling to raise money to pay off the uniforms." Groucho said, "Mr. Battle, why don't you have a donkey ball game?" I said, "I just don't have the time to do all it takes to pull that off." He said, "Mr. Battle, you just clear the date for me and I'll take it from there." The date was cleared and Groucho took over.

Sure enough, on the day of the activity, several long trailers rolled up to the school and unloaded their cargo of mid-size donkeys. Later, about twelve young men were directed to me. They said they were the riders and that Groucho had told them to report to me. I then issued them six gold tee shirts and six maroon tee shirts. That night both sides of the gym stands were packed and the cacophony of noise never let up. There were cheers for the yellow team (Douglass) and cat calls and cheers for the maroon players. The game was a huge success. Groucho turned all of the money over to the Band Booster Club, never asking anything for himself.

This was the way it went with anything I asked of Groucho. If I wanted to get one of the students' favorite bands to play for the Band Booster's dance, all I had to do was to ask Groucho and he would contact the band and have the leader call me. I'm very grateful and much indebted to him for all that he has done to help his band and his school. I was very gratified to learn that these days Groucho is putting his managerial skills and communication abilities to good use as the manager of an adult baseball team in the Upper Marlboro area.

Problems from within

We had won the support of the black community, and were winning the grudging respect of the white community and their schools. We were, through the help of the Band Boosters Club, able to overcome the lack of financial support given us by the county school administration. With our early successes, the band had established a strong foundation on which we continued to build interest in our program, attracting ample student participation and establishing standards of student commitment which would continue our tradition of excellence. Yet, there were still serious problems to contend with. The emergence of such a large instrumental music program over the first couple of years was not something the administration had anticipated or planned for. The logistical challenge of coordinating and balancing the regular class schedule and the band class was of paramount concern to all. An urgent problem arose because the concert and marching bands were not scheduled for regular periods of their own like mathematics or science. The only way I could rehearse either band was to get the teachers to permit band members to be excused from various classes Tuesdays and Thursdays of each week. For example, on the Tuesday and Thursday of the first week of the month, students would be released from their second period classes to attend band. Then, on the second week, students would be excused from their third and fourth period classes, rotating throughout the month. This took quite a bit of planning and book work to make the schedule work. All bandsmen had already given up one elective course to take band. The bandsmen were also required to find out what class work they missed and to get the homework assignments for each class. All of this put an extra burden on the band members, not to mention the impact of after-school rehearsals and an extensive performance schedule.

Problems started arising during the spring of 1955. I could never figure out the reason why, but the faculty, after a lengthy, heated debate, passed a draconian requirement aimed at all special activities. This new policy required each student participating in special activities to receive weekly passing grades in order to continue to participate in that activity. One could see at a glance how biased and unfair this ruling was. Because of our performance obligations and the year-round nature of our program, this policy was going to hit the band the hardest. Nevertheless, the policy was put in place. Special grade sheets with each student's name were passed around by the faculty. If a student received two "E's" in any subject(s) for that previous week, he or she could not participate in any facet of the activity for the coming week.

Miraculously, the band survived that winter without any major crisis, even though, as expected, several students received occasional "E's". However, spring was approaching and this did not bode well for the band. Spring was our very active time; often we would participate in a parade a week, sometimes two parades. I knew that any "E" received by one or more of my students could have a negative effect on our subsequent performance. It was at one faculty meeting that the cloud which threatened our band was lifted.

In the previous Fall, when the faculty first considered this policy, there had been a few teachers who were against the proposal. Their reasoning was that the band would be affected all year long, whereas many other activities only involved perhaps three or four weeks at a time. This logical thinking had nearly defeated the measure. While I realized that it was much more difficult for my band members to maintain their academic work in the face of the demands of the practice and performance schedules, I also knew that through being in the band they were getting some very valuable lessons that were essential to their education. The dedication and self-discipline required of them, the self-confidence and self-esteem they developed, and learning how to depend upon and cooperate with others were all part of those lessons, and I did not see how we could justify depriving them of those things. Besides, in many cases I suspect that being in the band helped some of the students academically, because of what they gained from the experience. However, a very compelling oration by a male teacher swayed the vote and the measure passed with a majority vote. I felt we were done in by our own teachers.

At a faculty meeting in the early spring the baseball coach announced that he would be unable to coach the baseball team for the upcoming spring season. Mr. Frisby began asking for volunteers to coach the team.

In the end, I don't recall if he volunteered or was appointed by Mr. Frisby, but the team was assigned to the same person whose very persuasive oration had swayed the faculty to vote for the restrictive grade requirement rule in the fall.

At this point the "orator" arose and said to the faculty, "I'll take the team, but you have to remember that this will be my first time doing something like this and I'll have to do a real effective teaching job with the team in order to get them in shape to represent Douglass on the field. All of the teachers were listening intently, some were smiling, others were nodding in agreement to what they were hearing. "And so," the orator continued, "I am going to ask you to rescind the grade requirement rule affecting participation in school activities." A gasp went up from the teachers. Nobody spoke. The speaker continued, "You know that many of these boys aren't scholars, and that's putting it mildly. The upcoming schedule requires that we play two games a week. If my main pitcher or catcher receives two or more "E's", this would automatically mean that we would lose two games that week." The monologue continued for the next ten minutes or so. Then Mr. Frisby said, "Ladies and gentlemen, are you ready to vote?" I looked down at my notebook. In fact, I tried to disappear. I didn't want to offend any teacher who might have been jealous of the band and any notoriety we received. Mr. Frisby intoned, "Kindly raise your hand if you are in favor of rescinding the grade activity requirement rule." I kept my eyes down, but weakly raised my hand. There was a slight pause as the secretary counted the hands and wrote the number down. "Those who want to keep the rule kindly raise your hand." I didn't even look up. I held my breath as Mr. Frisby said, "It's unanimous. The rule is rescinded."

At that moment I felt like the weight of the world was lifted from my shoulders. I remained cool. I didn't want anyone to yell for a recount. That was one of the happiest days of my teaching career, where the right thing was done, though in this case, for the wrong reason. We were able to continue the development of the band, and through it, the students, without the handicaps imposed by the shortsighted rules of our own making. And the bandsmen continued to maintain their academic work as well.

Rehearsal Bonding

The one factor above all that held the Douglass Band together was embodied in the phrase, "The Douglass Band Family." How we bonded together had its origin in how we practiced together. The Douglass Band consisted of five parts: Banner Bearers, Color Guard, Flag Corps, Majorettes, Bandsmen... about 110 bandsmen in all. The practice schedule of the band was long, inconvenient and arduous. The regular school day began around 8:40 a.m. and ended at 3:00 p.m. The school band's practice hours started at 3:45 p.m. and continued through to 6:00 p.m. All band members had to be in the band room at 3:45 p.m. No excuses were tolerated.

One of the important practical phases of the Douglass Band rehearsal took place during each of the three lunch periods during the regular school day. Two bandsmen in each lunch period would take the after-school food order for the other bandsmen. Hamburgers, hot dogs, soda, pie, etc., would be on the list. After the 3rd lunch period the orders would be compiled by the two lead majorettes and phoned in to *Cleo's*, a local restaurant/truck stop on Rt. 301 below Upper Marlboro. We had a special relationship with Cleo. It seemed that the local authorities were constantly trying to close up her business, but she was a strong woman who wouldn't let herself be pushed around. As the only black female business-owner in the area, Cleo was an important role model for our students. Anyway, Cleo would then see to it that the food was prepared and delivered to us at precisely at 3:50 p.m. The section leaders would hand out the food. The bandsmen would have until 4:15 to eat and clean up. At 4:30 all parade units of the band would go to their designated area of the school grounds and practice independently. The instrumentalists would remain with me to rehearse concert music. At 5:10 all units would automatically fall into parade formation. We would then practice marching until 6:00, at which time parents would arrive to pick up their bandsmen.

This procedure would go on each day of the week. It would not have been possible without everyone's cooperation, or without the leadership of the students who took responsibility for the various phases of the practice. The bandsmen would learn by doing. They were willing to sacrifice themselves for the good of the group. The bandsmen actually took special pride in being able to practice and perform on their own without adult supervision.

Douglass Goes National

Of course, it was not all self-sacrifice, discipline, and hard work. There was quite a bit of glory involved for the band at this time. In 1954 the Douglass Marching Band had achieved an outstanding record of winning over 14 first place trophies in less than two years, which attracted the attention of *Jet* magazine. It was appropriate that Barbara Parker, as drum major at that time, symbolically represented the entire band and school at our performances. It was Barbara who, as our leader, led Douglass into national recognition. Barbara was a very tall, beautiful, and talented drum major. Her commanding presence reminded one of Dorothy Dandridge or Pamela Green. In addition, Barbara played alto clarinet in the concert band. Perhaps one of the things that placed Douglass a notch above other marching bands in their class was the fact that, as I had promised the parents in the beginning, all auxiliary units (majorettes, banners, flag corps) had to play a concert instrument.

Jet magazine sent a photographer to Douglass where they took individual and group pictures of the bandsmen. The reporters spent close to two hours at the school, talking, interviewing, and observing the band's full dress rehearsal. After the reporters said their farewells, the bandsmen strutted around school, showing off their uniforms and recounting the events of the day. Three weeks later, a representative of *Jet* magazine came to school with the edition of *Jet* which we were waiting to see. The magazine had a picture of Barbara Parker on the cover. She looked elegant and sophisticated in her full dress uniform, tall white beaver head dress, and the lengthy official baton. *Jet*'s stock must have increased a little, because over three hundred magazines were sold in Upper Marlboro. It was awesome to us. Just imagine, our pictures and story going all over the United States. As a result, we received letters from all parts of America. Barbara received letters, Mr. Frisby received letters, and I received letters. Some letters were from schools wanting to know where we purchased our uniforms. Two schools even asked us for a donation. They said their parents were too poor to buy instruments or uniforms. I'm very proud to report that the band took up a collection and sent it to the needy bands.

Competition

It seemed that most of the Douglass "Eagle" Band's marching engagements took place in situations where we were the only Negro unit. From 1957 to 1959 one of our frequent rivals was Northwestern High School. Northwestern, at that time was in the "A" class because of the large number of students they had. Class "A" was the school with the most enrollment and there was a sliding scale down to "D" class. Douglass only had about seven hundred students which put it in the "C" class. One hot July night in 1959 stands out in my mind. On this occasion our band membership was about 75. Northwestern's band had about one hundred fifty members which included majorettes, flag corps, color guard and instrumentalists, and they made an awesome picture when assembled in their blue and white. The approach to the reviewing stand was downhill with a sharp turn at the bottom. The area was lit by flood lights. When the band turned the corner, the reviewing stand was on the left. As we awaited our turn on the side street to feed into the line of march, Northwestern's band, leading the parade, came into view. It seemed like forever before all of their units passed by.

We continued to wait as other units were fed into the line of march. Slowly I turned to look at my group. We weren't a large group but we were ready. Our new uniforms consisted of a black cap with a white bill, gold shirt with red and black trim, black trousers with white and red stripes, white socks, and white bucks.

Without my knowing it, a look of consternation must have crossed my face because my trombone player, Phillip Suggs, leaned over to me and said, "Don't worry, Mr. Battle, We'll take this tonight." I smiled and said, "Don't forget to keep your slides high." Meanwhile, Northwestern High was confidently winding its way along the parade route. Soon it was our turn to enter the parade line. Just before we started our cadence I called the drum major and head drummer over and told them, "Look, the Fire Convention parades can be very long and demanding. This section of Hyattsville is very hilly. Going up and down these hills while playing is going to be tough, so here's what I want you to do. Stagger the drums (half play, half rest, alternately) until we get within a half block of the reviewing stand, you'll be able to recognize it by the huge search lights moving back and forth. I'm going to hustle down to the reviewing stand so that when you come by, I'll be able to see what the judges see." With that, I was off. I did not have to march beside the band all of the time. My operating philosophy was to work with the band five days a week honing their skills. Then on the day of the performance I would turn it all over to the good Lord and to the bandsmen. In addition there were three Douglass Band Booster members who had special uniforms and they always marched at my side with the band. At these times when I would go ahead to observe, band boosters Gary Weems, Sr., Robert Pinkney, and Leo Brown would assume the responsibility and see to the immediate well being of the group.

That night our band was on a mission. My drum major was in charge. The thought was very comforting to me as I headed to the reviewing stand. Finally, I saw the glow of the lights and the pencil-like beams penetrating the night into the sky. As I went down the final hill the crowd was solid from the curb back to the buildings. There was hardly room enough for the marchers to make that important left turn to the front of the stand. I took my place in the stands that were reserved for visitors. It was nice being honored by the marching groups as they stopped in front and saluted the dignitaries in the reviewing stand. It was then that I heard them. There was no mistaking that driving beat. It was a little light, but then, they were not going full force. I heard the drummers roll-off and the band played "Under the Double Eagle" as they started down the hill. The song was over just before they reached the bottom of the hill. "Now," I said, "Now." And then it happened. All four bass drums kicked in as the band turned the corner. When the search lights shone on our band, the gold shirts became sunbursts, the ground was shaking from our devastating cadence, and the silvery air was punctuated with the flourish of Douglass High's instruments being set to the players' lips as the sounds of "them basses" echoed throughout Hyattsville. As my trombone players had predicted, Douglass High School was awarded the first place trophy. We had met and defeated the Northwestern High School Band on their own turf.

Another occasion comes to mind in which the Douglass and Northwestern High School bands faced off. "Maryland Band Day" was a celebration sponsored by the University of Maryland during a scheduled home football game which took place on a Saturday. This event involved some thirty Maryland-area bands. The bands were lining up on the football field awaiting their entrance into the stadium. It was a brilliant, sunny, fall day. The roar of the crowd could be heard as each band made its entrance and the band was announced by the commentator. It was one continuous movement, as one band entered the stadium, other bands were marching and practicing on the field. Our lead drum major lined the band up to practice our "column-lefts", and in doing so, this took us past the Northwestern band which was standing in a parade rest position. The Douglass band then executed a snappy left turn followed by a column front and halted very sharply when we were abreast of the Northwestern group. A few seconds later I glanced over to the Northwestern band and I saw a group of majorettes crowded around their drum major. I found out later that she was crying and was very upset because, once again, she had to compete against our lead drum major, Barbara Parker. I would like to name all of our majorettes, flag corps members, color guard, lead banner bandsmen, and instrumentalists, because all of them contributed unselfishly, blood, sweat, and tears, for the glory of the Douglass "Eagle" Band. Northwestern was a very, very good band. Douglass was quite fortunate to go head to head with them and be successful, at times. There was only one other stellar band around, in my estimation, that could duel Northwestern head to head. That was the Fairmont Heights H.S. Band under the very able direction of Isaac Cook. Ike, as we loved to call him was an outstanding black leader and brass instructor. Fairmont High, which was black, was in the same district as Northwestern.

Impromptu Visit to Board of Education

In the late 1950's, it seemed to me that all of the local "white" schools around us were getting tackle football teams. Flag football was fine but somehow it was pretty hard to become excited over flag football when you know there was another crucial step to be surmounted. One day during the lunch period, William Blount, the Industrial Arts teacher,

132

Benjamin Cumbo, the Physical Education teacher, and myself were outside seated on the benches eating our sandwiches and in general just "shooting the bull," when the subject of football came up. All three of us felt very strongly about the subject. We felt cheated that Douglass did not have a tackle football team.. Then I got one of those bright ideas for which I became noted. "Look," I said, "The county Board of Education is right there across the parking lot less than a football field away. How about the three of us going over there and letting the supervisor know that Douglass wants a football team as soon as possible." Cumbo and Blount looked at each other and then at me. "C'mon," I said, "Let's go." So the three of us strode with purpose over to the physical education entrance of the Board of Education. As we entered the building we were directed to the supervisor's office. We knocked and a heavy male voice from within said, "Come in."

The supervisor, who was white, looked at us with great apprehension. He barely nodded to Cumbo, but managed a weak, "What can I do for you gentlemen?" It was my idea so I spoke up. "We're here because we're asking you to see that things get started regarding a tackle football team for Douglass." The supervisor's eyes grew wide as saucers as he stuttered, "Wh, wh, what do you mean coming in here and demanding that the Board field a football team for you? I just don't go around half-cocked, spouting things I know nothing about. We support Douglass High School. Does Mr. Frisby know you're here? You have no right to come in here like this." I took a deep breath and said, "No, Mr. Frisby doesn't know we're here. You say you support our school. Well, that's all we came to talk about because, you see, our school does not have much. In fact, the set of books our Math Department received this past summer came from Hyattsville Jr. High. That school got new books and you, the Board, sent their used books to us. I could go on and on about what your kind of support is all about, but I know you know what I mean. And furthermore, we're not afraid and shaking in our boots, because we know that we are right and we're on very solid ground. You see, we're not asking anything for ourselves. We're asking for the children we teach." Then I turned to Cumbo and Blount and said, "C'mon, let's get to class."

The three of us never heard anything more about the confrontation, neither from the Board nor Mr. Frisby. However, when we moved to our new school building that following year, the School Board instituted a Junior Varsity-level tackle football program for our school. This was the first step toward a full-fledged football program for Douglass High School.

Music Department at the New Douglass

Douglass had a superb music department, which continued its, excellent traditions in the new school building, completed in late 1960. Walter Earl Pearson was the general music chairman and choral director. I was the instrumental music chairman and band director. From time to time, Pearson would ask me to send over some woodwind or brass instrumentalists to accompany a particular choral selection. However, the two big events the chorus and band members looked forward to during the year were the Christmas Concert and the combined band and chorus Spring Concert. For the Christmas Concert, the auditorium was gaily decorated with a huge Christmas tree. A teacher was volunteered by Principal Frisby to be Santa Claus. He handed out special gifts to students and parents who volunteered their time during the year. After that part of the program was finished, the combined band and chorus would render a concert. All of the participating students had to wear Christmas colors. The band and chorus would alternate their renditions, each playing or singing solos, duets, trios, etc. At the end of the program both groups combined and gave our version of the Hallelujah Chorus. After the program, the Home Economics Department served up cookies, hot and cold cider, and other confectionery goodies.

During the year for several years I was chairman of the enrichment committee at Douglass. It was my distinct pleasure to have arranged for the following groups to present concerts which were well received by our student body. These groups were as follows: The Ft. Meade Concert Band from the U.S. Army, The Airmen of Note from the Air Force, and the Sea Chanters representing the U.S. Navy.

National Competition

Following our victory in Hyattsville, Maryland over the Northwestern High School Band, we decided that we were ready for competition at the national level. The AAA sponsored a safety parade in Washington, D.C. each spring. This parade honored those members of the Safety Patrol, which had units in practically every school in the country.

In the weeks before the parade , we practiced after school each day for three hours. We would practice our marching maneuvers outside on the large parking lot next to the courthouse in Upper Marlboro. We chose that place because most of the county government workers were gone after hours. However, we did not count on some courts being in session, so from time to time an officer of the court would come outside and tell me to hold it down, that they couldn't hear the testimony because of the drums. I used that as an opportunity to play piano softly because it is difficult to get the band to play softly after they have been playing at the fortissimo level.

On the Saturday of the parade, as we unloaded in our formation area, an officer came up to me and said that we were in the category of bands of 75 units and under. This was welcome to me because some of the bands from Ohio had as many as 300 pieces. The nervousness really showed with our group because they just couldn't keep still or stay quiet, so I called them to attention and told them to save that energy for the parade. I told them to relax and not to burn calories. The short talk worked and we were ready when our turn came to flow into Constitution Avenue. Douglass took care of business. The majorettes kicked high, the band held their instruments high, and the drummers just wouldn't quit. When the reviewing stand came into view, we banded together and in one golden spirit, we launched into "Cherry Pink and Apple Blossom White." We were delirious when Douglass won the trophy for our category.

Catching the Spirit

Within several years of our move to our new building, integration came to Douglass High School too. Prior to the actual integration of the schools, our band had made plans to encourage those talented and interested "white" band members to join the Douglass Band. As a result, we did receive new members to the Douglass "Eagle" Band. Shortly thereafter the Douglass Band was preparing for an upcoming, and because of the distance, rather strenuous parade.

There were signs all around the school declaring in one way or another that, "once a Douglass bandsman, always a Douglass bandsman," or asking, "Did you catch the spirit?" or "Do you feel like a Douglass bandsman?"

While we were practicing long and hot hours for the upcoming parade, our principal, Mr. Frisby requested that the band, majorettes, and flag corps all perform at a short, welcoming dress parade to be held at the school. The parade and welcoming ceremonies were always a huge success. Drums were booming, flags were flying, and students and parents of both races were cheering. After the activities were over the band members were laughing and joking in the band room when one of the old members said to our newest majorette, who was white, "Do you have that Douglass spirit yet?" The new majorette replied, "No, I don't feel anything special."

Of the new white members who joined the band, three were drummers. Drummers held a place of high esteem in the Douglass Band and so it wasn't without reason that the old bandsmen, especially the drum-

135

mers, would point at the new drummers and laughingly exclaim, "You'll be sorry." Once a parade started, the only section that had to perform at top level at all times, and the only section which could not get a rest the entire parade route, was the drum section. Consequently, under ordinary circumstances, the drummers would get blisters on their fingers and hands where the sticks would cause friction. This ailment could knock out a complete drum line if those affected drummers were permitted to not play for that week. In the Douglass Band, drummers played through the pain and the bursting of their blisters. The Douglass drummers took special pride in baptizing their drums with the fluid that spattered over the drum head. This part was a little painful, but then the hand toughened and that meant no more blisters.

The day of the big parade rolled around. The bandsmen were both excited and a bit leery because the parade was a long one and there were about eight untested musicians on whom they now had to depend. The parade was held in Takoma Park, a community with a lot of hilly streets. It was just as difficult to march down the street as it was to march up. The distance was quite long and the competition tough. We were a very tired but proud bunch of musicians when it was announced that the first place trophy was awarded to the Douglass "Eagle" Band.

When the buses returned to school, the bandsmen straggled to the band room and just rested their heads on the backs of their chairs. All of a sudden, the new majorette charged into the room and said out loud, "I've got it, Mr. Battle. I've got the spirit. I'm a Douglass "Eagle" Bandsman." Her name was Joyce Friend, and she later excelled as a majorette and became known as the "Golden Girl". All of the other majorettes got up and surrounded her with cries of "See, I told you," or, "Yeah, you're really one of us now." Then my head drummer went over to the new drummers and said, "Let me see your hands." All three of the new drummers held out their hands. The head drummer examined their hands. Then he said for all to hear, "I think they're going to make it, Mr. Battle. The blisters are there." Such was the upbeat spirit of a Douglass "Eagle" Bandsman. It was good to see, at least in this instance, that even with the radical changes brought about by the integration of the schools, it looked as though the tradition of the Douglass "Eagle" Band would be able to continue on intact.

Taking a Stand

That first decade at Frederick Douglass was quite remarkable. We started an instrumental music program, virtually from scratch, and went on to win local, state, and national recognition. More importantly, we won the support of our community, and in return played a significant role in giving that community a renewed sense of pride in itself and the school. Most importantly, we gave hundreds of students the chance to grow in maturity and increase their self-esteem. Through it all, we were, as we needed to be, primarily focused on ourselves and our own community. We had much to accomplish and a lot to overcome. As a "colored" school, there was a tendency for us to be isolated from the "white" school system, and for us to turn inward and concentrate on ourselves. In the early 1960's, however, things began to change - social issues were swirling around us that we were at the center of, and that we could not very well ignore. The Civil Rights Movement was arousing the conscience of the nation, against much resistance, and the flurry of activities associated with that movement inevitably reached many of us and directly involved us in the struggle, a struggle that was not unfamiliar to me. A very memorable occasion during this period involved me and some of my students in a protest against racism. A very volatile situation in was developing in Danville, Virginia, where there was a bitter relationship between the Negro and white population. The Negroes there were attempting to integrate the public schools. The law was on the side of the Negroes, but the white population was determined not to let that interfere with their segregationist policies. Finally, in a last minute effort to circumvent the mandatory desegregation law, the Board of Education closed the public schools. The white parents set up private schools in homes, churches, or wherever. These private schools catered only to the white students, leaving the black children without a place to go. A call went out from the NAACP, to attend a gigantic rally to be held in Danville, Virginia in June, 1963 at the local armory. Al Winfield, the leader of the Altones - a local swing band I had joined - called us to a meeting to discuss the situation. Rev. C.R. McCreary, brother of band member Rivers McCreary, was helping to organize the protest along with Rev. A. Dunlop, Rev. L.W. Chase, Rev. J.H. Jones, and Rev. Elder L. Campbell. Rev. McCreary had asked us to bring the band to Danville to participate in the activities. In the end we made a commitment to appear on the program and do our part to help those Negro students being denied their education in Danville. Following one of the afternoon rehearsals of the Douglass "Eagle" Band, a few of the senior musicians inquired about the Altones going to Virginia. I explained the situation and they said, "Mr. Battle, take us please." I then explained that there were really too many complications in trying to take a full band out of town. The students accepted that statement and left. However, there were three senior trumpet players in my office before class the following morning. "Mr. Battle," they said. "You won't have to take the band to Virginia next Friday." I said, "I already know that, fellows. You came in here just to tell me that?" They said, "No, Mr. Battle. We three trumpets could go and we would wear our band uniforms and contribute to the program by playing Leroy

137

Anderson's 'Bugler's Holiday'. We each know the parts from memory."
Then another bandsman chimed in. "Billy's father is willing to take us
in his car." Well, they certainly gave me food for thought, so I said to
them, "Look guys, the first bell is about to ring. Suppose I get back to
you after lunch." They left, but not before getting a time when I would
meet with them.

All during morning classes I pondered the problem and finally came
up with a plan. That afternoon I met with the trio of trumpet players. I
was dead serious. I told them that those brave students in Danville
needed to see and hear the positive side of life from their own age
group as well as adults. I also told them that we would be in a strange
neighborhood and that sometimes we may not be among friendly faces.
In fact, things could get a bit rough down there. I asked them if they
wanted to reconsider going. "No", they said. "If you go, we go." I thanked
them, and further said, "One more thing before you leave. I'm not
telling the Board of Education or Mr. Frisby about your participating. If
either one finds out, my name will be mud. Not only will both forbid us
to go, but the Board could give me my walking papers." "Don't worry,
Mr. Battle. We won't let you down."

Early Saturday morning of the following week, we, the Altones, met
with the students and their parents. I had a brief conference with the
drivers. I told them to stay alert, to observe the speed limits, and that
we would only eat at "Mickey D's". Some time later when we entered
Danville, we were met by the State Police who directed us to the armory, after they warned us not to start any trouble by trying to picket.
When we arrived at the armory, we found that it was already jammed
with people. It seemed as if all of the students were seated in bleach-
ers, taking up the whole side of the armory. There must have been
about two thousand students cheering and clapping hands as we strode
to the opposite side where the piano was placed. The Altones quickly
set up. Before we started to play, a very beautiful, classy female came
over to us and introduced herself. "Hello, my name is Maxine Sullivan."
(She had that mega hit *Loch Lomond*.) I introduced the Altones, then
the trumpet trio and their parents. I then asked Maxine for an auto-
graph. She obliged, then she handed out the charts to the songs she
was going to sing, among them was *Loch Lomond*. The signal for the
start of the activities came in the form of lights blinking. A pastor stepped
up to the microphone, asked all to bow their heads while he prayed.
After that the participants were introduced to the students to rounds
of generous applause. The school girls went wild when the trumpet
trio of Theodore Hawkins, Orville Harley, and Anthony Thomas was
introduced. They looked magnificent in their jet black coats and trousers trimmed in the state of Maryland colors, and their white Sam
Browne belts, West Point style. The musical selections were interspersed

between speeches of encouragement to the students. The loudest response went to the trumpet trio for their rendition of "Bugler's Holiday." I was truly proud of them. They looked and sounded so professional, executing those lightning runs and doing all of this with no stands or sheet music.

After the concert, the students came out of the stands and gathered around all of the musicians. Conversation was very lively. The Danville parents ushered the participants over to the refreshment tables. The pastors and their civic action committees expressed their profound thanks to all of us for our unselfish contribution to the cause of freedom. It was very sad to see all of those faces, eager to learn, having to struggle so hard for an opportunity that should have been theirs without asking. Like the motto of the United Negro College Fund says, "A mind is a terrible thing to waste." Of course, there was no miraculous conversion of the local population. The struggle to ensure our civil rights in many ways and in many places continues even today. But we demonstrated that we were not about to quietly tolerate the injustices of segregation - not in Danville and not anywhere else. We also accomplished something very important between us. We demonstrated our commitment to each other in this time of need, a commitment from which we could always gather strength because at its heart was respect for each other, respect for ourselves, and the faith that those on the side of justice would persevere.

from former students –

"LeRoy 'Boots' Battle taught me the rudiments of the trumpet as well as he did with each student with their own instrument, and I am proud to have been one of the original buglers of that (first) Drum and Bugle Corps, and the first 1st trumpet of the original Douglass High School Band.
"Boots" Battle was my inspiration to go on to college and to be a confident and motivated person, and I want to thank you "Boots" Battle, for being a positive role model in my life."

Earl E. Tolson, Jr.

"Your teaching will always stick with us... Believe me, you are the best"
— Harold Eugene Hawkins

"His caring and training in the Douglass High School Band was a beautiful experience that we have carried with us throughout our lives."

— Margaret A. Walls & Doris Burroughs

"I was a senior at Douglas High School when Mr. Battle arrived as a music and band instructor... I can remember my buddies and I wanted out of class one day so we decided to be disruptive in Mr. Battle's class. Sure enough, he did exactly what we knew he would do, gave us an opportunity to stop or leave his class. Four of my buddies got up and walked out and I was supposed to walk out too, but I just couldn't do it. So I stayed and didn't cause any more trouble... the next day when I went to class again he pulled me aside and told me how he admired what I did and that it took a lot of strength to do . (before) I saw myself as a

139

follower... but from that moment and from that day I decided that I was going to think for myself. I believe that experience made the greatest impact on me growing up and becoming a man. The thing about it, I never took time to tell him, and it's really a shame to have to wait so long before your know if you made a difference... I always thought of Mr. Battle and his music, but what he did for a bunch of country students... went far beyond the music.

— Walter Savoy

"At some point after I'd obtained my undergraduate degree, I began to reflect on who, of all the teachers I had, was the best... First, you expanded all of our horizons, especially, of course, in music... (second) you always pushed us to excellence. You _never_ accepted less from _any_ of us... However, many of my other teachers did these things... the reason I chose you as the best of all my teachers was the fact that, while my sisters and I always knew that we were going to college, many of our schoolmates in southern Prince George's County did not. No one in their families had _ever_ gone to college, no one encouraged them to go, and there was no money to pay for it. In spite of this, I can name many band members who were the _only_ child in their family to go to college, who went on music scholarships, and thus, who went solely because of your foresight, inspiration, and influence... I was blessed to have had many excellent teachers over the years... but of all the teachers I had... you were the best. Thanks for all the things which you knew that you were doing for us, and for the things which you may not have known that you were doing for us... just THANKS!"

— Agnes C. Powell

Douglas Drum and Bugle Corps – 1953

Calvin Wallace, on Sousaphone, and Paul Huff, on piano, receiving individual practice – 1964

Mr. Battle, Vice-Principal of Suitland Jr. High, with Brig Owens of the Washington Redskins.

141

Linda Adams, Ann Tolson, and Lauvenia Moore, 1st Clarinets practicing at the Navy School of Music, 1956

Doris Walls attends a band clinic at the U.S. Naval Receiving Station Auditorium.

Yvonne Simmons, outstanding drummer, 1956

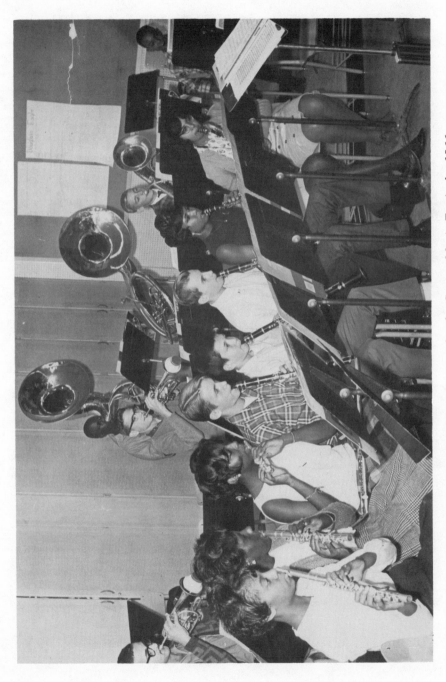

The instrumental ensemble rehearses for the County Music Festival – 1966

143

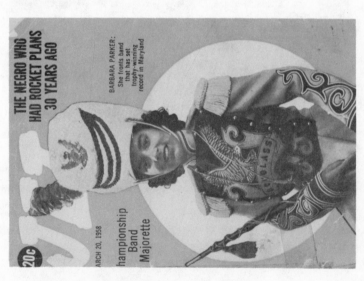

Barbara Parker accepting first place trophy on behalf of the Douglass High School Marching Band – Indian Head, Maryland, 1959

National recognition for Douglass High School and Barbara Parker – 1958

PRETTY, 15-YEAR-OLD MAJORETTE

Up to a point, Upper Marlboro's Douglass High is much like any other high school in Maryland. That is until one views the amazing antics of the marching band—an aggregation whose fancy arrangements and top musical selections have made the school one of the most-talked-about in the state.

The band set a phenomenal record by capturing 14 trophies in predominantly white competition during the past two years in Prince George's County, where the school is situated.

Last spring, the assemblage was invited to march in the reception in the nation's capital for King Saud of Saudi Arabia and President Ngo Dinh Diem of Vietnam. This year marks the first time the group is slated to high-prance in the Cherry Blossom Parade in Washington, D. C.

And when the award-winning band is on parade, one of the first persons to capture the eye of spectators is a high-stepping, fancy baton-twirler who fronts the band as lead drum majorette. She is 15-year-old Barbara Ann Parker (see cov-

Barbara Jean, Director Leroy Battle and Barbara Adams admire trophies.

PUTS MD. SCHOOL BAND ON MAP

High-prancing during practice, cute Barbara Jean leads the award winning Douglass band during outdoor rehearsal.

er), a cute sophomore who is now in her second year as leader of the six-member drum majorette squad.

The director of the group is Leroy Battle, a former Don Redmond drummer who quit the bigtime whirl to take over the post in the small farming town—located 17 miles from Washington, D. C. In just six years he has organized a 40-member "A" band, with 30 "under-studies," in a "B" group, and firmly planted them in the ranks of the state's best.

Spring always finds the group busy—preparing for their annual concert and making guest appearances.

Recently, the Douglass band received its biggest distinction when group became first Negroes to appear in the *First Chair Of America*, the yearbook honoring the nation's finest high school bands, orchestras and choruses.

Douglass High featured in Jet Magazine, as one of the nations top high school bands.

Principal ROBERT F. FRISBY (Right)
Vice Principal SPICER PETERSON (Left)

The various sections of the Douglass Band, featured in "First Chair of America", honoring the best bands in the country.

SANDRA MIDDLETON, Snare Drum; ALBERTA ADDISON, Co-First Clarinet; BERNICE PROCTOR, Alto Saxophone; EUGENE SMITH, Tenor Saxophone, All-County Band; THOMAS ADDISON, Trombone; LAWRENCE NEWMAN, Baritone, All-State Band 2 years; WARREN PINKNEY, Sousaphone; CAROL HAWKINS, French Horn; EVERETT TOLSON, Trumpet.

(Top) 1st Chair members of the Douglass "First Chair Band". (Bottom) The entire band – first Negro band to be so honored.

147

Douglass High School Band Boosters Club – 1956. Seated in front: Gary Weems, Vice President; Mrs. Ruth Tolson, President; Mrs. Eugenia Brown, Secretary; Nelson Lee, Sgt. at Arms.

(Above) "Swing Band" members – 1952
(Left) Mr. Gary Weems, President of
Douglass High Band Boosters Club,
with Roy Battle – 1964

(Above) Performing at Indian Head, Maryland, for the Fire Safety Parade – 1959
(Left) Senior Band Ensemble – 1953

LeRoy Battle and Walter Pearson, choral director, working together on a music program at the "new" Douglass High School – 1963

151

Douglass majorettes at summer camp in New York, 1964 (top);
Glendora Davis, achieved "high honors" in 1964 (left); Phillip and Sandy
preparing for Memorial Day Parade in 1967 (right).

152

SILVERENE JOHNSON	JUANITA HOLLEY	CYNTHIA DOUGLAS	THEODORA BROWN
Drum Major	Special Twirler	Majorette Leader	Best Majorette
BRENDA TOLSON	BEVERLY WELLS	JACQUELINE PINKNEY	JOYCE LEND
JOANIE JOHNSON	PAMELA WALLS	LINDA HARLISS	SHIRLEY SAVOY

The Douglass majorettes – 1966

*Douglass Eagle Band, led by Color Guard, opens the
Marlton subdivision – 1966.*

The Douglass Band at Bowie State Teacher's College homecoming – 1962

*Roger Pinkney, Thomas Addison, and Raymond Powell take
trombone lessons from Navy instructor – 1956*

Promotion Day, 1956 – new members of the "A" Band

Benjamin Cumbo; Physical Education teacher and friend.

Part 2
My Friends

My wife, Alice H. Battle, in 1955.
...she is the wind beneath my wings

Continuing to Grow

(Some of) The Rest of the Story

While I called this an autobiography, I know there is much I've left out. I have concentrated so far on those things which I thought were most prominent in affecting my character and in giving my life the direction it had. In some ways this has simply been a reflection on my relationship, first with my family, and second, with my music, as I followed it through its role in my own self-discovery, to sharing it, both as a performer and as a teacher, with others. There was also an important digression into my military career along the way. There are many other things that I have forgotten, and some that I have chosen to overlook, but I do not intend to overlook the many friends and acquaintances to whom I owe so much and who continue to shape my life. The remainder of the book is devoted to them, as well as to several loose ends that otherwise did not fit neatly into the purposes of the first part.

Getting My Car and My License

I never thought much about getting my driver's license or owning a car in New York - most people didn't. The public transportation system made day-to-day driving irrelevant, and you could usually catch a ride with someone who did have a car whenever you really needed one. At Morgan State I didn't worry about getting my license either, being from out of state, and fortunately, there was usually somebody "going my way." So when I started teaching at Frederick Douglass, at the age of twenty-nine, I still didn't know how to drive. I lived about 15 miles from the school, and I was fortunate enough to be a part of a transportation pool. A car would pick me up each morning. However, because I stayed late to rehearse the band, I had to find another way home. It was the Band Boosters Club which solved my problems. The parents would take turns transporting me home after rehearsals. They would also take me anywhere that was required. While all of this was very convenient for me, I knew that a lot of people had to sacrifice a great deal to enable me to operate. This fact bothered me to no end so I resolved to somehow get my driver's license. Two of the teachers came to my rescue. They were George Walls and Benjamin Cumbo. These teachers were uniquely responsible for my being able to operate what

159

I called my "freedom machine," my car. Ben and George owned different make cars which they basically showed me how to start and stop. So there it was. This was how I learned to drive. I would await the arrival of either Ben or George at the entrance gate to the school grounds. Whichever of them arrived first, would move over and let me get into the driver's seat. I would then drive either Ben or George to the front door of the school, a distance of approximately forty yards, before driving the car to the parking lot. I did this each morning for about a month. Then they said to me, "Starting tomorrow, you are to back our cars into the parking places." After about a week it was time for me to take my driving test, which was given each month in town.

In my hurry to own a car, I got the cart before the horse, so to speak. Now get this. I purchased my new car, a green Chevrolet, at 10:00 a.m., and took my driving test at 11:00 a.m. The salesman had to ride with me to the testing center. Mr. Frisby was very understanding about my situation and had arranged for me to miss my morning classes. Word had spread throughout the school that I was being tested for my driver's license. The salesman exited the car and the examiner climbed in and told me to make a left turn. I jammed my hand trying to put my left arm out of the window (the window was halfway up). After that inauspicious beginning, I do not remember much because I was totally focused. Finally, we wound up back at the starting point and the examiner said, "Congratulations."

The car dealer had seen to it that all my paperwork was done, and I received my temporary license. I drove less than a mile to school and parked. Lunch was just about over and in the lunch room, all of the students and teachers applauded me. It seemed that someone had called the school's office from the test site. I immediately went to both Ben and George, hugged them, and further expressed my profound thanks. My feeling good about purchasing a car and then passing the driver's test was short-lived when Ben said "Tell me something, Boots." I said "Yeah?" He said, "Just what would you have done if you had failed the test?" I said "Huh?" Then we both burst out laughing.

Mr. Frisby, who lived close to me, happened by then. He said, "Battle, I'll trail you home today, so don't leave before me." I thanked him and then a dark cloud seemed to pass over me. I just realized that I had to negotiate fifteen miles in order to get home. It was soon time to leave. Mr. Frisby was ready and he honked his horn for me to get going. Now to get home I had to navigate a long winding route called Ritchie Road. I am not going to tell you a lie. I drove that road, all 15 miles of it, straddling the center line. Mr. Frisby was honking at me and waving his arm, telling me to get to the right, but I wasn't about to move. Approaching cars blinked their lights and had to swerve to the shoulder to miss me, but I rode that center line all the way home. When we stopped and

I got out, Mr. Frisby called me over to his car and started to explain. He started out with "LeRoy". Then he stopped and said, "Good luck, son. Be sure to notify your drivers not to come by for you." And with that he drove off, slowly shaking his head.

The Little League Story

In the early 1960's the Anne Arundel County Little Leagues were not integrated. The black teams in the southern part of Anne Arundel were from three general areas: Shady Side, Galesville, and Edgewater. Shady Side, whose colors were red and white, was coached by Bernard Powell. Galesville, whose colors were blue and white, was coached by Orville Hutton. Edgewater, whose colors were green and white, was coached by Harold Brown. Now I give these teams and coaches a great deal of credit. When master schedules were made up, they did not include the black teams. In fact, many local white fields had rules which specifically prohibited black and white teams from playing together. The black teams rose above this pettiness and formed their own athletic association, called the Southern Anne Arundel County Athletic Association.

It was about this time that I became involved with the Little League because of my son, LeRoy Jr. The first year he played, as I was observing the black teams playing each other, a thought came to me that a fourth team would even things out. So I set about making plans for this yet to be organized team. There was a tobacco field in front of where I lived that was owned and farmed by Daddy Holt. He, in reality, was the Rev. Harrison Holt, lay speaker and local preacher for the church, and the father of my wife, Alice. I asked Daddy Holt if he would agree to let me use the field for the baseball team which I was going to organize the next year. Dad Holt said "Yes", and we, with the help of my wife's brothers, cleared the field, leveled it, added clay, and after about a month had put it into baseball shape.

In early spring, I put up notices in and around the black churches and schools announcing that tryouts would be held for the "Lothian Clippers" baseball team. Within two weeks there were 30 aspiring baseball hopefuls. We went through the usual procedure of asking the boys where they wanted to play. This idea was soon abandoned because every boy wanted to either pitch or play first base. I, along with several parents, divided the boys into small bunches and went to different parts of the field to start our tryouts. After several days of hard practice, we were able to field a team to represent Lothian with style.

Our next task was to get equipment and uniforms for the boys. We held bake sales, asked the merchants for donations, and received cash contributions from the parents. We raised enough funds to buy fifteen uniforms. We asked the local men's semi-pro baseball team, the *Drury Giants*, to donate the catcher's equipment, bats, and balls. The parents purchased the individual gloves needed by the rest of the players.

During my tenure as little league manager, a span which covered 15 years, many, many, positive experiences come to mind, and, I might add, a few negative ones, also. One particular game against the Edgewater team gave us Lothian Clippers great satisfaction. Now Edgewater was tough. The boys were quite large for their age, they had crafty pitchers, a strong catcher, and their bats could sing. At the time the Lothian Clippers entered the league, Edgewater had been league champion for five out of the last seven years, and to make matters worse, they hadn't lost a game in the past two years running. Lothian played fairly well that season, albeit in a losing cause. We had only won seven of seventeen games. However, we never lost heart, and our en- thusiasm was still as strong as when the season started. We had a good, strong battery, but our bats had been silent for the past 3 games. Well, to get to the point, on this day, Little Beaver, our pitcher, "had it." This was the last game of the season. He was throwing hard and accurate and was only allowing grounders. Our infield was airtight, but we were trailing by a score of 3-0. It was two outs and the last of the 7th and final inning. Edgewater had previously beaten us 3 times this season, and you could feel that they were already celebrating, because they were woofing loud and strong to our batters as they came up and popped out. Well, as had been previously stated, there were two outs and the top of our batting order was due up. The leadoff man was walked. The number two man got hit by a wild pitch. Harold Brown, the wily coach of Edgewater, signalled his pitcher to walk the third man, thus enabling his infield to be able to make a play at any base. This brought Kenny Smith, our heavy hitter, to the plate. The first pitch to Kenny was a scorching strike, right down the pike. "Time," I called to the plate umpire. Then I waved to Kenny for a conference. I put my arm around him and said, "Kenny, all this pitcher knows is how to throw fast strikes or pitch outs. Now, they are not going to play games with you. They want you out and fast. So if his next pitch doesn't look like a pitch-out, feel free to put the fat of the bat on that pill and send it for a ride." "Play ball," the umpire said. Kenny stepped up to the plate, wiggled his bat, and waited for the ball. He didn't have to wait long. No sooner had Edgewater's pitcher let fly, that Kenny, with a level swing supported by his whole body, put the "fat of the bat" on the ball, and I want to tell you that ball is still rising. Lothian won, 4 to 3. That was the first time I had seen so many boys crying. Edgewater took it hard.

The fact that Anne Arundel County had one Department of Recreation, yet separately sanctioned and operated the baseball leagues, one for the white youth and the other for the black youth, concerned me deeply. The coming of spring and of the baseball season in the black community was observed with a very colorful parade in Galesville, Maryland. I, herein, take my hat off to all of the black parents who made up the Southern Athletic Association. These parents here mentioned, in particular, were the cornerstones of this progressive black organization: Mrs. Harriet Hull, Mrs. Theresa Fountain, and Mr. Melvin Booze.

These three persons and many others were involved in organizing the various units of the parade. Each of the four teams marched wearing their colorful uniforms. There were also decorated bicycles, baby carriages, convertibles, and a very talented drum and bugle corps.

After the parade, everyone would gather in and around the community hall, eating hot dogs, ice cream, drinking sodas, and playing games. In the evenings, the second part of the festival would begin, namely, the dance. By this time the young athletes had left for their homes and the older people would start arriving in their cars. Later came the band, and soon, as Fats Waller would say, "The joint was jumping." The admirable thing about these affairs was that all of the money that was taken in was divided equally among the four teams from the named communities.

During my years of working with the Lothian Clippers, there were persons who worked with me to help make the initial idea which I had come to fruition. When I say, "We did this" or "We did that," it is to these dedicated persons whom I am referring, maybe not for the total period which I worked, but sometimes during that time, they contributed their 100% to the little league team.

Billy Harried and Forrest Holt were very involved persons in the organizing of the Clippers, reaching out to the boys, interesting them in the activity, and molding them in becoming excellent players.

There were mothers who were always there. Mrs. Pauline Garrett's enthusiasm for the team and the game always kept the boys aspiring. I recall one "away" game when I couldn't be there and I asked Mrs. Garrett to be responsible for the team. She took over as coach and did a splendid job. We won that game. Mrs. Ruth Sesker was our tireless, working, secretary-treasurer. She always kept her records right up to date. Ms. Helen Anderson, with her knowledge of the game and her willingness to always go the extra mile, helped tremendously with the successful operation of the team. The list of involved parents continues: the Harry Brown family, the Tommy Wallace family, the Sammy Smith family, Mrs. Elizabeth Smith's family, Mrs. Estelle Johnson's family, and Mrs. Mable Thompson's family. Other families who had boys participating always pitched in where there was a need. I am speaking specifically of the Cornell Hugh family, the Clifton Sharps family, the Arthur Pratt family, the Rice family, the Thompson family, the Kenny Smith family, the Waters family, the Harry Wingo family, and the backbone of our group, Mr. Buck McGhee.

There are other parents and support persons whose names are not mentioned but who helped in many ways with the operation of the Lothian Clippers Little League Team and to whom we owe continual thanks.

As time went on it came to my mind continually about this dual setup. I thought more and more about the hodge-podge, hit and miss manner in which black and white teams were kept separate. It just seemed that the black coaches and parents were giving their tacit approval to this setup. I know with all my heart that this was not the case, but we were lost by not knowing the correct course to take. We certainly wanted to avoid confrontation or at worse, violence. Before the start of each season, the county Recreation Department would hold meetings for baseball coaches in each part of the county. At these meetings, there would be a free flow of information to and among all of the coaches, black and white. There was plenty of goodwill and banter. However, everyone steered clear of the race situation. It was after the second meeting as I was driving home when a plan began to develop in my mind. By the time I reached home, the plan was forged in my head and I knew exactly what course of action I was going to take the next day.

About three miles down the road from my house was the Patuxent Manor Trailer Court. The residents were all white and for the most part "blue collar." That evening I put on my gold "Little League Coach's jacket and baseball cap emblazoned with a royal blue "L", climbed into my freedom machine, and headed down the road to "Patuxent Manor." As I made a right turn into the entrance of the "trailer court", I saw twelve or fifteen boys and a few girls playing a pickup game of softball. They were of all ages and completely disorganized. A few more yards from where I turned in I noticed a group of young and middle aged adults. They were gathered around a car with the engine hood up. Some were holding cans of beer, others had their heads under the hood. As I slowly drove up, all of their attention was on me. As I turned the engine off, one of the men said, "Yeah man, Can I help you?" I smiled and said, "Hopefully, I can help you." I then introduced myself, explaining to them that I was manager of the Lothian Clippers just up the road. I told them that I couldn't help but notice all of the children trying to play softball, but that they did not have the space, equipment, or skills needed. I then told them that there would be practice the next day on the Lothian Clippers' field and that I would like their permission to talk with the group playing out front and invite them to try out for the team. At that point, the hostile looks changed to smiles. The men said they would talk to the other parents for me. I thanked the men and drove over to where the children were playing. I got out of the car and asked them to gather in front of me. Then I explained everything to them and let them know that they would be welcomed with opened arms.

In my mind I just couldn't believe that the white coaches had not attempted to recruit from "Patuxtent Manor". It was like finding a gold mine. I wound up my presentation and said my good-byes. As I turned and drove off, I noticed in my rearview mirror that quite a few of the kids were smiling and waving. It's the little things that count. I felt pretty good about my sojourn into uncharted waters.

When I arrived at Lothian's field, practice was just winding down. I went over to the catcher's plate and motioned for all players, coaches, and parents to please gather in close. I knew in my heart that I had taken a chance opening up our ranks to the white players without a discussion. However, I strongly felt that such a discussion could lead to heated debates, which in turn could involve personalities, etc. Consequently, I decided to bite the bullet. After all, leaders, at times, must act in an autocratic style to further a democratic cause. So when I met with the youngsters, coaches, and parents, I told them it was a "fait accompli." Many of our ball players already knew which white players would be good, from playing together at school. They started yelling to get this person, or that person. I asked our secretary to take down those names. Before dismissing the group, I asked them to please come early tomorrow and to do their best to be businesslike.

Later I explained the situation to my wife, Alice. Alice always welcomed the chance to serve as my "sounding board." If ever I had a plan or idea, and could stand the "awful truth", all I had to do was to ask Alice for a critique of same. The big question was, after all of the pleading and cajoling, "would anyone from the trailer court show up?"

That night was quite a restless one for me. I hardly ate any breakfast. Alice had prepared my favorite too, waffles. Finally, the late afternoon practice time arrived, 4:00 p.m. The regular Lothian players were on the field going through a very spirited practice. I kept looking anxiously down the road, looking for cars. Then, it happened. At 4:15 I heard horns blaring and saw a caravan of about five cars. There was a lot of waving back and forth. I offered a silent prayer of thanks. As soon as the cars were parked, we got right down to the business of practice. It wasn't long before we had our pool of players divided into: pitchers, those boys who naturally threw hard; catchers, those who could throw from a crouch, first basemen, left handers, etc. At the end of practice we found that we had enough youngsters to field three teams, two 8 to 10 year old teams and one 10 to 12 year old team.

Not only did Lothian's teams benefit from integration, so did the parent support organization. We were very fortunate to obtain the services of Mr. and Mrs. Jabe Truitt, long time residents of the Lothian area, along with their children and their in-laws, doing everything possible to help support the Lothian Clippers. Mrs. Truitts' parents came up on their vacation, and while here, built the utility/refreshment stand down on the field. Mr. and Mrs. Robert George were on call each and every day of practice and every game day. The Harold Shaws, the late Dr. Billy Graham, and others who were long time residents and short time residents of Lothian became involved with the Little League baseball teams.

It was beautiful and inspiring to see the camaraderie that developed between the black and white players, parents, and coaches. As we started this particular season, Lothian was the only club that was integrated. It was very interesting and educational to see how the white parents adjusted and relaxed as Lothian went from one black playing field to another. The black parents also enjoyed the close contact with the white parents. In fact, later in the season, one would notice both groups sharing food and treating each other to sodas. In the middle of the schedule, when the coaches of the segregated teams selected their players to take part in the all-star game, I suggested that both of our teams attend that game, even though we were not allowed to participate. There was "a method to my madness", because I was going to see that Lothian took part the next year and I wanted them to get the feel of real pressure and how to perform on cue. It was wonderful to see both black and white players piling into cars for transportation regardless of who was driving. Lothian had a pretty good summer and we won our division.

Later that summer at the end of the season's coach meeting, our area supervisor attended and I said to myself that now was the time to do something about this ridiculous scheduling situation. So I asked for the floor and then I preached about all of the stupidity, wastefulness, and senselessness of the way the Anne Arundel County Recreation and Parks Department conducted their little league baseball. I then told them, "For those of you who do not know, the Lothian teams are integrated and we want to be included in the big picture." Then I turned to the supervisor, looked him directly in the eye, and said, "We want you to schedule us like you do all of the other teams." To which the other coaches clapped their hands, whistled, and otherwise showed their approval.

166

Well, that phase of racism was torn down in Southern Anne Arundel County. Soon, other black teams were integrated and then sooner or later the question was asked, "What's all the fuss about?"

Through the years leadership and skill instructions were provided by the following coaches: Helen Anderson, Benny Ellis, Rickey Halsey, Ronald Harris, Cornell Heigh, George Jones, Terry Pott, Leila Smith, assistant, James Thompson, Jabe Truitt, Rickey Truitt, and Tommy Wallace.

Also, we could not have functioned without the support of the many persons, down through the years. Special thanks are hereby given to Carol Harris, Betty Collinson and Barbara, Vashti Holt, Mrs. McNamara, Mr. and Mrs. Hall, Mrs. Owens, Mrs. Maxson, Mrs. Ellis , Mrs. Smith, Mrs. Thompson, Mrs. McVey, Mrs. Lane, Mrs. Mary Belle Holt, Claude Holt, Jimmy Holt, Mrs. Virginia Walker and Mr. Jesse Walker, Jean Truitt, and Rebecca and Bobby Cole.

A successful ball team needed all facets to operate at a high level. Therefore, in addition to the above persons I pay tribute to our "Angels" who tackled the "nuts and bolts" of the running of the refreshment stand and all that it entailed: Robin Garrett, Colette Owens, Diane Mangus, Sheila Truitt, Mrs. Robert George, and Mrs. Jake Truitt.

Mr. Robert George, Sr., also contributed his talent of artistry and printing by publishing our newsletter on a regular basis.

My Redskins Band Experience

Because of where I lived, it was quite natural for me to follow the Washington Redskins football team, and given my background, it's not surprising that I also was a fan of their marching band. But for quite some time I had contemplated looking into the one obvious negative aspect of the Washington Redskins Band. There weren't any black members, and this bothered me to some degree because I truly admired their musicianship and uniforms. Actually, what I wanted was for a few of my top bandsmen to make the band. I made telephone calls to every number listed in the book connected with "Redskins" but to no avail. I could not find out when and where practices were held. So I decided to play my one trump card and write to Sterling Tucker, who was then the Executive Secretary of the Urban League, Washington chapter. Within a few weeks Mr. Tucker answered my letter, instructing me to have my students at the District Armory on a particular Wednesday night. I did not know on what the bandsmen would be tested. However, I did know that all quality requirements would include the chromatic scale, a major and minor scale, a prepared selection, and sight reading. Needless to say, that was a very busy, demanding, week for my two trumpet hopefuls. We were met by roll takers who checked our names off. We then continued through the huge drill hall and were directed to a special section.

I was both shocked and happy to see Mr. Tucker there. He came over, we shook hands, and I introduced him to the two bandsmen. Soon, one of the Redskin drum majors came over to us. He announced that all persons taking the test should follow him to another room at the end of the hall. Within thirty minutes I saw both of my bandsmen going where the band was playing. Both turned around and gave Mr. Tucker and I the "thumbs up" sign. We were quite proud and they were big hits at school, but for some reason they only stayed one season with the "Redskin Band." They graduated from Douglass, and for the most part, that was the last I saw of them.

Later that year, I was urged by several of my friends and cohorts to try out for the Redskins Band. So, one Wednesday night in August, I showed up at the armory, took my test which included marching while playing, demonstrating the various rudiments, and sight reading. I passed with colors flying. Then I was told to go to a certain equipment truck to get a drum. From there I went directly up to the drum line. We were not marching yet. Rather, we were working on a show tune which was to be played at the game that week. After we had gone through the show piece, the director felt comfortable that we would be able to play it Sunday. He then blew his whistle and said, "Let's hit the floor."

I got up and started to follow the rest of the drummers to the band forming up when one of the bass drummers said to me, "Hey man. This doesn't mean you. You're a reserve. You just stay here and watch." I didn't understand that at all. I went back to the stands. There were about twenty forlorn looking bandsmen there. I said to no one in particular, "What gives with reserves?" A gray haired trumpet player looked my way and said, "I'll tell you what gives. A reserve ain't ——. The only way you'll become a regular is if somebody dies and you're the only one left." Everybody broke into laughter. " Seriously though," he continued, "reserves fill in if a regular is absent. Reserves get only one free ticket to each game. The regulars each get two, and on Sundays when you come to the armory to change into your uniform, the reserves do not have a locker, but you still have to be in uniform and carry stuff to the band section where you would watch the pre-game show put on by the band."

I was very happy to have made the Redskin Marching Band, but I was a little sad because I couldn't participate as a full functioning member. I now realize that may have been a bit narrow-minded and perhaps petulant of me. However, at that time, I wanted a locker with my name on it and I wanted to march with the band in that pre-game show. My big break in advancement came one night at rehearsal when

168

I least expected it. The band was getting ready to run through the Christmas Show formation. If a regular bandsman is absent when a letter is formed, this empty spot is very glaring. At this rehearsal, one of the sousaphone players was absent so the line chief said, "OK., Battle, get a horn and fill the space."

I went over to the equipment truck and they gave me the sousaphone, but no mouthpiece. I said to the equipment man, "Hey, where's the mouthpiece? C'mon, I'm in a hurry." Just then someone called him away, but he turned to me and said, "It's OK., you won't need a mouthpiece. They just want you to fill in the regular spot. Reserves aren't expected to play each position."

As he disappeared around some cars, I quickly checked the truck to see if I could find a mouthpiece. No luck. I then looked into the cab and fate smiled on me. The mouthpieces were kept in an open box on the floor. I had no sooner picked one to my liking when a voice rang out, "Battle, get in the damn formation." To which I responded immediately. The director said, " First we will warm up by playing the Christmas carols we're going to perform on the show. As the music was being passed out, the librarian started to skip me. I stopped him and asked for the bass part. He looked at me, shrugged his shoulders, and handed me all the parts.

It was while we were playing the second carol that I noticed all the other bassists had stopped playing and were looking at me. I kept playing to the end of the selection. After the rehearsal, the line chief and a few other bassists said they wanted to talk with me. As it turned out there was a permanent opening in the bass section because the regular bass player had to move to another state. The section chief said to me, "Battle, we heard you tonight. You were sight reading and you have a good tone. We're offering you a place in the band as a regular." My heart was jumping with pure joy as I said, "I accept, on one condition.:

"And what would that be?" the line chief said. "That I'll be transferred to the drum section just as soon as an opening occurs." "You've got a deal," he said. That Sunday, I definitely had the feeling of walking on cloud nine when I went into the band room and read my name over my locker.

Thus began my relationship with the Redskins Band that lasted for sixteen wonderful years.

I Meet the Altones

During my first year as a teacher, I was so busy that I did not have too much time to play with other bands. It was around 8:00 p.m. one Friday night when I received a phone call from someone named Al Winfield. Al said his combo was playing at the Cotton Club on Kenilworth

Avenue and he needed a drummer immediately. He said that he had gotten my telephone number from another leader with whom I had played. He also asked if I could play that night and if I could get there soon. I answered yes to both questions. Then he told me to take a cab, that he would pay the cost. When I arrived at the club I noticed a man coming out. What got my attention was the fact that the man was carrying a drum set. He had the bass drum on one side and his trap case on the other. I said to myself, "What gives?" When I entered the club, I had to pause to get my eyes used to the darkness. Then someone came up to me and said, "Hi. My name is Al. Man, am I glad to see you." As he helped me to the bandstand, I noticed immediately that there were five musicians on the stand, all with their instruments out and ready to play. The combo consisted of two saxophones, one trumpet, bass, piano, and me, the drummer made six. Nobody said anything, so I went about setting my drum set up as quickly as possible. As I sat down and was doing some last minute tuning, I saw Al go over to someone whom I assumed was the club owner. Al nodded and then came over to the bandstand and said, "Because of what happened, we'll have to play fifteen minutes overtime, Boots. I'll explain to you later. OK., let's get rolling. You all set to go, Boots?" I nodded and Al said, "Let's start off with Perdido." Then he proceeded to stomp the time off. As soon as we hit, I was all over those drums, heavy beat on the bass drum, syncopated rhythm with my left hand on the snare, and a sizzling, driving, Ride cymbal. In a word, we were cooking.

That's when I noticed Al. He actually stopped playing. He took his horn out of his mouth, turned around, and looked at me. He then broke into a wide grin, turned back around, and continued to play with increased enthusiasm. Later, Al explained to me that the other drummer had a very big ego and was always at odds with the rest of the band. Tonight his temperament got the best of him and he just packed up his drums and left.

After the gig, Al asked me to be a regular with his group and I agreed. In fact, our association together lasted until Al passed away, thirty some years later.

The Altones Today

The current combo I'm fronting is "Roy Battle and the Altones". The group is a four piece instrumental unit with a female vocalist. The other members of the band are Marilyn Carlson, Jack King, Dennis Davis, and Blake Cramer or Dick Glass.

Marilyn Carlson - Vocalist-a seasoned performer whose feeling, clarity, and range are outstanding. She is a crowd pleaser and is always in demand. Marilyn is a very dedicated band member who has to drive at least 3 hours from her home in Virginia to make each gig.

Jack King - On Acoustical Bass, is without doubt the best and finest bassist around. You just can't keep still when you hear his melodious, driving beat. In addition, the strengths of Jack are his loyalty, dependability, and truthfulness. It is Jack's caring and help that has kept me going. Jack and his wonderful wife, Helen, are always there for me. Many, many thanks!!!

Dennis Davis - On tenor saxophone, is an unparalleled musician. He can read fly specks and the term "solid as a rock" fits him like a glove. Dennis is a retired member of the U.S. Naval Academy Band. Both loyalty and dependability are his trademarks.

Blake Cramer - The consummate musician with "ears" as big as a house. He plays a lively keyboard and exciting vibraphones.

Dick Glass - A musician's musician. When Blake has a conflicting date, Dick fills in. He has mastered the keyboard, trumpet, bass, and guitar. Both Dick and his wife Judy (a great singer) always willingly back the Altones.

Judy Willing - Vocalist, whose throaty, driving and swinging style of interpretation is always a welcome addition to any Altones performance. Whenever Marilyn can't make it, Judy Willing is always willing.

Artie Dix - Vocalist. Tall, handsome, and suave, plus a very soothing baritone voice all add to the joy of hearing him sing.

The Altones feature music of the 30's, 40's, and 50's. We are very dance and swing oriented. Our home base, up to the writing of this book, is the Annapolis Yacht Club. When we play for a dinner dance there, it is like stepping into a Hollywood set of luxury. To see the glamorous ladies all bejeweled, swirling around, and the men, self-assured and confident, is to leave the troubles of the world behind.

Thanks also to:

Joseph Boswell - manager of the Annapolis Yacht Club. I am extremely grateful to Mr. Boswell for having faith in the Altones.

Dr. Stephen Hiltabidle - Commodore of the Annapolis Yacht Club, and his wife, Mrs. Hiltabidle, for their support.

Former members:

Al Winfield - deceased, was the original founder of the Altones in the 1940's, hence the name. His voice was a cross between Joe Williams and Frank Sinatra. Al's melodious approach to playing his tenor saxophone matched his carefree style of living. He was also an avid aviator. His wife, Bea, always supported us.

Bill Medley - His carefree style and love of life blends well with his outstanding musical abilities on the electric bass. For many years he was a regular member. Now he fills in occasionally for Jack.

Dee Ballard - Songstress. It's always a joy when Dee performs with us. Her enthusiasm and talent are something to behold.

Mike Thompson - Everybody's favorite keyboard player. Mike can do it all. He swings like he invented the form.

Icke Tilghman - One of the most talented entertainers around. Icke knows how to move an audience, whether with his soulful singing or driving piano. It's always a joy to gig with him.

Tim Johnson - He let's his instrument (bass) do the talking for him. Tim's beat is one you cannot ignore. Tim does it all-Disco, jazz, Latin, you name it.

Otis Winfield - He is the brother of Al Winfield (the original Altone). Otis has the tone that lets you know immediately that he was born to play the tenor saxophone. No if's and's or but's, when it comes to musicianship and performance, Otis is the man.

Lonnie Carnegie - A great keyboard man. When Lonnie sits down at the grand piano he's Duke Ellington, Carmen Cavellero, and Billy Taylor all wrapped up into one.

Buck Hill - Easily one of the best tenor saxmen ever.

Dave Kasals - A wonderful guitar player, he always adds a sparkle to the Altones.

Harry Pender, **Harold Mann** - Both are tremendous drummers with different styles. Whenever I had an operation or emergency that prohibited me from playing a gig, either drummer would gladly fill in for me.

Rivers McCreary - One solid entertainer who always enthralls audiences by playing his trumpet or harmonicas and singing.

Hope Clayton - vocalist-A classically trained singer who can emote and swing with the best.

Loretta Holmes - vocalist-a cool and vivacious chanteuse whose sultry delivery of any song would literally "bring the house down".

Al "Hot Pappa" Carter - deceased, top guitar player, whose dynamite chords and unique sense of rhythm lifted the Altones to new heights.

Saved by the Guardian Angels

This incident took place in Manhattan during the early 80's. I had gone to Brooklyn, N.Y. from Maryland to visit with my mother and aunt for a few days. On this particular day my Aunt Bert and I decided to go downtown to do a little shopping at Macy's Department Store. We had made quite a day of it. We had purchased numerous gifts which we were taking back to Brooklyn. We had a good time shopping and looking at the numerous sights which Macy's had to offer. Then we wound up our stay there by having a sumptuous lunch. We then made our way to the 8th Avenue subway at 34th Street.

We had no sooner taken our seats on the subway when something happened to the electrical system. Suddenly all of the lights went out. The coach was plunged into darkness, that is, except for one small light that cast an eerie glow over the faces and forms of that jam-packed subway car. We did not know just what to do, whether to sit there and wait until the problem was fixed and then we would be on our way, or should we get up and leave the car. The doors were stuck in an open position. We decided to stay because we were riding in the lead train on the track.

I could tell that the whole coach was rather apprehensive. As I sat there in the dark, I imagined all sorts of evil things happening. However, I kept my fears hidden and carried on a soft conversation with my aunt to keep her calm. It was then that it happened. Three tough looking, burly, unkempt men walked into the car. I couldn't see their faces but I heard one of them say, "Alright people. You're going to give it up or your asses belong to us." With that statement they went to the back of the coach where they planned to rob the passengers as they worked their way up to the front of the coach. I was just about to tell Aunt Bert that we should get up and leave when one of the unruly three yelled out, "Nobody move or it will be your last."

My heart sank. I felt abused, as if my manhood had been taken away. There seemingly was no way out. I felt sorry for Aunt Bert and I took her hand and gently squeezed it, not really knowing what our immediate future would be. It was one bleak moment, and getting bleaker.

Just as one of the thugs jostled a passenger, two guardian angels entered the coach. Each angel entered through a separate opened door. The guardian angels seemed so young and good looking. They didn't say a word. They just stood at "parade rest" with one arm behind their backs. They wore red berets, white "T" shirts with the words "Guardian Angel" emblazoned on the front in red, khaki pants sharply creased, and combat boots with spit shines. As I said before, they said nothing but stared straight ahead. One of them was so close that I could have touched him.

The hoodlums all uttered expletives as they left the subway car. I had never seen anything like that before. I was so happy. Aunt Bert looked and smiled. Shortly thereafter, the lights came on. The train lurched and started to roll. The two Guardian Angels rode with us for two stops and then got off.

When I returned to Brooklyn, I immediately wrote a letter to then mayor Koch, extolling the heroism of the Guardian Angels in that situation. I wrote the mayor because as I recall, he was raising questions as to the value or need of the Guardian Angels.

The Tuskegee Airmen

At this time I will pay tribute to those stalwart, brave men who fearlessly paved the way for what I called the Third Wave which engulfed the U.S. Air Force, namely, the 477th Medium Bombardment Group. The first wave of black airmen to be officially recognized in the Air Force scheme of things was the 99th Pursuit Squadron. The second wave was the 332nd Fighter Group, which was composed of four pursuit squadrons; the 99th, the 100th, the 301st, and the 302nd. The Derring-Do exploits of these pursuit squadrons are well documented in the annals and archives of modern aerial warfare. In fact, if one listened very carefully at that time, during 1944 and 1945, one could hear the collected sighs of relief of the white bomber crews in the European theater of operation when they sighted the "Red Tails" of the Black Eagles of the 99th and/or the 332nd Fighter Group, coming up to escort the bombers to and from the appointed targets during World War II, and not without reason. The famed "Red Tails" never, ever, lost an airplane for which they were responsible. These Fighter or Pursuit Squadrons were then under the very capable leadership of Col. B.O. Davis, Jr.

Lt. Gen. Benjamin O. Davis, Jr.

Words cannot properly express the respect and awe in which we hold General Davis. His leadership ability guided all phases of the "Tuskegee Experiment" to a successful conclusion.

It was Gen. Davis who saved the 99th from being abolished. Through his factual, frank, and impassioned presentation of our case, he convinced General George C. Marshall to allow more than just ninety days for the 99th Pursuit Squadron to continue fighting in the European Theatre and to prove themselves worthy and deserving to be called pursuit pilots.

It was Gen. Davis who commanded the four-squadron 332nd Fighter Group to unequalled heights as professional warriors, by protecting our U.S. bombers on their missions. Under his capable command, not one bomber of ours was lost to enemy fire while under their protection. The bomb group leaders were very, very happy to see the "Red Tails" and "Spinners" of the 332nd Fighter Group meet them at their rendezvous point.

Lastly, it was General Davis who was again called back from the front to take charge of an embattled 477th Medium Bombardier Group that was placed under arrest at Freeman Field, Indiana for disobeying an unlawful order given by Col. Selway.

Gen. Davis replaced Col. Selway and with his chosen officers who he brought with him, reorganized the 477th to the point where they became a first class Composite Bombardment Group alongside the 99th Pursuit Squadron.

Mrs. Eleanor Roosevelt

Also, while I am at it, I would like to pay tribute to Mrs. Eleanor Roosevelt, wife of the then president, Franklin D. Roosevelt, for the strong, unyielding, positive stand which she took by insisting to the president that the airmen of the 99th Pursuit Squadron, and their support personnel, were truly talented and had the intelligence and skill to operate each and every component of an air unit, from the pilots and all that it took to keep them flying.

My Co-Workers At Douglass

My eighteen years of teaching at Frederick Douglass Jr.-Sr. were mainly filled with the joy of teaching. I am, however, keenly aware that cooperation is the operative word when one considers being a part of a teaching family. There are many teachers over the eighteen years whom I would like to acknowledge because of their unselfish contribution to my individual success. They are listed as follows:

Elaine Blackwell - A fiery, dedicated, competent, Physical Education teacher who always helped me with my majorettes. She was quite petite but nobody messed with her. Elaine definitely had her act together.

Hazel Rich - A warm, caring, teacher who to my knowledge was the first to use behavior modification in her Reading classes. It opened my eyes to what setting reasonable goals combined with love could do.

Walter Pearson - My counterpoint in General Music. He always strove for excellence in behavior and performance.

William Blount - A kind yet tough teacher who knew how to light the fire of learning in the Industrial Arts students.

Benjamin F. Cumbo - A great Physical Education teacher who always had a ready smile and kept us laughing. Ben was a dynamite influence on the boys' P.E. program at Douglass.

John Myles - The brain of Science and Physics, he could figure anything out, abstract or concrete

Oliver Davis - Unselfish and giving, never a discouraging word in music.

175

Delores P. Smith - A wonderful bundle of energy in Physical Education, very creative, always willing to help me with my majorettes. Her classes were quite large but she always had total control. Many of my majorettes got their start in her dance classes.

Joseph Stephenson - The philosopher of History. A solid, dependable person who taught Social Studies.

Alice Tolson - Never too busy in Art to help. A great person. She was always on the cutting edge of Art. If any new procedure or theory came out and it was beneficial, Alice always inculcated it in her classroom.

Ralph Amis - A straightforward, no-nonsense but fair teacher of Science and Physics.

Thelma Thomas Daley - A visionary in the field of Guidance. She could do it all. Thelma was way ahead of her time.

Mozella Lawing - Smart, tough, and caring. Mazella was living proof that beauty and brains go together. She was frequently selected by the U.S. government to carry out their experimental Science projects at Douglass.

Geneva Wade - Not afraid to experiment. Permitted me to teach rhythms to her third grade pupils.

Ethel Walker - A very cooperative Home Economics teacher, always willing for her girls to prepare refreshments for performers.

Wilbur Hawkins - Driver's Education instructor. He was a great favorite and a wonderful, concerned teacher who was always willing to help me.

Marguerite Simpson - Always in my corner. Possessed a very quiet strength, maintained a no-nonsense approach, but fair. A great Social Studies teacher. I owe a great deal to this unselfish person.

Joseph Ennis - Was one fine Math teacher who developed a super drill squad that brought Douglass honors. Joe is solid as a rock... you can depend on him.

Martha Duckett - A champion for the students. Always willing to assist me. A great counselor. Martha knew her profession.

John Griffith - I'm very proud of John. He was once a Douglass bandsman. John was a very good shop teacher who did all he could to help the band.

Janie Moore Goldsten - Smart as a whip. An excellent Math teacher. Never failed to back me.

Virginia Dyson - I could always depend on her for support. She was a great business advisor and possessed a wonderful sense of humor.

Goldie Smith - Vivacious fashion plate of Douglass. Held nothing back. I was very grateful for her active involvement. She was a former Douglass student who returned as an excellent science teacher.

Zether Willis - Special Ed "to her bones." Supported me always.

Catherine Flowers - It was always a joy to work with her and her Special Education classes.

Frances Spencer - A strong, quiet, very effective Home Economics teacher who never failed to assist me.

Dora Halton - She ran a tight ship in Math, very competent, always ready to help me.

Willa Bowers - A quiet no-nonsense teacher with a heart of gold. Always in my corner.

George Walls - A very good-natured shop instructor who never failed to assist me when needed.

Lina Bowers - One of the most efficient and knowledgeable teachers in her specialty of Business Education around. She made certain that those bandsmen who missed her classes for rehearsals never missed their assignments.

Leo Hill - A very imposing Physical Education instructor. He was well versed in his subject and how it related to the total school program. Leo always cooperated with me.

Elinor Ford - A strong, dedicated Math teacher who always tried to help me by permitting her pupils to come to rehearsals.

John Butler - An excellent core teacher who never failed to help me.

Clara Martin - A very good, no-nonsense Art teacher who never stood in the band's way.

Violet French - A wonderful English teacher who stood for student progress.

Geraldine F. Williams - She may have been small in stature but she was a giant of an English teacher. I always appreciated her support.

Laverne Timus - Was a very positive, no-nonsense Core Teacher. I always appreciated her cooperation.

Harry Williams - Was an effective, caring agriculture teacher who always presented the latest improvements to his students... We saw eye to eye on the subject of band.

Charles Pinkney - A very good Science-Math teacher who was very cooperative towards the band.

Laura Burke - Was a very classy, demanding English teacher who turned out knowledgeable students.

David Washington - Also known as "Mr. Drivers Education". He possessed the students' keys to freedom in the form of a Driver's License.

Milton Mack - He was a very dedicated Core teacher who stressed reading through phonics. Mack was always cooperative.

Thelma Gardner - A Guidance Counselor supreme who made many class changes to help the band students.

Frederick Davis - A quiet giant of a History teacher who always volunteered to help me.

Ida Pinkney - A wonderful core teacher, very helpful to me.

Fannie Timmons - A very able core teacher who cooperated with me on the complex schedule.

Robert F. Frisby - Was a father figure to me. He never let me go too far astray. He was well versed in the "Cinnamon Bible" (the Book of Rules and Regulations provided by the Maryland State Department of Education for use by all secondary school principals). Mr. Frisby was transferred from Douglass to the Board of Education of Prince George's County in July of 1967.

Lawrence W. Jackson - My final year at Douglass was under the very able leadership of Mr. Jackson. Mr. Jackson could always find humor in any situation. It was this quality of leadership coupled with a solid understanding of how to work with students, parents, and teachers that made him an extraordinary leader.

Peggy Bethel - A very competent elementary school teacher who always encouraged her students to take pride in the Douglass Band (in 1950, Frederick Douglass included grades 1 through 12).

I shall also be eternally grateful to the staff members of the "Douglass Family".

Cafeteria Staff: Ruth Tolson, manager, Mary Franklin, Laura Curtis, Berlyn Brooks, Mildred Curtis, Shirley Curtis, Burlean Brooks, and Mildred Wedge.

Custodial Staff: Robert Hawkins and Carlos Pinkney, building supervisors, Hattie Colbert, Carroll Pinkney, James Spencer, Charles Duckett, Katie Pinkney, Barbara Ann Pinkney, and Mabel Barnett.

Secretarial Staff: Alma Ruth, secretary to Mr. Frisby, Ella Greene, secretary to the principal, Blandine Walls, secretary to their administrators, and Myrtle Jones, secretary to the guidance counselors.

The Douglass Bus Drivers: John Davis, Gary Weems, Jr., Thomas Contee, Sidney Brooks, Mrs. Tommasina Young, Warren Pinkney, Gary Weems, Sr., Eugene Johnson, Thomas Brooks, Ellsworth Watson, William Hall, Nelson Lee, George Hill, Sidney Griffith, et al.

First Stage Band At Douglass, 1950-1953

Because of the fact that we did not have a balanced instrumental setup to start a concert band, my first year of teaching I composed special arrangements to suit the instruments we did have. The following students were the front runners who paved the way for those stellar musicians who, later in the history of Douglass, set so many records, won so many trophies, and who made the "Douglass Eagle Band" a household name known and respected by high school musicians and the public in general. I beg forgiveness if I have omitted any names – our band records are not readily available for that time:

Chester Adams	Walter Curtis	Clifton Oden	Earl Tolson
Linda Adams	Vincent Curtis	Aubrey Perry	Gilford Tolson
Mary Booze	Charles Dent	Marcel Pinkney	Melvin Tolson
John Briscoe	Joseph Deville	Julia Proctor	William Tolson
James Brown	Donald Diggs	Evelyn Savoy	Lawson Veney
Roland Brown	Jack Griffith	Lucy Savoy	Harrison Walls
Anthony Butler	Phyllis Harper	Walter Savoy	Eleanor M. Wedge
Donald T. Butler	Alice Harper	Vivian E. Sherbert	Gary Weems, Jr.
Paul Butler	Lorraine Harper	Albert W. Smith	Clemmie Weems
Winfield Butler	Clarence Hawkins	Susie Smith	Rose Weems
Edward Carroll	Lavel Holmes	John Stewart	Camilla Wilson
Marvel Chapman	Austin Humbles	Ann Tolson	Roland Wilson
Frank Crawford	Patricia Humbles	Donald Tolson	
Charles Curtis	Pearl Medley		

The Parents of the Bandsmen

I would like to give special thanks to the parents of the bandsmen who always assumed the responsibility of "getting the bandsmen home". The students rode to school on the bus, but following practice, which was held on a regular basis after school, the parents had to be responsible for seeing that they got home. I depended on the parents assuming that role. I further depended on the parents to get the bandsmen to the school prior to parades, trips, performances and then to be there to pick them up when they returned to the school or when the performance was over. The success of the Douglass Band Program depended on the consistency of the parents assuming this responsibility.

Further, I would like to pay special thanks to those Douglass Band Boosters who went "above and beyond" the usual. These are the band boosters who tirelessly trudged with the band up and down steep hills when they paraded in all types of weather. These same dedicated members willingly chaperoned all of the band affairs, including dances, bake sales, dinners, etc. These were the Douglass boosters who gave some of their time to accompany the band on an overnight trip to Delaware University. It was these booster members who rode with the band to the World's Fair in New York City and to Atlantic City, N.J. The activities listed above represented only a small portion of the sacrifices made by the Douglass High Band Booster Club for the safety and well being of the bandsmen.

I recall a special trip the band took to Atlantic City, N.J. We had raised a certain amount of money and were able to pay off a uniform debt. To our surprise, we had quite a bit left over, so a decision was made to just give the bandsmen a "trip and treat" where they did not have to be concerned with marching or performing. Rather, all they had to do was show up and the club would take it from there.

We must have made quite a sight rolling up Highway 301, five buses in all. The bandsmen and chaperons alike were singing and clapping their hands all the way up to Atlantic City. When we arrived at the boardwalk, the parents set up headquarters on the beach by making a circle with beach chairs and large sun umbrellas. The bandsmen organized themselves. Some changed into bathing suits for swimming, some planned to hit the boardwalk and ride in the carts, others checked out where to buy taffy and eat. The most wonderful part of it was the fact that money was no problem, all a bandsman had to do was ask any one of the five designated band booster members for what he or she needed. Everyone slept on the trip back and we even had a few dollars left over.

Band Boosters Club of Douglass High School

I would like to acknowledge the group of people who, because of their total unselfishness, commitment to support and outright love of Douglass Jr.-Sr. High School, played a very large part in the equation responsible for the tempering of LeRoy A. Battle... "The Douglass Jr.-Sr. High Band Boosters Club."

The Adams Families	The Curry Family	The Harley Families
The Addison Family	The Curtis Families	The Hawkins Families
The Archer Family	The Cusik Family	The Henson Family
The Armstrong Family	The Dade Family	The Hill Family
The Arvin Family	The Davis Families	The Hinson Family
The Baird Family	The Day Family	The Hodge Family
The Banks Family	The Dent Family	The Hoffman Family
The Barnum Family	The Deville Families	The Holley Families
The Bateman Family	The Diggs Families	The Holliday Family
The Bell Families	The Douglas Family	The Holmes Family
The Belt Family	The Driver Family	The Horn Family
The Bixler Family	The Duckett Families	The Huff Family
The Blake Family	The Dyson Family	The Humbles Family
The Blackwell Family	The Ellis Family	The Hunt Family
The Bolden Families	The Ervin Family	The Hushbeck
The Booze Family	The Estep Family	The Hutton Family
The Brannon Family	The Eure Family	The Isenberg Family
The Briscoe Family	The Ferrell Family	The Jackson Families
The Bryson Family	The Fletcher Family	The Jenkins Families
The Brooks Families	The Ford Family	The Johnson Families
The Brown Families	The Franklin Family	The Jones Families
The Butler Families	The Friend Family	The Nelson Lee Family
The Campbell Family	The Galloway Family	The Keehn Family
The Carroll Family	The Gantt Family	The Kidwell Family
The Chase Family	The Garner Family	The Kirkpatrick Family
The Chapman Family	The Goebel Family	The Kirsch Family
The Chesley Family	The Gordon Family	The Krenzler Family
The Clark Family	The Gray Families	The Lindsay Family
The Coates Family	The Greathouse Family	The Lohr Family
The Colbert Family	The Greene Families	The Marbray Family
The Colby Family	The Griffith Families	The Marshall Family
The Contee Families	The Hagen Family	The Mason Family
The Cottman Family	The Hamilton Family	The McCloud Family
The Cowan Family	The Harliss Family	The Medley Families
The Crawford Family	The Harper Family	The Mehrer Family

The Meyers Family
The Middleton Family
The Miller Family
The Molock Family
The Moore Families
The Myers Family
The Netherton Family
The Newman Families
The Oden Family
The Owens Family
The Parker Family
The Patterson Family
The Payne Family
The Perry Family
The Pinkney Families
The Polhamus Family
The Proctor Families
The Ragsdale Family
The Ramsey Family
The Randall Family
The Raymond Family
The Reed Family
The Rich Families

The Riley Family
The Rogers Family
The Salerno Family
The Savoy Families
The Selby Family
The Shade Family
The Simmons Families
The Skipper Family
The Slater Family
The Smith Families
The Spicer Family
The Spriggs Families
The Staubs Family
The Stewart Family
The Suggs Family
The Swann Families
The Tavel Family
The Taymen Family
The Thomas Families
The Thompson Families
The Tolson Families
The Turner Family

The Veney Family
The Wade Family
The Wallace Family
The Walls Families
The Walters Family
The Washington Family
The Watkins Families
The Watson Families
The Webb Family
The Weems Family
The Wells Family
The White Family
The Williams Families
The Wills Family
The Wilson Families
The Windsor Families
The Wines Family
The Wiseman Family
The Wood Family
The Worthy Families
The Wright Family
The Young Families

Nelson Lee - Nelson is a very caring person who literally became the official Douglass High School "Eagle" Band bus driver. For over 20 years, Nelson, who was also one of the town policemen of Upper Marlboro, faithfully transported the band to all away games, concerts, etc. Nelson would take great pride in wearing his uniform, including holster and pistol. You know how the state police stay close to the head football coach at the Saturday games you see on T.V.? Well, that's how Nelson made me feel. Nelson stuck close to me and was always ready to assist the band any way he could.

Benjamin Foulois Jr. High

My assignment to Benjamin D. Foulois Jr. High in Morningside, MD was my first adventure as Guidance Counselor after leaving Frederick Douglass where I was a band director. I'm very grateful to **Mr. Harold I. Bayes** who was my principal. Mr. Bayes was very cool and methodical in his approach to problems. His motto seemed to be, "Sleep on it." I still find it very useful.

Other persons at Benjamin Foulois to whom I should pay tribute are:

Charles Kinser - A fine Physical Education instructor. He had a way of bringing out the best in boys, no matter how uncoordinated they were. Chuck also was a great role model for his young charges.

Pat Patterson - Was a core teacher who demanded respect from students, mainly for each other. Pat was always in control of her classes.

Suitland Jr. High

In all of my 28 years as an educator, I can truthfully say that my assignment as vice principal at Suitland Junior High School located in Suitland, Maryland was the most challenging. I think the location of the school (just inside the Beltway) contributed to some of the difficulties. The Junior High School was also located directly behind the Senior High School. We had a problem of the Senior High students taking short cuts through our school to get to their school. Local gangs seemingly would plan to settle their differences at our school. Then, to top it off, both schools used the same athletic field which was midway between them. Consequently, on game days held by the Senior High, there was always a constant flow of unwelcome traffic in the Junior High School. With the above as background to my particular situation, I am paying tribute to the following teachers because of the way they stood by my side and responded accordingly to either prevent or stabilize each situation:

Charles McMillan - French teacher who personally took it upon himself to keep order in his upstairs hall area. He supported me and my philosophy of "tough love". In addition, both he and his wife Melba opened their home to me and fed me, which gave me a place to relax while awaiting night meetings.

Fred Hawkins - Mathematics teacher who unselfishly and consistently volunteered time to help maintain order at the school. Fred was one teacher whom I could count on to stand at my side in the face of seemingly insurmountable odds.

Jan Stocklinski - Core teacher who in a word explains her success in working with students termed "out of control", and that word is "fearless". She did not hesitate to look the student "eye to eye" or to put her caring arms around them to calm or reassure them. Jan was definitely part of my unofficial "cabinet".

Nancy Meyers - Girls' Physical Education teacher who operated on a "preventative" basis. Nancy could see many problems before they became full-blown. Her contribution to preserving the sanity at Suitland Junior High was invaluable.

Arthur Curry - Boys' Physical Education teacher whose commanding presence demanded instant fear, then respect. Art took it upon himself to patrol the main halls, counsel students, and free me up to deal with the "urgent" situations.

Thelma Boyd - Guidance Counselor whose quiet, yet firm approach to helping the students was a very significant factor in the equation of success.

Bill Farrell - Was a wonderful band director. He always kept his students focused on their techniques and phrasing. We both were together in the Redskin Marching Band.

Linda Campbell - "Toughie" was my nickname for this dedicated science teacher.

James Madison Junior High

During my second year at Suitland Jr. High, plans were made by the Board of Education to open up a new school, James Madison Jr. High in the Upper Marlboro/Clinton area. Later that year word got out as to who would staff the new school. It was no secret at Suitland Junior that my name was among those slated to go to Madison. I was both embarrassed and happy to learn that a petition was started by the faculty to keep me at Suitland. Another contingent even went to the superintendent and said that my talents would be sorely needed at Madison, which unfortunately turned out to be true. The following two teachers, through their dedication, proved to be invaluable allies in our quest for superior education in a wholesome setting:

Ella Edwards - Guidance Counselor extraordinaire who taught me restraint and "grace under fire". She was the one person at Madison who, with her keen, uncanny clues as to just what made our youth tick, and how to effectively work with them, made her a very welcome ally in my fight against ignorance.

George Barnwell - Band Director at Madison who really captured the cooperation of all of his students in a way that was wondrous to behold. He went about his work in a quiet, yet very efficient way. The students loved him and it was inspiring to hear them master their technical exercises and then to transform this technique into a stellar performance group. In his quiet way, George Barnwell added to the smooth operation at Madison Jr. High.

Margaret Mackenzie - A very effective Math teacher who had a winning smile and attitude, but did not tolerate any nonsense from her students.

Mary Pannell - An excellent Science teacher who made my job easier because of her being able to control her students while encouraging their growth in the subject.

Mary Anne Raysich - Her piano playing, singing, and knowledge of adolescent psychology all came together to make her a stellar teacher of General Music and Chorus.

Surrattsville Junior High

After two years of serving as vice-principal at James Madison, I decided to re-enter the field of Guidance at Surrattsville Junior High School in Clinton, MD. Frankly, I had wearied of dealing with the two percent of the school population presenting most of the problems. At Surrattsville, the 7th grade students were my responsibility.

The persons to who I shall pay tribute are:

Marsella Mesarick - Was a very effective 9th grade counselor. She really saw to it that her students were well prepared for high school.

Bonnie Tooley - Took care of the 8th grade students in a first class manner. Bonnie really understood what it took to give good guidance and counseling. She was a solid, caring counsellor who knew how to ply her profession.

Ruth Conley - Was the Guidance secretary who took her position very seriously. She always managed to do a first rate job on any clerical work required of her.

Arthur Hay - A wonderful art teacher who never failed to challenge his students to be and do their best.

Mohican Bowmen

Archery was one sport that I was very active in from 1950 to 1960; field archery to be more specific. The club with which I was affiliated was the "Mohican Bowmen". We had our club Archery Course on the Henry Butler farm in Cheltenham, MD. **Al Winfield** and I were the force behind the start-up of the Mohicans. **Andrea Toliver** was the visionary who guided us in the construction of our range. Another strong architect in the Mohican formation was **Bill Hinds** who knew where the technical things we needed were, and how to get them. We were a very competent and skilled organization (which is still active today), and we are proud to have been the first Negro Field Archery Club in the nation. **Bea Winfield** was one of the most loyal, involved members of Mohican Bowmen, male or female. In addition, Bea drew a great bow, reaching the rank of Bowman first class.

Charter members of the Mohican Bowmen:
LeRoy A. Battle, 1st President
Ernest N. Bishop
John Henderson
Milton O. Holmes
Walter M. Reid
Andrea F. Toliver
Alonzo L. Winfield

Bowling - still emerging, still tempering

It was around 1965 that bowling actively entered my life. My niece, Carol Chaney Holt, and my brother-in-law, Sidney Holt, urged me to take part in a bowling party that she, Carol, and her friends were giving. I told Carol that I had never bowled before. In fact, I knew zilch about the subject. "No problem," she said, "Sidney and I will teach you." To make a short of it, I was hooked by the time I finished my first game. I was real proud of the 85 that I made. Since that wonderful day of my having "discovered" bowling, I have left a trail of wonderful highs and heartbreaking lows at the following establishments: Bay Bowl, Annapolis; Fair Lanes, Clinton; Odenton Bowl, Odenton; Bowl America, Odenton; Fair Lanes, Glen Burnie; Parkland Bowl, District Heights; and Bowl America, Kent in Landover.

It was at Bowl America that I really learned from the splendid examples set by Bob Hill, president, and Rose Jones, secretary, of what good officers mean to a successful league. It was at Parkland Bowl in District Heights that Duke Drew, Ed Brady, and postman James Tibbs became my bowling friends.

My wife often states that "music and bowling are your therapy". It's true. I love to both work with my combo, the Altones, and to bowl. About 7 or 8 years ago I used to bowl at Parkland Bowl in one of the popular Post Office leagues. The average age of this league was about 25 and I just couldn't keep a decent average. Both my team captain, Tommy Hill, and the league secretary, Florence Hill, were on my team. They encouraged me and supported me but I could see that I was holding them back, so I decided to join a Senior Citizens league at the Crofton Bowling Center in Crofton, MD.

I have received much satisfaction being affiliated with this senior bowling group. The sense and level of competition is extremely high and I find that there is so much to learn about bowling. There are several guys in this group who have 190 averages or better. Right now my best average is 158 in league play.

I am grateful to the following for assisting, instructing, and technically helping me:

Corinne and **Elmer Call** - Thanks to Corinne for showing me how to make a 10 pin. I call Elmer the house "pro". He's very willing to share his technique with me. One of these decades I'll catch on. Elmer's a "preservation Jazz aficionado."

Dan Carlos - Another house pro whose average is near the 200 range. Dan shares his skill with all willingly. He is a born teacher who gets great satisfaction out of the high scores of his pupils. Dan is also knowledgeable about Jazz.

James Woods - Is known as Mr. T. He is a very dedicated bowler who works diligently to improve his game. Mr. "T" also sponsors the annual Crofton Senior Bowling Tournament.

Roger Vargas - He never fails to correct me when I miss a spare. Roger is one tough bowler. It's uncanny as to how quickly he can read the lines.

Al Keitel - The captain of my bowling team. Al, to his credit, never expresses disappointment if I miss a spare. I respect Al very much because he helps me and tells me the truth. Al knows my ball and if I try to help it too much, he gets me to slow down and move into a more rhythmic flow.

Mark Lyers-A young, strong, Afro-American member of the Prince George's County SWAT team. This brother can bowl. Mark checked my bowling ball one day and suggested that I get a certain ball. I did, and I want to tell you, my average has increased by 5 points. Thank you, Mark.

Thomas McCormack-I have the utmost respect for Tom. He critiques my bowling honestly. He can be ten lanes away and can tell by my delivery whether I am bowling well or not. Tom is forever reminding my to keep my swing smooth.

Howard Cobb- Kudos to one of the best league secretaries ever. Howard and his lovely wife, Ruth, turn the technical side of bowling to love.

I would like to tip my hat to those wonderful people who contribute to the warm, effective functioning of the Crofton Bowl: **Butch, Turtle**, **Sandy**, **Sue**, **Cindy**, **Blanche**, **Pat**, **Bubba**, **Steve**, and **Greg**. These are the people who dedicate their skills to maintain order, comfort, cleanliness, and the overall well-being of their patrons.

I would like to make a special mention of the fact that **Pat**, though petite, has a heart as big as can be. Pat, on her own, will bake cakes to honor birthdays for the senior bowlers. Also, I'm forever grateful to her for giving my mother the "Red Carpet" treatment when she visited the bowling lanes.

Sandy - The wonderful, caring, manager of the Crofton Bowling Center. From the very first day I started at Crofton, Sandy went out of her way to make me feel welcome.

Crofton Tuesday Afternoon Senior League

Charles Rogers - Watch out for this southpaw; it looks like his ball is going into the gutter, then POW, he's got a strike.

Bill and **Orma Caves** - Talent and courage personified.

John Davis and **Barbara Currier** - My two teammates who should be commended for putting up with a burden such as my erratic play.

Jim and **Charlotte** - Always a cheerful earful, he keeps you laughing.

Jim Bennett - A gentle giant with a bigger ball yet.

Janie and **Bob Conner** - They're both deadly bowlers - don't say you weren't warned. If he pulls out his gold ball and she rolls that purple blaster, just give up.

Ursula Bull - She'll sweet talk you, then bowl you into the ground.

Julia Shai - A very tough competitor. Don't let that cherubic face fool you.

John Painter - Always in there giving you his best.

Rubye Richards - You have no idea what happiness is, that is, until you've seen Rubye get a strike.

Jo Britten - Never gives up. She's my former teammate and she is a toughy.

Emily Brooks - A very gentle lady, that is, until you bowl against her. Then look out.

Toy Corrado - Never, never make the mistake of counting her out.

Leonard and **Sallye Finley** - It's all his fault that my average isn't 200. Sallye's OK., but that Leonard.

Sadie Gallagher - Mrs. Congeniality with a very tough ball.

Anna, **Happy**, and **Susie** - They are always a joy to be around. I feel sorry for you if you have to bowl any one of them and you are not prepared. You'll get blown out of the water.

Frank Herrelko - A talented bowler and a true champion of the youth bowlers.

Luther Howard - If you miss a joke that was told, don't worry. Luther will retell the same. Look out for his ball.

Reba Garnder - Hey Babba Re-Bop. This gentle lady can bowl.

Vic LeRoy Jones - Solid as a rock. His piranha will kill you.

Jack Marion - Don't let him use that green ball or your goose is cooked.

Ada-Mae and **Harold** - A very caring couple. Always willing to lend a hand.

Bud and **Alma** - You're in for a long afternoon when you play them.

Esper Spry - A challenging year for Esper. But her spirits are high.

Paul Winchell - I like this guy. He travelled a long way to hear my band.

Buck and **Mona** - A very talented and caring couple who take their bowling very seriously.

Charles and **Mernie** - Don't let her sweet smile throw you off, she's mean with that ball. He's no slouch either.

Tom Conner - A very deadly south paw. He tries to smooth talk you and he swears that any strike he may make, and he makes plenty of them, is luck. Ha!

Dick and **Peggy** - Where form and technique meet to spell doom for the competition.

187

Esther and **James** - Queen Esther will bury you under all the wood she knocks down.

Helen Kohlmann - Doesn't say much, but beware, her ball does the talking.

Sally Wolf - She bowled a 217 game on me and I haven't recovered yet.

Mary T. Hayes - A very warm person who always has a kind word.

Marty and **Mary Mann** - Both mean trouble. Let the competition beware.

Barbara Caffey - She's always sharing. A wonderful person.

Dale Dunn - Deadly with his ball. Need I say more?

Robert and **Donna Lauffer** - Your name is mud if she ever gets that curve ball doing right.

JoAnn Atchison - will fight you tooth and nail for each spare.

Cal Squires - Don't let him use that gold ball. That's all I have to say.

Eiko and **Phillip** - Both are very dangerous. Watch out for their "Shadow Ball".

Dan Danchik - If he pulls out that Quantum Ball, forget bowling. Just pack up and go home.

Marge Reed - Don't let her gray hair fool you. Her ball will give you gray hair.

Eileen Ennis - She may laugh and talk but she doesn't play when it comes to bowling.

Pat Murphy - That pink ball of hers will keep you in the red.

Dorothy Key - When she's on she'll burn you good. Ignore her sweet smile.

Luigi Vagnoni - Not only can he bowl but he plays a great tenor saxophone as well.

Oscar Krakat - A very, very, tough and capable bowler.

Roland Ceola - You've got a scrapper here, he'll battle you all the way.

Ralph and Ray - My former teammates. They always keep trying.

Tom Horeff - Long and tall with a devastating ball.

Helen and **Dred** - They're a dynamite pair. Let the bowler beware.

Dick Callahan - Quiet Dick with the noisy ball. He'll bury you with a lot of strikes.

Eunice Bartlett - She'll battle you to the bitter end.

Margie Burke - Don't overlook her ball, she'll beat you before you know it.

Fran - Has a back-up ball that is murder. You cannot relax if you play her.

Pat Rubilotta - I made the big mistake of selling him a ball. He repays my generosity by beating up on me with that same ball.

Stan Haft - Some balls make the man. Like Gyro-Pro.

Don Hoffman - A very unselfish, likeable entrepreneur who can really make his ball talk, it only knows one word... strike.

Jim Perkins - A friendly fellow who is always ready to help you out by subbing. The league needs more like you, Jim.

Big Al and **Sandy Raynor**-Honest Al will string out 5 strikes in a row and claim that he dropped the ball or it was a bad delivery, etc. Don't say I didn't warn you. He has a built in cheerleader in Sandy.

Notice to the League

If your name was omitted, please forgive me and take it out on me next time we bowl each other.

Special People

Tony Kornheiser - Special columnist for the Washington Post, and host of the WTEM Sports Show. Tony embodies the meaning of loyalty. He has made me one happy man by making "Roy Battle and the Altones" the official house band of the Gary "Big Time" Brown show. Thanks to Tony's playing of our tape, the Altones have gone nationwide, along with his show.

Jim Bohannon - The nationwide Talk Show host interviewed me on air in March 1995. Jim is one of the most knowledgeable men I have ever met. I will be ever grateful to him for playing the Altones's tape on his show.

Leo P. Heppner - Publicity specialist who always goes out of his way and travels great distances to cover our band and take "promo" pictures of us for brochures and newspapers.

Credella Matthews, **Evelyn Jones**, and **Dorothea Dennis**...Three wonderful, close friends of the family who took it upon themselves to literally assure that the communities of Shady Side and Churchton would receive the word about "Easier Said...". A friend in need is a friend indeed.

John Saunders - I'm very grateful to this talented drummer who graciously welcomed me to Morgan State College by permitting me to sit in on the drums... an act of kindness I shall never forget.

Karl Koenig - A fellow band director who truly helped me over a very difficult time when I was working on my Master's thesis. Theoretically, I had "hit a brick wall" at a certain point. It was Karl's encouragement that eventually caused me to persevere and solve a particular problem. Also, it was Karl who consented to be my guest conductor at the spring concert of 1964.

Gary Braun - a true cosmopolite who daily plays my band's selections on station WTEM for the Tony Kornheiser Sports Show. Gary can hold his own whether it be front of the microphone or behind same.

189

Greg Garcia - was one of the very first Board Control Technicians at WTEM who took a liking to my band's music. He was very instrumental in having our sounds played on the Tony Kornheiser Sports Show. Greg is now a successful television/screenwriter in Hollywood.

J. Matoka Altemus, R.N., Ph.D - When my class of aviation cadets reported to Midland Army Air Force Base for Bombardier and Navigation training, it was the guidance of Matoka that helped us keep our collective acts together.

The following persons were instrumental in helping me specifically with my recovery after a very serious operation: **Alice Garrett**, **Helen Harried**, **Ruth Williams**, **Barbara Tongue**, **Irene Holt** (family), **Charlotte Downs**, **Irma Howard**, **Alice Boothe**, and **Charles E. Garrett**.

My Community - I would like to take this opportunity to acknowledge the wonderful support given to me by my community. Since the first day that I married one of their beautiful girls, they have always accepted me like a close friend. I have never felt like an outsider. I could and can always depend upon some delicacies to be set aside for me by some very special ladies. When I was ill and subsequently recovering from an operation, it was the community which came over to give my wife relief and to help in my recovery. I know that it is a very precious blessing to be a part of such a caring community. I would also like to express my special appreciation to the Owens family, whose daughter Tierra delivers our mail to us, and whose sons Sean and Demetrious were kind enough to shovel me and my car out of a terrible ice and snow storm last year. Both young men have taken a protective interest in Alice and me.

Tribute to My Doctors

I would like to publicly pay homage to those individuals who collectively further contributed to my tempering, my physicians. I am and shall be ever grateful and indebted to them for calling upon their vast training and knowledge to enable me to meet each day. Errol A. Phillip, M.D., James M. Blake, M.D., Stephen B. Hiltabidle, M.D., Anthony W. Greer, M.D., H. Logan Holtgrewe, M.D., Jim Levy, DDS., Charles E. King, M.D., Dorothy Powell, M.D., Aris T. Allen, M.D., William Matory, M.D., John Seaman, M.D., Lisa P. Battle, M.D.

People Who Helped With this Book

Marguerite Simpson - Always going out of her way to assist me. Marguerite is completely unselfish. I cannot praise this gentle lady enough for the way that she pitched in and helped me in my quest for information.

Ira O'Neal - "What do you need? How can I help you?" These gentle words from this kind, unselfish, giant of a man truly served to calm the troubled waters of my mind when I was wrestling with a particular problem. Thank you for your wisdom, my comrade in arms.

Al McKenzie - A solid, knowledgeable person who always takes time to respond to my queries. He was my comrade in arms when we were arrested (101 officers) at Freeman Field.

C. Gordon Southall - I cannot say enough to let you know how much I owe to this kind, jovial, caring individual who so willingly took it upon himself to walk me through the process of realigning myself with Tuskegee Airmen, Incorporated. He is a fine fellow and Captain with the Tuskegee Airmen, is a one-in-a-million guy. He knows what needs to be done and how to go about same. Gordon was my personal "Internet" of information and procedures.

Marlboro Copy & Printing - Thanks to manager Kathy Livingston, assistant manager Ginger Miller, and staff members Chris and "Liz". They were always 'there' for me to take care of my copying and faxing needs.

I think I started writing this book the day I was born. Who can deny that all of our moments of sorrow and joy are forever imbedded in our living computer to be recalled later. After 45 years (from my first year of teaching) my computer sometimes skips or just plain "goes down". Consequently, I had to call upon the following kindhearted people to assist me in ferreting out the current addresses of my former bandsmen, their parents, my former co-workers, etc.: Cleo K. Sesker, Barbara Baden Bentley, Leo Brown, Mozella Lawing, Marguerite Simpson, Duke Simpson, Cynthia Douglas Orr, Delores P. Smith, Agnes C. Powell, Ira O'Neal, Al McKenzie, Elaine Blackwell, Mary Franklin, Howard Cobb, Laurence W. Jackson, Sue Southall, Cleo M. Whitley, John Saunders, Raymond Blake, Earl Tolson, Sr., Earl Tolson, Jr., Mabel Crawford, Saundra O. Middleton Benjamin, David R. Smith, and Dr. Earl O. Embry.

My Extended Family

I would also like to thank the members of my family for their never-ending, tireless support of the Lothian Clippers Little League teams when I was coach and later manager. I could always depend upon them to help in whatever ways they could, whenever and wherever they were needed. They are listed as follows: **Mom** and **Daddy Holt**; **Claude** and **Dot Holt** and kids; **Jimmie** and **Irene Holt**; **Jimmy III**; **Forrest**, **Bruce**, and **Chaney**; **Sidney** and **Mary Holt**; **Gantt** and **Ann Holt**; and **Jim Dandy**, **Vashti**, and **Novene**.

In addition, I cannot even begin to thank my family for the faithful support rendered to me in other facets of my life. Many times, if I had to play a gig in Annapolis and there was little or no parking near where I played, I would park at Vashti's house. She would then drive me to the job, go home, and then return to pick me up at 2:00 a.m. or 3:00 a.m..

One time, after I had finished playing a gig around 1:00 a.m., I discovered that one of the other musicians had mistakenly taken my keys home. So I immediately phoned Jimmie, told him the problem, and he was at the club within the hour to pick me up.

Vashti, who is a registered nurse, has more than once completely disrupted her busy schedule so that she could be here to stay with us making it possible for her to change my bandages every day.

Yes, I could go on and on about the caring and generosity directed my way from my wife's family. All this too has been a part of the tempering of LeRoy A. Battle. In closing, I would like to say that what you have read portrays only a portion of my life. As the average person passes through this veil of tears, he or she is confronted with literally millions of decisions which involve the quality of life and morality. In spite of the brutal, frontal assault on America's value and cultural systems which occurred in Oklahoma City, I firmly believe that mankind is basically "good". Man is definitely equal to more than the sum of his parts. Each day I am confronted with decisions that demand addressing. I am reminded of the saying, "Man or woman cannot solve all the problems that he or she faces. However, man or woman cannot solve any problems unless he or she faces the same."

Sometimes I get downhearted or down on myself because of a stupid, wrong decision to a problem. This feeling does not stay with me long, however, because of strength that I find in my good Lord and in my wife. Alice is a veritable fountain of strength. She has been fighting M.S. for over twenty-five years and refuses to give in to this scourge of a disease which attacks and drains the strength of youth. Alice would look at me and say, "Bad decision or not. You've got to keep going." Yes, Alice is living testimony to that saying, "You cannot un-ring a bell".

Final Thoughts

Finally, I firmly believe in the saying that "Education in and of itself cannot make leaders of us all, but a good education should teach us which leaders to follow." I recall that my father-in-law, Dad Holt, quoted a "Persian Proverb" which still serves as a guide for me. I'd like to share it with you.

He who knows not, and knows not that he knows not, is a fool, Shun him!

He who knows not and knows that he knows not, is a child, Teach him!

He who knows and knows not that he knows, is asleep, Wake him!

He who knows and knows that he knows, is a leader, Follow him!

Mohican Bowmen …First black field archery club in the U.S.
LeRoy A. Battle, 1st President, kneeling on far left.

LeRoy Battle with his mother, Margie, upon receiving Master's Degree in Music Education from the University of Maryland in 1961

LeRoy Battle with wife Alice at her retirement banquet in 1980. She had been serving as Principal of Shadyside Elementary School.

Sons LeRoy Jr. and Terry

*Son Terry in his recording
studio.*

Lisa, age 5; LeRoy Jr., age 2

*Daughter Lisa P. Battle, M.D., at Honors Program on her
graduation from Howard University School of Medicine in 1985.*

The "Early" Altones, circa 1960, featuring (l. to r.) Bill Medley, Al Carter, Roy Battle, Al Winfield, and Charles Branch

The "Present" Altones, 1995, featuring (l. to r.) Dennis Davis, Marilyn Carlson, Roy Battle, Jack King, and Blake Cramer.

Mr. LeRoy Battle today –
still "swinging" after all these years.